LEXICROMICON
A BLUFFERS GUIDE TO THE WRITINGS OF H P LOVECRAFT

Copyright © 2022 by Mark Hayes

All rights reserved. No part of this publication may be reproduced, distributed or transmitted in any form or by any means, without prior written permission.

Steampowered books
11 Saltholme Close
High Clarence
TS21TL

Publisher's Note: This is a work of fiction. Names, characters, places and incidents are a product of the author's imagination. Locales and public names are sometimes used for atmospheric purposes. Any resemblance to actual people, living or dead, or to businesses, companies, events, institutions, or locales is completely coincidental.

Book Layout © 2022 Steampowered books

/ Mark Hayes. -- 1st ed.
ISBN ISBN-13: 9798420451946

For Cal and Jon
And everyone who ever rolled a pair of d10's

Contents

Introduction: A Failure to Beware
The Beast in the Cave
The Alchemist
The Tomb
Dagon
A Reminiscence of Dr. Samuel Johnson
Polaris
Beyond The Wall of Sleep
Memory
Old Bugs
The Transition of Juan Romero
The White Ship
The Street
The Doom That Came to Sarnath
The Statement of Randolph Carter
The Terrible Old Man
The Cats of Ulthar
The Tree
Celephais
The Picture in the House
The Temple
Facts Concerning the Late Arthur Jermyn and His Family
From Beyond
Nyarlathotep
The Quest of Iranon
The Music of Erich Zann
EX Oblivione
Sweet Ermengarde
The Nameless City
The Outsider
The Mood-bog
The Other Gods
Azathoth
Herbert West-Reanimator
Hypnos
What The Moon Brings
The Hound

The Lurking Fear
The Rats in The Wall
The Unnameable
The Festival
The Shunned House
The Horror at Red Hook
He
In The Vault
The Descendent
Cool Air
The Call of Cthulhu
Pickman's Model
The Silver Key
The Strange House in The Mist
The Dream-Quest of Unknown Kadath
The Case of Charles Dexter Ward
The Colour Out of Space
The Very Old Folk
History Of The Necronomicon
The Dunwich Horror
Ibid
The Whisperer in Darkness
At The Mountains of Madness
The Shadow over Innsmouth
The Dreams of the Witch House
Through The Gates of The Silver Key
The Thing on the Doorstep
The Evil Clergyman
The Book
The Shadow Out Of Time
The Haunter Of The Dark

INTRODUCTION:
A FAILURE TO BEWARE!

A year ago I discovered an oddly entertaining fact. I was born on the day Howard Philip Lovecraft died. Why I found this oddly entertaining is a long story, but in essence, I've joked for a long time that I was born the day Julius Caser was assassinated, but my birth and his murder were unrelated. Which of course, is evident due to there being almost two thousand years between these events, but why let the obvious flaw in the logic get in the way of a good anecdote?

This day, or to be more correct date, is the Ides of March, or the 15th. Which is also not entirely correct as the term Ides refers to the first full moon of a given month and actually falls between the 13th and 15th it just so happens when Julius got knifed in the back by half the senators of Rome it fell on the 15th that year.

If you want another odd fact about the 15th of March, if you express all time, from the birth of the universe to a week last Tuesday, as a single year, (the big bang happening at 00:00 on January the first and it now being midnight on the 31st of December) then the sun and by extension the whole solar system was born on, you guessed it, the Ides of March. Though of course there was no moon at the time, full or otherwise.

So Caser dies, the sun is born, I'm born, and Lovecraft dies, all on the 15th of march, and it's always a full moon…

Werewolves, I'm just saying…

None of this is the reason I found the date of Lovecraft's death oddly entertaining. The reason I found it entertaining was simply because I had spent almost three years by this point writing a blog about Lovecraft and only just bothered to look up when he died, and lo and behold, it was on the ides…

As to why I had spent three years writing a blog about Lovecraft, that's another story entirely. The origin of my Lovecraft blog, which was based on the premise that I would read each story in the order he wrote them then write about that story is simple enough. I had, like many writers before me, for a long time been enamoured of the strange worlds of Lovecraft's mythos and all the things his writing has led to, but I'd actually read very little Lovecraft. Then my girlfriend bought me a folio edition of the complete works for Christmas. Now all things considered had she bought it for me as a birthday present and presented it to me on the Ides it would have made for a better story, but we work with what we have, and this is nonfiction.

But having been presented with a folio edition of the complete works of Old Tentacle Hugger what possible excuse did I have not to read them?

Well, plenty of reasons, not least of which is that for all his imaginative genius for peculiar ideas, strange worlds and bizarre creations, Lovecraft's writing is, well, Lovecraft's writing. Dry to the point of arid at times, Lovecraft could, as one wag put it to me once, write the humanity out of anything. But the problems with his style are minor compared to other issues with Lovecraft's stories He was a misogynistic, racist, right-wing, homophobe who had no compunction against expressing his less than desirable political leanings in his writing, be it fiction or a considerable amount of non-fiction essays on a multitude of subjects.

It's an unfortunate truism that for many modern readers the most horrifying aspect of Lovecraft's stories are not descriptions of cosmic isolation, the elder gods, the deep ones, or his general nihilism. What horrifies modern readers is instead the political leanings of the writer and so many choose to avoid his work entirely. This is something of a shame because there is much to love about it. If that is you can pick a path between the dross, the over written, the dull and the distasteful, to the gems buried among them.

What I needed, I determined, was for someone who had read the complete works and filtered them through the eye of a modern reader. Someone who could point out the stories to avoid, the ones that need to be read, the little-known gems and the overblown twaddle. Someone who could perhaps supply the odd, interesting fact that I could borrow to sound knowledgeable, and who knew which stories have most influenced various bits of modern culture, artist, writers and musicians. Someone who had perhaps supplied a simple ranking system as a guide, say in quantities of tentacles, so I could see at a glance which stories were worth reading and which I should avoid like a blood splattered copy of the Necronomicon.

Sadly, no such guide appeared to exist. There were plenty of academic texts on Lovecraft, but they all seemed to be trying there hardest to be 'worthy' or written by self-styled Lovecraftian scholars. Which is to say they all seemed either assured of their own cleverness or written by the same kind of devoted fanboy that would tell you despite all evidence and that song about the lawnmower, that every Genesis album was a masterpiece…

So, I was stuck with three things, a blog in need of content, a folio edition of the complete works of H. P. Lovecraft and no guidebook to the dark twisted woodland path that is his works. Frankly at that point I had no choice, if I couldn't find a readable guidebook, I'd just have to write one…

This then is that guidebook. Welcome to the Lexinomicon, a bluffer's guide to the writings of H. P. Lovecraft.

Mark Hayes 2022

THE BEAST IN THE CAVE

Howard Phillips Lovecraft wrote 'The Beast in The Cave' at the tender age of 14, way back in 1905. It is the earliest of his work ever to be published, though that did not happen until over a decade later in 1918 in the 'The Vagrant' a New England amateur press journal. The story was not, however, the first of Lovecraft's stories to be publish. That honour lays with another tale, 'The Alchemist'. It wasn't even the second, that one was… well, we will come to that in a while.

This is, however, the story we start with, because when I first decided to undertake this little project of mine almost four years ago, I decided that as I am a writer, I should do them in the order they were written. Because how better to understand how another writer develops over the years than to read his stories in chronological order? At least, that was what I told myself at the time. If this little project has taught me anything about Lovecraft the writer, then it's that knowing him better is not necessarily a good thing… But let's not get ahead of ourselves. Instead, let's do this one story at a time, starting here, lost in the darkness, with the disturbing knowledge, we are not alone…

As you may expect 'The Beast in the Cave' is a fairly simple story. Young Howard was not the most precocious youth. His father had been committed twelve years before when Howard was merely a toddler and he was raised by an overprotective mother, his aunts and his maternal grandparents, who were affluent for much of his youth, but the family's fortunes were definitely on the wane. It was his grandfather Whipple (yes that really was his name) who instilled a love of literature in young Howard. So, if we have anyone to blame for Lovecraft's literary endeavours, it's Whipple… Now there a sentence that no one should ever have to write with a straight face.

The synopsis for 'The Beast in the Cave' is a man finds himself lost deep within a cave complex, his torch batteries fail and plunge him into absolute darkness. The man quickly comes to the conclusion he is beyond rescue and tries to reconcile himself to a slow death by starvation alone in the dark. That is until that is he realises he is not alone after all. There is something lurking in the darkness near him, something hungry…

As I said, it's a fairly simple story. It is, however, a surprisingly good allegory for much of Lovecraft's later fiction because it holds within it one of the central themes that run through so much of his work. The idea of isolation. Of being alone in an unforgiving, uncaring cosmos. Or rather wishing you were alone in the dark and hoping that other things within that endless night will not notice your existence.

There are other hints of Lovecraft developing his style in this story. It is written from the point of view of a single voice recounting his tale and fears. The man (he is never named, a common trait with many of Lovecraft's narrators) recounts his fear for his own sanity in the face of a slow, torturous demise, or worse, a quick and painful one at the hands of 'the beast'. It is the narrator's fear of his mortality, of the darkness, of the unknown and the unknowable, that is central to this tale.

What's perhaps surprising is just how well Lovecraft uses that theme of fear, expressed through the narrator's emotions, so it grows steadily as you read the tale even before the introduction of the beast itself. That beast which he encounters as a presence in the darkness of the cave takes on an ultimate sense of menace for the narrator. A presence that he can only hear and feel; blind as he is in the pitch black of the cave. A presence the reader feels as well as you turn the pages. For all this is written by a young Lovecraft and lacks maturity it still manages to get that sense of horror across to the reader surprisingly well…

But then there is the final twist and it's a disappointing anti-climax in so many ways. A dreadfully predictable one, which is written quite clumsily as well. In a last-minute rescue, the light of the narrator's rescuers torches reveals the beast itself, and all is well. There is nothing supernatural about it, in fact it's just another man, one who has been lost in the dark far longer, and all the tension that was built up just dissipates away like the darkness in the torch light.

Before that reveal the beast could be anything and in the context of the story that's what keeps you reading. What draws you onward is how its presence makes the main character feel, and what he fears it could be. The whole story hangs on that unknown factor, revealing what it is at the end softens the story and takes away its impact.

If we are going to be fair to young Lovecraft, and perhaps we should be, he was still finding his feet with a pen and paper at the time. He was in essence still to develop his soul as a writer and knowing his later work you can only suspect that if this had been written later in his life the beast would never have been revealed. Instead, the tale would have ended a paragraph or so earlier, rather than grasp towards some comfortable resolution. Which is not to say this is not without worth. It's a well written story for someone of any age. It just lacks something, and what it lacks is the cold calculated chill of a Lovecraft ending. That said, it's also lacking some other things that crop up in Lovecraft's later fiction and is better for their omission.

THE SCORE: 2 OUT OF 6 PROBING TENTACLES

MYTHOS CONNECTIONS: None

LOVECRAFT TWATTRY: None

SHOULD YOU READ IT: Probably not, unless you have an academic bent towards reading authors early works.

BLUFFERS FACT: Lovecraft's original manuscript for his first draft of 'The Beast in the Cave' still exists, in handwritten form and is full of his crossings out and deletions.

THE ALCHEMIST

While it is one of the better-known early Lovecraft stories 'The Alchemist' like 'The Beast in the Cave' is still one of his Juvenilia works, written as it was in 1908 when he was still only 17. Like 'The Beast in the Cave', Lovecraft did not find a publisher for the story until several years later when he submitted it to 'The United Amateur' in 1916. 'The United Amateur' was another New England small press magazine, far from a big noise in publishing circles and boasting only a tiny circulation. It does, however, have the distinction of having been the first magazine to publish and feature a story by the young unknown Providence author when it featured 'The Alchemist' in its November issue that year.

If the publishers ever became aware of whom they unleashed on the literary world we will never know. If so, they have a lot to answer for ('Celephais' for one thing), but best not to get ahead of myself...

It's tempting to compare 'The Alchemist' and 'The Beast in the Cave' as they are both works written by a young Lovecraft, the former of which is a far more accomplished work, with a darker edge to it than latter. Rather than being a simple tale of a man trapped in a singularly terrifying situation, 'The Alchemist' is a story with depth that can be read on different levels. It is far more recognisably Lovecraft, and it suggests, perhaps not unsurprisingly, that he had matured a lot as a writer in the three years between these stories. But then while it was only three years, the years between fourteen and seventeen tend to be big years in terms of development for anyone. A littler more maturity is only to be expected, and in terms of writing Lovecraft certainly had that.

The scope of 'The Alchemist' is much more ambitious than the first story. It's a tale that spans hundreds of years of a family's history. It begins, however, with us being welcomed into the crumbling dust-laden world of the young Count Antoine de C-. It is through the eyes of the Count that we learn of the dwindling fortunes of the de C- family, and the crumbling family pile which mirrors that demise.

(Note: Lovecraft is fond of the device of hidden surnames, it's one he uses often in his early fiction. The affection stems from the practice in use by the scandal sheets of his day which often involved redacting names to avoid being sued.)

The Count resides in the last solitary tower among the ruins of the family mansion with a single aging family retainer and when that servant dies the Count is left alone brooding on the history of his family and its sadly depleted line. It is then he first comes to learn of the family curse. A curse both cruel and desperate. Each son born of the family is, it seems, cursed to die before they reach the age of thirty-two. Spurred by this discovery, the Count dedicates the rest of his ever-shortening lifespan to discovering the secret behind the curse, ultimately seeking a way to evade its impending embrace.

And so, there begins a tale of obsession, the kind of story that Lovecraft excels at. Told by the Count himself, there is little outside perspective on his plight but then the Count is the one obsessed, so his perspective is by nature a grim one. Faced with a curse which gives his life the equivalent of an expiry date, the Count choses, rather than living the life he has to the full, to hide himself away in the ruined house that was once the hub of his family fortunes desperately seeking a way to break the curse, by discovering its cause.

It never occurs to the Count (or Lovecraft) that the Count would have been better off taking what little fortune remained and living hard and fast in the streets of Paris, London, Vienna or even Rome. But then even the young Lovecraft was a tad obsessive about fate, so living fast and leaving a good-looking corpse as a character's raison d'etre probably never occurred to him.

The Count's obsessions drive him to delve into the family library, which hold an interesting collection of treatises on alchemy, dark arts, and other oddities, as well as scraps of the de C- family history. It's a collection that suggests he is not the first Count de C- to seek an answer to the curse, and while pursuing his goal he discovers the root of the family curse lays in the murder of one of a pair of black magicians by one of his distant ancestors.

Viewing the world through the eyes of one in the grip of obsession is where Lovecraft's writing often excels, even this early on in his career. Through the Count's narration you feel the crumbling remains of the castle around him, the layers of dust on the ground he walks through, the dark passageways and secret ways within those ruins through which Antoine explores his obsession, which almost naturally turns to madness as the clock on his life ticks slowly and relentlessly down…

And that's where an older Lovecraft would have ended this tale.

Unfortunately, he doesn't. The ending again is a disappointment. Much like the ending of 'The Beast in the Cave' the ending and its big reveal are lacklustre. Though it is carefully crafted it has a jaded predictability about it. Disappointingly so, as if you have read other Lovecraft stories before you would naturally be expecting a sharper twist. But this remains a Juvenilia work. Lovecraft was still finding his feet and his style when he wrote this. The darkness and edge to his stories was not quite there yet. But there were signs of something more. Certainly, it is a far more engaging and troubling tale than 'The Beast in the Cave' - full of promise of darker more disturbing things to come.

THE SCORE: 3 OUT OF 6 TENTATIVE TENTACLES

MYTHOS CONNECTIONS: None

LOVECRAFT TWATTRY: None

SHOULD YOU READ IT: Your life will not be unfulfilled if you give it a miss, but it has a certain charm as a window on a young writer developing his style.

BLUFFERS FACT: The story is referenced in the Blue Öyster Cult song 'The Alchemist.'

THE TOMB

Madness, and fear of encroaching madness, are themes that Lovecraft visits time and time again in his stories. This was, given his family history, a subject that is close to his heart. He also suffered a nervous breakdown in his formative years and was afflicted by parasomnia and pareidolia (sleep paralysis and seeing faces in dark shadows) all his life. Indeed, a fair degree of his later work can trace its inspiration back to these afflictions.

While Count de C-'s obsession in 'The Alchemist' touched on the subject, it was in 'The Tomb' written nine years later that Lovecraft first used the fear of encroaching madness as a device by using a narrator of questionable sanity. The narrator in question, Jervas Dudley, makes no bones about it as he tells his tale, repeatably informing the reader that his word is questionable. Dudley also claims he is privy to a world more mysterious than the mundane one other pass through. He talks of dalliances with dryads in the woods and ghosts in spectral masons. Alluding more than once to his possession of some form of second sight and claiming he has a touch of the fay about himself.

When he wrote this story in 1917 Lovecraft was at the very beginning of his publishing career. 'The Alchemist' was published in November the year before, so he was probably disappointed when this story wasn't picked up for publication for another five years, by which time Lovecraft was firmly established in small New England press magazines.

Despite what Dudley tells us, the question of his sanity is an open one. In the story Lovecraft pushes the idea that what society believes to be the ravings of a madman could hold more than a seed of the truth behind them. In typical languid prose, the narrator vouches an opinion that Kipling summed up more succinctly with, 'There are more things in heaven and earth than are dreamt of in your philosophy.' Which is a concept at the heart of much of Lovecraft's work when he writes about sanity or the lack of it.

Lovecraft's laboured prose is, I find, occasionally a problem with his writing. He will at times stretch a sentence around all kinds of strange geometry to say something in the least succinct way possible. Ironically, this style is also something of the joy of reading Lovecraft, but it is all too easy to get lost in his sentences at times. In 'The Tomb', he really finds his stride in this respect, weaving long tracks through the woods, where shorter paths exist. However, there is a depth to that style which draws you in and gives voice to his narrators. The story, quite intentionally, reads as slightly deranged ramblings, wandering around strange roads and trails. It gives a certain authenticity to the faltering sanity of its narrator.

As a tale within itself, 'The Tomb' draws you along, in mild bemusement at the narrator's wanderings. The hints of madness mixed with obsession are all there. Jervas Dudley, on one of his long fanciful walks through the woodland, comes across a locked tomb hidden in a grove. The grove is overlooked by the remains of a burnt-out mansion. The mansion, once home to a wealthy family named the Hydes, was struck by lightning years ago. Local folklore has it that it was struck down for the decadence of its inhabitants by the Lord above. The tomb Dudley discovered is the Hyde family crypt and having discovered it he becomes obsessed with the tomb, the family interred there and how it may connect to himself.

When, some weeks later, he finds a porcelain figurine with the initials J.H carved upon it in a box which also holds a key, Dudley comes to believe he has found the way into the tomb. He returns to the tomb, not for the first time, and is elated when the key fits the lock.

Within the tomb, he finds the coffins of the long dead and one empty one. An empty coffin the right size and shape for himself. Such is his obsession with the tomb and the Hyde family he takes to sleeping in the dusty tomb each night, within the coffin he believes was left there for him.

Eventually, Dudley is undone when his nightly wanderings are discovered, though those who discover his strange behaviour try to convince him that he actually sleeps outside the tomb, and the padlock on the door has never been touched. Dudley of course knows they are wrong about this, even when they are showing him the rusty locked padlock, that has not seen a key in many years.

Lovecraft almost ends the story there. A story told by a man in an asylum, believed to be mentally unstable, telling us a tale that even he admits in his own recounting has questionable validity.

Yet one final twist remains…

This tale has long been a favourite of Lovecraft fans, there have been several comic book adaptations of the story, which follow the plot to a greater or lesser degree. It is also certainly closer than a movie released in 2007 called 'The Tomb' which was publicised as 'H.P.Lovecraft's The Tomb'. Ignominiously it went straight to DVD and had no actual ties to the Lovecraft story at all.

This tale has also long been a favourite of mine. Its strength lays in its narrator, and the choice you are given by the story to believe in all he says or believe instead the story is merely a window into his insanity. In that regard it is the essence of a good Lovecraft short story, leaving you with the slightly unnerving suspicion that thinking the narrator is mad is the most comfortable alterative.

THE SCORE: 5 OUT OF 6 MADNESS INSPIRED TENTACLES CLAWING AT YOUR MIND...

MYTHOS CONNECTIONS: None

LOVECRAFT TWATTRY: None

SHOULD YOU READ IT: Yes, you probably should, but avoid the movie... Really, avoid the movie...

BLUFFERS FACT: As well as the movie, the character of Jervas Dudley even managed to inspire a few musicians and is the name of a track on an Album by 'The Order of the Solar Temple' (the quality of which I cannot speak to as it's hard to find a decent copy), and a track on the Proxeeus album 'In the throes of a nightmare', which is excellent ambient rock if you like that kind of thing.

DAGON

Lovecraft was born, raised and spent the majority of his life in the port town of Providence, Rhode Island. Perhaps therefore it's no great surprise that mysteries of the sea feature so often in his fiction. Even now it remains an oddly bizarre fact that humanity knows more about the universe beyond the thin shield of our atmosphere than we do about the depths of our own oceans. Back in 1917 when 'Dagon' was penned this was even more of a truism than it is today.

What may lie in the inky black abyss beyond our shallow shores had long caught the imagination of both writers and readers alike. It is, after all, the last great terra incognita of our own world. Stories of sea monsters have abounded among sailors since man first put out on to the oceans.

I can understand Lovecraft's attraction to the mysteries of the ocean. I live close to the sea; my local beach is a short twenty-minute walk from the house. It's a deserted stretch of sand bordered by sea grassed dunes on the shore side. Beneath the bay are the remains of a primeval petrified forest that washes up like black ash on the sand. I have on occasion walked along that beach at midnight, alone in the oppressive heat of a summer night, my only company the sound of the waves crashing against the shoreline. There, the cold sea water lapping at your feet, a still deadness to the night air, hearing strange noises you can't account for, barely audible above the sound of the surf and the sinister nature of the sea is never far from your consciousness.

That is why I find it of little surprise the ocean inspired Lovecraft to some of his darkest and best loved fiction. The shore is in many ways a medium between one world and another. The comfortable known world of the land and the unknown abyss below the waves. It's only natural to speculate what may lay beneath the ocean, in the inky darkness no sun ever shines upon.

What is more interesting is the maturity of the writing in 'Dagon' one of the first stories Lovecraft wrote as an adult, which was also one of the first to be published, and remains one of his best-known, as well as still being one of his most disturbing tales.

'Dagon' is narrated by a former sailor who admits he's become addicted to opiates he started to take in a vain attempt to forget what he has experienced and the terror that still gnaws at his mind. Penniless, and soon to be drugless, he tells us he has decided to end his torment permanently by taking his own life, but not before he first decides to write his story down. His last testament of the experience that has driven him towards oblivion.

The tale he writes down tells of how he ended up alone in a lifeboat after his ship was taken by the German navy. He'd managed to escape in the small craft but found himself cast adrift somewhere in the mid-pacific far from land. Forced by circumstance to spend his last few days eking out limited supplies, fighting off the effects of sunstroke and delirium, his prospects look grim. Until that is, he wakes one day from a fitful sleep to find his craft is no longer adrift in the ocean but has somehow now run aground. Rather than the middle of the ocean he is now on a strange, black, slimy plain with a rotten stink in the air. A stink so putrid that even gulls would not dine upon the corpses of the dead fish that litter the plain.

Eventually, he starts to survey the strange land he has found himself stranded upon and comes to the conclusion it was, until recently, part of the ocean floor. A vast segment of it which, he posits, must have been forced upwards by powerful geological forces or some other unknown cause. Short of options, he sets out to find out more, as he is faced with the likelihood his supplies will soon run out and before long he would be joining the rotting fish that litter the plain.

Eventually, he comes across a range of hills in the otherwise flat plain and heads towards it. When he crests the largest of these, he discovers that beyond it the land falls away into a canyon, so vast and deep he cannot see down beyond the shadows of its walls. But what truly disturbs him is what he finds at the lip of the canyon. A great basalt monolith, carved with strange markings, carved by hands, which may or may not have been human, carvings of things that most certainly were not. A strange cyclopean relic of some long-lost civilisation hidden from the eyes of men within the ocean depths.

It is then that out of the inky darkness of the canyon, a hand reaches up and grasps the lip by the monolith. A gigantic, webbed, inhuman hand. But it is what follows that hand that haunts the marina's nightmares ever after, driving him to the dulling effects of opiates. He turns and runs as the very land he is standing on starts to shake from an enormous earthquake, but it is not the earthquake that causes the terror he feels.

Sometime after these events the man is found, adrift once more in an open boat, by a passing merchantman. He is delirious from heat stroke, and they tell him he was raving of things that could not be. He only finally comes to his senses weeks later in a hospital bed.

Is the land from the sea bottom some fever-induced delusion or did the events he claims to have witnessed happen as he describes? Does it matter either way? Even to the mariner the truth is, he is sure, somewhere in between, and as so often Lovecraft's narrative invites the reader to draw their own conclusions.

I adore this particular story, perhaps because I live by the shore, I have an affinity with the idea of the darkness below the waves, but it has always inspired a somewhat guttural reaction in me. It is with this tale that, for me at least, Lovecraft comes of age with his writing. It is the first truly Lovecraftian tale, and the first in which he begins to explore the mythos for which he is most famous.

THE SCORE: 6 OUT OF 6 TENTACLES COMING OUT OF THE OCEAN DEPTHS TO DRAG YOU DOWN TO THE ABYSS

MYTHOS CONNECTIONS: The deity Dagon (whose worshipers crop up a lot) and the first suggestions of the Deep Ones civilization were born here.

LOVECRAFT TWATTRY: None

SHOULD YOU READ IT: Most definitely, preferably after a midnight walk along an inky shore.

BLUFFERS FACT: Dagon is actually a biblical demon/god worshiped by the Philistines, he is also mentioned in Sumerian text and associated with merman motifs in Assyrian art dating back to the late Bronze age. Lovecraft however most likely first came across the name in John Milton's Paradise Lost.

A REMINISCENCE OF DR. SAMUEL JOHNSON

This story is something of an oddity. It's not the usual Lovecraft fare. It is in fact no more, and no less than exactly what the title claims it to be, albeit a fictional account told to us by a narrator who claims to be over two hundred years old - which is the only fantastical part of this story.

What 'A Reminiscence of Dr, Samuel Johnson' is, however, is a rare, somewhat awkward piece of Lovecraftian comedy and much like its Shakespearean equivalent, it really helps if you have read the background material if you wish to spot any of the jokes.

Written in 1917 and published in the same year under the pseudonym 'Humphrey Littlewit Esq.' it was written with no small wit intended. Surprisingly, for the normally po-faced Lovecraft he managed to poke fun at both his own writing style, which had been referred to by contemporary's as antiquated, and at the amateur press in which the story ultimately appeared. All of which has an unexpected irony when you know that Lovecraft himself was also a major player in the New England Amateur Press Association of which he was president for a short while.

No one expects humour from Lovecraft, and the story's jokes are certainly a little flat. That said, the observations on the wit of Dr Johnson, famous for creating the first dictionary as well as his rapier-like retorts is well written. Though it does make you wonder why Lovecraft's narrator doesn't punch the good doctor on their first meeting and instead becomes firm friends, given how Dr Johnson belittles him.

What is clear from this story is that Lovecraft had a high degree of respect for Dr Johnson, as well as several other literary lights mentioned in the story. Which is part of the problem - it's hard to lampoon someone you respect. I suspect Lovecraft would have been far from enamoured at the portrayal of Dr Johnson in the third series of Black Adder, which is where I personally first came across the good doctor with Robbie Coltrane's rambunctious portrayal. Lovecraft's Dr Johnson somewhat pales in comparison, as does the humour. For all the craft of this story, Lovecraft is not secretly a Terry Pratchett or Douglas Adams when he tries his hand at humour.

In the end, the thin humour cannot save this dull tale and not simply because it is not what I expect from a writer of horror and delver of the dark places of the human psyche.

THE SCORE: 0 OUT OF 6 TENTACLES THAT DON'T EVEN MANAGE TO BE LIMP AND FLACCID...
(It does get 4 out of 6 Johnsons as a work of pomposity and vague humour however if you like that kind of thing)

MYTHOS CONNECTIONS: None, unless Dr Johnson was a Deep One, which I missed if that was the case.

LOVECRAFT TWATTRY: None

SHOULD YOU READ IT: Only if you're the kind of completist fool who would write a blog on every piece of fiction Lovecraft's published.

BLUFFERS FACT: Littlewit, the narrator, is born August 20, 1690 – 200 years to the day before Lovecraft's own birth, making him nearly 228 years old as he writes a memoir.

POLARIS

'Polaris' is the name of the north star, that single static point in the ballet of the northern hemisphere's night sky. The star long beloved of navigators as it is always there on a clear night, hanging due north, and guiding their way.
'Polaris' is also the first of a group of Lovecraft's stories known collectively as 'The Dreamlands Sequence.' These stories all relate to one extent or another to Lovecraft's greater mythos. Though this is truer of some of the stories than others. This first Dreamlands story was written by Lovecraft in late 1918 and was published a couple of years later in 'The Philosopher', another of those ubiquitous New England amateur press magazines that were his main stay in the early years of his career.
According to Old Tentacle Hugger 'Polaris' was inspired by a dream, though this could have been part of Lovecraft's pitch as he was no more above cheap theatrics than any other aspiring author. The claim of its dream inspired genesis, however, does play into the story itself. Effectively 'Polaris' is about a dream. Which begs the question where does the dreamer end and the writer begin...?
A slightly less ethereal theory on the genesis of this story among scholars of Lovecraft states the tale was inspired in part by Lovecraft's frustration and deep-seated guilt about World War One. Howard was rejected when he tried to enlist. Olathoe, the narrator's alter ego in his dreams himself is similarly rejected for military service.
Lovecraft's keen interest in astronomy also played a part in inspiring the story. Choosing 'Polaris' as the object of his narrator's obsession and dreams, has much to do with both the stars fixed nature in the sky and precession. Precession is the name given to the strange rotational wobble the Earth goes through upon its axis, the 'period of precession' being the time it takes for this wobble to complete one full rotation.
At the start of the story, our unnamed narrator is lying awake staring at 'Polaris' through his bedroom window, feeling at once uneasy and mocked by the ever-present star blinking at him in the sky. It is not until he falls into sleep's grasp that we discover why, as he starts to recount his dreams.
In his dreams the narrator is taken back to another time and place, before the dawn of recorded history. There he finds a city at the heart of the fading Empire of the Lomars that existed, at least in the

narrator's dreamings, around 26000 years ago. He knows this because 'Polaris' is hanging in the same place above the horizon as it does in the view from his bedroom and the period of precession just happens to be 25765 years, or close enough to 26000 as makes no odds.

Precession has been known about since at least the time of the ancient Greeks, though theories on who first discovered it vary, there is more than a little evidence it was known about by the Mayans, ancient Egyptians and other cultures. Measuring precession, however, requires a lot of complicated maths of the kind Lovecraft never mastered, which was one of the reasons he was denied his childhood ambition to become a professional astronomer. Astronomy's loss was literature's gain, however, not poetry's…

> *Slumber, watcher, till the spheres,*
> *Six and twenty thousand years*
> *Have revolv'd, and I return*
> *To the spot where now I burn.*
> *Other stars anon shall rise*
> *To the axis of the skies;*
> *Stars that soothe and stars that bless*
> *With a sweet forgetfulness:*
> *Only when my round is o'er*
> *Shall the past disturb thy door.*

This 'enchanting' poem above is spoken to the narrator, or at least so he imagines in his dream, by 'Polaris' itself. The reference to precession is far from subtle, and the less said about the mangled 'revol'd' the better… The subtext is more interesting, though no less crowbarred into verse, in that it suggests that the narrator dreams of his own past life, revisiting in his dreams the actions of that life, and also reliving the shame his soul feels because of those actions.

In his dreams he knows the inhabitants of the city and feels a sense of familiarity that is almost sublime. With each nightly revisit to these dreams that sense of familiarity becomes stronger until, rather than merely observing the city, he inhabits it himself, becoming Olathoe. A weakling who is both feeble and given to strange faintings, who curses himself as such that he is left behind while his fellow citizens go off to war, which echoes Lovecraft's own experience in the years of the first world war. Desperate to serve his city Olathoe takes a post as a guard, watching the high passes from a tower. He is charged with the lighting of a beacon that will summon the warriors should the invaders arrive. Wherein lays the shame the narrator feels for this 'past life' knowing that in the end Olathoe failed in this duty too.

Taken purely as a story 'Polaris' has a lot to recommend it. It is reasonably original as a tale of a dreamer's dream, leaning towards an unknown mythical history of humanity. It is, however, not without issues which need to be considered with some context. It is a story of firsts for Lovecraft. The first Dreamland story, his first attempt to write myth and the first really personal tale in some respects. However, it also has a more unfortunate first about it. It's the first of Lovecraft's tales that gives the readers unsettling feelings in the wrong way.

This all comes down to the invaders faced by that ancient and mythical city. The invades are named as Inutos, a name Lovecraft derived from the modern word Inuit. The Inutos are described several times as small, yellow, barbaric, and referred to as being a lesser race to that of the proud and seemingly Caucasian Lomars. The racism inherent in this description is unfortunate, to say the very least. Lovecraft was hardly alone in his era in portraying Asiatic people as a threatening presence, but it's the use of that word 'lesser' which is most troubling, it's the first inclination of Lovecraft's racist views though some little context is needed, which is perhaps a little forgiving here. His imagined Lomarian empire is firmly placed in North America, and the migration of the Inuit peoples from Asia to North America happened somewhere around 26000 years ago. To the people of his imagined lost empire, the Inuit would indeed be barbarous invaders. As the narrator identifies himself with the empire's citizens, his views on the Inutos holds water there. But that doesn't excuse that 'lesser' in the description given by the narrator, or indeed the lack of the narrator's real self taking issue with the way his dream-self describes the foe.

That is, I will grant, a harsh criticism of one small aspect of the story. Some would see it as picking at a small scab in the context of when this was written. It also, on this occasion, has no impact on how I scored the story as a whole (Unlike the poem). It is a solid well-crafted tale and this first Dreamlands story is one I enjoy despite its issues. But it would be remiss of me not to point out the problems with it and, while it may be the first Lovecraft story to have such issues, it is sadly far from the only one, and those issues are more pronounced in some of his later words.

THE SCORE: 3 OUT OF 6 TENTACLES, POINT REMOVED FOR BAD POETRY...

MYTHOS CONNECTIONS: Minor, though the first of Lovecraft's tome's, 'Pnakotic Manuscripts', is introduced in this story. One of the manuscripts credited to 'The Great Race' it turns up again several times in later works

LOVECRAFT TWATTRY: Relatively minor racist connotations, but they are clearly there.

SHOULD YOU READ IT: Yes, if you can put the mild racism to one side, and get past the poetry.

BLUFFERS FACT: On his rejected enlistment form Lovecraft was described as 'feeble and given to strange fainting fits when subjected to stress and hardships' (sounds familiar) This apparently was not the stuff that Uncle Sam's finest were made of.

BEYOND THE WALL OF SLEEP

'I have an explanation of sleep come upon me.' – Shakespeare

From the first of the Dreamland mythos in 'Polaris', we move straight on to a second, the much lauded 'Beyond the Walls of Sleep'. It is a story that inspired many, writers, musicians (including 'Black Sabbath') and Hollywood. Though referring to the 2004 movie of the same name as 'inspired' stretches the definition.

Written and published in 1919, in an amateur publication called, of all things, 'Pinecones', Lovecraft claimed the story was partly inspired by an article in the 'New York Tribune' in the April of that year. From that article he took the 'backwards' Catskills population, which his narrator likens to 'white trash in the south'. From that same article he also took the family name of the lunatic featured in the story 'Slater'. Quite what the real 'Slater' family thought of this was never recorded, but we can be certain Lovecraft was sure they would never read his story themselves, considering his opinion that the residents of the Catskill mountains were New England's hillbillies ...

Lovecraft is once more showing his prejudices in this tale, though again he does so through his narrator. It isn't exactly racism; however, it is more an intellectualism which is a more forgivable prejudice. That said, it is clear Lovecraft had opinions on 'the backward and inbred,' descendants of Dutch settlers living in the mountains of New York State in the 1920's. More amusingly, however, his narrator, a man obsessed with trying to understand dreams, also displays his own (and possibly Lovecraft's) prejudices against that other great interpreter of dreams, Sigmund Freud, with the wonderfully dismissive-

'Freud to the contrary with his puerile symbolism.' - Lovecraft

Clearly Lovecraft's narrator has little respect for the Austrian psychotherapist. Which if nothing else establishes that he is a man of opinions...

The narrator, unnamed as so often in Lovecraft's fiction, tells the reader of his time working as an orderly in the state mental institution. It was there he came into contact with a man named Joe Slater. Joe had been incarcerated on the grounds of insanity after committing a string of murders. What interests the narrator about Slater is not so much the crimes but the murderer's state of mind when he committed them. Slater claims to have no recollection of the killings, only of 'awakening', for want of a better word, to find blood, quite literally, on his hands.

Slater's story is a strange one; a member of a remote hillbilly type clan, he has little education and possesses an intellect that is none the worse for it. Except that is when he has his 'episodes'. Occasionally, so it would seem, when he sleeps, he awakens as someone else entirely, and when that 'other' takes charge of the body of Joe Slater there are bloody results. Little wonder then the courts determined he was insane and condemned Slater to an asylum. Our asylum orderly narrator, however, thinks otherwise.

In many ways this story is the reverse of the one told in 'Polaris'. Rather than the sleeper travelling in his dreams to inhabit another, in this case, the 'other' comes to occupy the sleeper and take control of his body. In effect it is a tale of possession, but not by such simplistic tropes as the devil. Lovecraft seldom writes about such prosaic demons. The narrator is also not one for naive concepts like simple insanity explaining Slater's condition. He studies Joe Slater long enough to understand the 'other' personality that possesses him when he sleeps is just that, an 'other'. A conclusion he reaches because he cannot attribute the things the 'other' says and describes to the mind of a backwards backwoodsman like Slater.

A mere orderly though the narrator claims to have been, he is also a scientist, of the slightly barking mad variety. As such he devises a device which allows him to commune with the dreams of others, a way to get a sneak a peek inside the head of Joe Slater. But what he finds in the mind of Slater is not in any way what he expects and his attempts to look into Slater's mind leads to a strange form of communion between the narrator and the 'other' mind, which ultimately leads him to see the universe in quite different terms.

It's at this point the real strength of Lovecraft's writing shines through. That glorious descriptive tone that eats away at you, draws you in and makes you see a universe that is at once strange and yet he manages to make it seem real at the same time. In these passages the impossible becomes reality and 'Beyond the Walls of Sleep' is a minor masterpiece in this regard. Much like 'Dagon', it is the kind of story that Lovecraft excels at. For all his flaws the unworldly is where his writing has its greatest strengths and most disturbing power.

I could explain more of what the narrator discovers when he communes with the 'other'. But unlike some other stories to explain further would detract from the story itself and this is one that needs to be read and experienced within your own imagination. All that said, however, I don't quite love this tale in the way I love 'Dagon'. For me it is weaker, lacks impact, and wanes somewhat towards the end. But many would disagree with me and consider it a triumph.

THE SCORE: 5 OUT OF 6 TENTACLES, DESPITE THE SLIGHT UNFULFILLING ENDING

MYTHOS CONNECTIONS: Minor, there are hints of things to come but nothing solid

LOVECRAFT TWATTRY: A certain distain for the less educated

SHOULD YOU READ IT: Definitely, if only for the latter half of the story

BLUFFERS FACT: Stephen King quotes from 'Beyond the Walls of Sleep' in 'On Writing', his non-fiction guide to the art of the novel. Somewhat obtusely King uses a passage from the tale to demonstrate how 'not' to write dialogue, which was never Lovecraft's strongest suit. However, King does so with genuine affection for both this particular story and Lovecraft's work in general.

MEMORY

There are short stories, and there are shorter stories, and then there are micro stories. 'Memory' is the shortest of all H.P. Lovecraft's tales. In modern terms it is flash fiction, it is also a masterpiece of flash fiction before the term flash fiction had even been conceived as a term. It is among the most beautiful, insightful and chilling bits of writing Lovecraft ever undertook. Written in 1919, it was published in 1923 in 'The National Amateur', it takes up no more than a page, yet manages to convey a terrifying vision of eternity and humanities place within it, in a mere 353 words. The bleak nature of humanity's existence, in a cold, uncaring cosmos, is a constant theme in Lovecraft's work and in 'Memory' he wastes not a single word of those 353 while giving us a truly unsettling context as to our place within that cosmos and eternity itself.

'Memory' is also one of the many works of Lovecraft that is entirely within the public domain. So rather than talk about it, I shall instead urge you to just read it in full. Reading it will not take you long, but if doing so does not send a shiver down your spine... Well, then you probably need to read it again and think upon it for a while.

MEMORY: BY H.P. LOVECRAFT

In the valley of Nis the accursed waning moon shines thinly, tearing a path for its light with feeble horns through the lethal foliage of a great upas-tree. And within the depths of the valley, where the light reaches not, move forms not meet to be beheld. Rank is the herbage on each slope, where evil vines and creeping plants crawl amidst the stones of ruined palaces, twining tightly about broken columns and strange monoliths, and heaving up marble pavements laid by forgotten hands. And in trees that grow gigantic in crumbling courtyards leap little apes, while in and out of deep treasure-vaults writhe poison serpents and scaly things without a name.

Vast are the stones which sleep beneath coverlets of dank moss, and mighty were the walls from which they fell. For all time did their builders erect them, and in sooth they yet serve nobly, for beneath them the grey toad makes his habitation.

At the very bottom of the valley lies the river Than, whose waters are slimy and filled with weeds. From hidden springs it rises, and to subterranean grottoes it flows, so that the Daemon of the Valley knows not why its waters are red, nor whither they are bound.

The Genie that haunts the moonbeams spake to the Daemon of the Valley, saying, "I am old, and forget much. Tell me the deeds and aspect and name of them who built these things of stone." And the Daemon replied, "I am Memory, and am wise in lore of the past, but I too am old. These beings were like the waters of the river Than, not to be understood. Their deeds I recall not, for they were but of the moment. Their aspect I recall dimly, for it was like to that of the little apes in the trees. Their name I recall clearly, for it rhymed with that of the river. These beings of yesterday were called Man."

So the Genie flew back to the thin horned moon, and the Daemon looked intently at a little ape in a tree that grew in a crumbling courtyard.

And that's it, the whole of it, and in my opinion, for whatever it is worth in this cold, uncaring eternity, is that it is a work of near perfection. And oh, oh, so cold... I could say more, but I believe the tale speaks for itself better than I ever could. Indeed, it would seem odd to write more words to describe and critique it than exist within the work itself. It is, however, joyful in its bleak wonder. The universe existed without us, it will exist long after we are gone, and the best we can hope for is that it remembers us, if only fleetingly as a moment of 'Memory' in some demon's mind.

THE SCORE: 6 OUT OF 6 TENTACLES, BECAUSE IT IS A SLICE OF THAT RAREST OF THINGS, PERFECTION.

MYTHOS CONNECTIONS: None.

LOVECRAFT TWATTRY: None.

SHOULD YOU READ IT: You just have, but you should read it again.

BLUFFERS FACT: The cosmos is cold, eternity is long, and the entire span of recorded human history stretches less than 10000 years, we are a blink in the eye of a god we cannot perceive. Sleep well…

OLD BUGS

Lovecraft tells stories of ancient star beings lurking under the oceans. Insect intelligence watching human life from the outer planets. Strange monsters in the darkness waiting only to prey upon those foolish enough to call attention to their fleeting existence. Tales of strange and incomprehensible beings that were here before us and wait only for the stars to be right before they come again from the dark, cold places of the world. Stories that are often chilling, uncanny, occasionally just a little on the weird side, but all with a kind of darkness at their heart, an understanding that, as Lovecraft put it...

"Fear is the strongest and oldest emotion of mankind."

So then, when you come to read a tale by the Old Tentacle Hugger entitled 'Old Bugs', one assumes, quite naturally, that this is a tale about ancient insect intelligences lurking in the dark waiting to consume humanity, or at least, something along those lines...

It may therefore, come as a mildly disappointing to realise that the 'Old Bugs' in the title of this story is an itinerant alcoholic in an imagined version of the 1950's. A man who is earning his poison by doing odd jobs around a particularly disreputable Chicago speakeasy.

Of course, you then might make the understandable leap and expect a twist in the tale. After all there is the question of what drove 'Old Bugs' to the demon drink in the first place, what horror had he witnessed that he needed to drown it in cheap rotgut moonshine... Is that the twist? Did an encounter with some ancient insectoid intelligence from another world drive 'Old Bugs' to the bottle, in a clever play on words? Well, no...

The only thing that drove 'Old Bugs' to drink was, his own low character and lack of moral fortitude, and while there is a tale here, it is a morality tale about the evils of drink, with a twist that is telegraphed early on, and comes as little surprise and doesn't involve ancient insectoid intelligences. The only really interesting thing about this tale is not in the tale itself, but how, and why it was written, which has much to do with Lovecraft's opinion on prohibition.

Old Tentacle Hugger was a lifelong teetotaller who believed firmly in the 18th amendment and the corrupting nature of drink. It was these firm convictions that led to 'Old Bugs' being written after his friend

Alfred Galpin suggested to Lovecraft they try alcohol in the month before the prohibition laws went into effect in January 1920. It was written exclusively for Alfred himself rather than public consumption. The original manuscript contains a note at the end directed at Galpin which simply said, 'Now will you be good?'

That note and the use of both Alfred Galpin, and his fiancée's real name in the story makes Lovecraft's motivation in writing it entirely overt by the end. The question of why Lovecraft was evangelical in his teetotalism and steadfast in his belief in prohibition is more open to conjecture. He was known to declare on numerous occasions:

'I have never tasted intoxicating liquor, and never intend to.'

The truth of this declaration has, however, on occasion been a matter of debate. Some have pointed to his breakdown as a teenager and posited he flirted with drink in that period of his life. Prohibition was very much a central facet of American political life in Lovecraft's formative years even before it came into effect in 1920, and the temperance league were as powerful a lobby in their time as the NRA are now. Lovecraft's home state of Rhode Island was one of only two which opted not to ratify the Prohibition Act, which made it a particularly hot topic in Providence when Howard was coming of age.

'Old Bugs', atypical though the story is, has many Lovecraft's hallmarks. The dispassionate nature of the prose. The unsympathetic nature of his characters. The tinge of distaste for their lives and weaknesses. That he presents the vision of his friend Galpin, projected thirty years in the future, succumbing to the demon drink with some contempt is obvious. Despite all this, the tale hangs together, its preachy moral message (while far from hidden) takes second fiddle to the story itself - for which we should perhaps be thankful. But it has a twist that you can see coming even if you do not know the story behind the story, and while it hangs together well enough, it has little to inspire interest about it.

In the end, 'Old Bugs' is what it is. A morality tale on the evils of drink. Which is fine, if you want to read such a thing, but it isn't what you read Lovecraft for. It's a strange vision of the 1950's - no Thunderbird's, no bright colours and no rock n roll, I suspect Lovecraft would have hated the real fifties, though I am glad we never had to live through his. That aside, it's enjoyable in and of itself, it just lacks the Lovecraft we read his works for.

THE SCORE: 2 OUT OF 6 TENTACLES, WHICH SEEMS GENEROUS NOW I THINK BACK BUT I OPENED A BOTTLE OF RUM WHILE READING THE STORY SO THAT MAY HAVE HELPED THE SCORE

MYTHOS CONNECTIONS: None.

LOVECRAFT TWATTRY: While you could make the argument the whole story is twattry of the first order considering why it was written, there is surprisingly little.

SHOULD YOU READ IT: God no, have a drink instead, I recommend a brightly coloured cocktail.

BLUFFERS FACT: 'Old Bugs' was first published long after Lovecraft's death by 'Arkham House' in 1959. Making it the last of all of Lovecraft's stories to make it to publication apart from a discarded early draft of 'The Shadow Over Innsmouth' that was published in 1994. One could question in both cases why they were published at all.

THE TRANSITION OF JUAN ROMERO

'The Transition of Juan Romero' is a strange fish, like 'Old Bugs' it was first published posthumously by 'Arkham House'. Lovecraft himself disavowed the story, refusing to allow it to be published in his lifetime. Which raises a couple of questions, firstly about the morality of publishing houses choosing to ignore the wishes of a writer, and secondly why Lovecraft disavowed it in the first place. The former is one of those questions that come down to the lure of the greenback winning out over a writer's wishes. The latter is a story all of its own and an insight into Lovecraft's bitchy attitude to some in the amateur press circles he frequented.

'Transition' was written over the course of a single September day in 1919. The sixteenth of September to be exact. We know this because of the reason Lovecraft wrote it in the first place. Old Tentacle Hugger had got into a discussion about what he described as a 'dull yarn' written by a contemporary under the pen name Phil Mac. Phil Mac was actually Prof Philip Bayaud McDonald, whose most notable contribution to literature is the ponderously titled 'A saga of the seas: The story of Cyrus W. Field and the laying of the first Atlantic cable'.

The 'dull yarn' in question was a short story by Mac set in a desert, which is now sadly, or not as the case may be, lost to the world. The only lasting result of this 'dull yarn' was that Lovecraft decided he should show what could be done with a story set in a desert. Thus, he set out to write what became 'The Transition of Juan Romero".

Professor McDonald's story well have been dull, though as it is lost to the ages so it would be an act of conjecture at best to say Lovecraft managed to prove his work was superior.

'The Transition of Juan Romero' is far from a masterpiece, however, which probably explains why when it was written to try and prove himself more capable than another writer it was quickly dismissed by Lovecraft himself. He did send the story to a few friends, after they badgered him to do so, for which we should perhaps be grateful because if he hadn't done so, it is unlikely the story would ever have found the light of day. Most collections of Lovecraft's work do not even bother to include it.

'Luckily' for me, mine does...

Bearing in mind Lovecraft's own assessment of 'The Transition of Juan

Romero' when I sat down to read it my expectations weren't high. I'd never read it previously because of the backstory to its creation. If an author disavows his own work, why bother? But as this is a guide to the 'complete works' of Lovecraft I had to read it and having forced my way through 'Doctor Johnson' it would be remiss to avoid this one. At least 'The Transition of Juan Romero' is more in the right tentacle pit than his ramblings about 17th-century literati, I told myself.

As I've already said, 'The Transition of Juan Romero' is far from Lovecraft at his best, but as it turns out it's also far from his worst. Its narrator tells us the tale of his time as a miner in the mid-west. He is an Englishman who had spent time in India before coming to the States, and he has a lurking past of some description. Lovecraft manages to make him a little on the mysterious side, though this seems more forced than usual, as does the MacGuffin Lovecraft employs of a Hindu ring that the narrator brought with him from India.

Juan Romero himself is described as of Incan descent, again this comes across as a bit clumsy in the way it's written. The plot involves a bottomless abyss discovered in the middle of a gold mine and a thunderous night when the narrator's ring begins to glow. Strange chanting in the darkness, coyotes howling in the night and mysterious voices on the wind all of which combine to draw the narrator and his Incan friend down into the depths of the mine. This is a story chock full of atmosphere, because Lovecraft threw atmosphere at it in every way he could, if anything it feels like he is trying too hard. The biggest fault with the whole story is the sudden rush towards an ending that uses the oldest of old tropes. The narrator wakes up in the cold light of morning to find the world has more or less reset itself. Except, that is, for poor Juan Romero, who has died, without a mark on his body, the narrator's ring having disappeared.

And that's the story...

But here's the thing, trope-ridden though it is and a grasping hack job of a read, this ultimately is a first, and only draft. It's a story Lovecraft threw together in a single day, chucked in a cupboard and forgot about. As a writer, if my own first drafts turn out half this good then I'd be a happy man - and I have all the advantages of a word processor in front of me. The story needs a second draft, a few bits of it need scrapping, others need working on and it needs a stronger ending, but if Lovecraft wanted this story out there in the world he would have done all that. In the end, this may not be as good as you expect a Lovecraft short story to be, but it is still worth the ink on the page, though I would not suggest this to anyone as their first Lovecraft story unless I did not want them to read any more.

THE SCORE: 2 OUT OF 6 TENTACLES, WHICH MAY BE GENEROUS, BUT WHEN I SAT DOWN TO READ IT THE FIRST TIME I EXPECTED IT TO BE LUCKY TO SCRAPE A SINGLE ONE, BUT HELL ITS BETTER THAN I EXPECTED, ALL BE IT NOT BY MUCH AND KNOWING THAT IT WAS NEVER MEANT TO BE OUT IN THE WORLD, I FEEL LOVECRAFT IS OWED A LITTLE LEEWAY WITH THIS FORGOTTEN CHILD.

MYTHOS CONNECTIONS: None.

LOVECRAFT TWATTRY: Lovecraft uses the archaic spelling Hindoo, a spelling which is latterly considered derogatory. In Lovecraft's defence spelling Hindu this way was much more widespread in 1919, and for once is perhaps not attributable to his unfortunate opinions.

SHOULD YOU READ IT: Probably not, unless first drafts interest you, but for writers it's an interesting window into an early draft.

BLUFFERS FACT: Huitzilopochtli, a Mesoamerican deity associated with human sacrifice, is mentioned, suggesting the events may have involved a sacrificial ritual.

THE WHITE SHIP

Mankind seeks utopia but upon finding that utopia, mankind fails to recognise it for what it is and seeks something else instead, leading to that utopia's destruction.

Lovecraft's 'The White Ship' is often presented as an allegory for the human condition. That may not have been his intent when it was written and published in 1919 but it certainly works as one. This somewhat goes against an oddly popular opinion I've both read and been told (presumably by people who have read the same commentaries and repeated them verbatim) that Lovecraft's writing takes the humanity out of everything. This is a remarkably common complaint about his fiction but one which I suspect is often as not reiterated by people who'll go on to admit to having read little of his work. In my own view, if the oft repeated myth of Lovecraft's lack of humanity were true then the 'The White Ship' and the allegory at its heart would never have been written, for in essence it is the most human of all stories.

Basil Eaton is a lighthouse keeper who stands vigil on a lonely shore. Year in year out he watches the ships sail past. Eaton is a third-generation lighthouse keeper, which suggests that the shore has not always been as lonely as he would have us believe. As he stands his lonely vigil, watching the tall ships pass by in declining numbers each year, it is perhaps no surprise he dreams of something more, and that those distant exotic shores the ships visit speak to him, offering him their wonders.

Then late one night 'The White Ship' comes, and its bearded master beckons the lighthouse keeper to join him aboard his craft. Basil does just that, leaving the lonely shore and the lighthouse behind, as the ship sails off to other lands. Lands that do not exist in any real world, lands with strange names and their stranger inhabitants.

Upon 'The White Ship', Eaton sails past many lands, strange places with names like Zar, a green and remarkably pleasant seeming land where '"dwell all the dreams and thoughts of beauty that come to men once and then are forgotten', Thalarion, a city of a thousand wonders, and an unfortunately equal number of demons, Xura, the land of 'Pleasures Unattained' which viewed from a distance seems nice enough, but reeks of death and plague as they sail close to its shores. Each of these places, Eaton is warned by the bearded captain, are lands 'From which those that enter them, never return.' Each of them could also be translated to some portion of the human id. Which is often posited as Lovecraft's intent. Though they also seem as much to be ideas of the different dooms that could befall a man, as of states of mind.

'The White Ship's' course follows the flight of a blue 'celestial bird', which adds to the eeriness and dreamlike quality of the journey. Then finally, as they travel westward they come upon Sona-Nyl, the 'Land of Fancy'. Sona-Nyl is also a perfect society, a utopia where 'The White Ship' and its passengers stay for 'many aeons', living lives that are full of joy and wonderment. 'Land of Fancy' may seem an odd name for a utopia, but the connotation is that it is a land where you have what you need, rather than what you lust for in Xura, grasp for in Zar, or search for in Thalarion or any of the other cities 'The White Ship' passed by. In the 'Land of Fancy', you can be whimsical, for the land has all you truly need…

But, and here is the human failing behind this tale, what you truly need is never truly enough. In time, in this happy utopia, Eaton learns of Cathuria, the 'Land of Hope'. A land that is more perfect still, where the grass is no doubt greener. Lovecraft's message in this story is that no matter how perfect things may become, man will always long for more. So, even in utopia, Eaton is haunted by his desires. Eventually, he convinces the bearded captain to take to 'The White Ship' out once more and sail on westward, following once more the 'celestial bird'. And so, they sail on through storm-dashed seas, until the ages they spent in utopia are nothing but a distant memory. In search of Cathuria the 'land of hope'. And in the end the ship takes them to the very edge of the world, and plummets to its doom. As it was always apt to do, chasing the ego of men.

Of course, this is a Dreamlands tale, and like all such tales, the twist is Basil Eaton wakes at the end. Yet, as is also often the way of such tales, he finds himself not in his bed but on storm-lashed rocks next to his lighthouse. A lighthouse with no light, as its keeper has forgotten to tend it, and upon the rocks there is a great wreck. Then in a final twist, in the morning nothing remains. Except, that is the corpse of that same 'celestial bird' which 'The White Ship' followed ever westward, and a single broken wooden spar. White, of course.

To sum up, 'The White Ship' ends with a typical, 'it was all a dream, or was it' ending. Yet the tale is better than that. It is the journey, the imagery and the analogy behind it that make this such an interesting work. It has something of a parable about it, and for me at least is one of Lovecraft's most human stories. A tale about the soul of what it is to be human and the quest for utopia that can never be satisfied, even when it is achieved. Of course, that's just my interpretation, there are many others for this particular story.

THE SCORE: 5 OUT OF 6 OF THE OLD KRAKEN SUCKERS. BUT THEN I AM A BIT OF A SUCKER FOR THIS KIND OF TALE...

MYTHOS CONNECTIONS: None.

LOVECRAFT TWATTRY: None.

SHOULD YOU READ IT: It has an eerie beauty, and a depth beyond the tale itself, so yes, you should.

BLUFFERS FACT: Some contend Lovecraft's choice of vessel was inspired by the infamous real ship that bore that name. That vessel, 'The White Ship', has the distinction of causing more death, destruction and war than any other vessel in history. It sunk with all hands, save a lone survivor, while crossing the English Channel. Aboard the ship at the time was the heir apparent to the English throne in 1120. Its fate brought about a period of brutal civil war in England known as 'The Anarchy'. British folklore would have it that seeing 'The White Ship' abroad in the channel at night is an omen of the worst kind. But while that's all a nice idea, the prosaic truth is its more likely he just thought the name sounded eerie and fitted into the supernatural nature of his tale.

THE STREET

This story always leaves me a little uneasy, and not for the good reasons a Lovecraft story will sometimes leave you such. This was not an unease at considering humankind's place in the cosmos. Nor was it an unease about what the shadows of my room might hold, that itch at the back of your mind after being drawn into a tale. This was another form of unease.

'The Street' is the story of a street, so bonus points for the title telling you exactly what to expect. It is told from the perspective of a timeless observer, which may well be the street itself, and follows the streets beginnings as a few rude huts occupied by first European settlers, right up to Lovecraft's present. It also manages to be the story of the rise of the United States from the humble beginnings of small British colonies. The story incorporates the wars of independence, the civil war, right up to men going off to fight the first World War. But mostly it tells how the nature of the street and its inhabitants changed over time. While it is never mentioned directly, it is safe to assume 'The Street' is part of a New England city. There is a consensus among Lovecraft's fans that the city in question is Boston, as Lovecraft took some inspiration for the story from the Boston police strike of 1919, just after which Lovecraft wrote the story.

To a degree, my problems with this story really begin towards the end. By the time the story gets to Lovecraft's present, 'The Street' has gone from being the fashionable heart of the city, to a down at heel part of town in decline. Dilapidated buildings with cheap rents have made 'The Street' the haunt of immigrant families, clustered in small communities. Accents no longer native to the city are heard in the street. Strange religions and political ideas that seem alien to the street become prevalent from the standpoint of the timeless narrator. The story twists into something xenophobic, in all the worst ways.

'They went in pairs, determined-looking and khaki-clad, as if symbols of the strife that lies ahead in civilisation's struggle with the monster of unrest and bolshevism.'

The above quote is not from 'The Street' itself but from a letter Lovecraft wrote to the fellow author and early collaborator Frank Belknap Long while he was writing the story. He was talking of the national guardsmen drafted in to keep the peace during in the Boston police strike. It is the latter part of the quote that is the most relevant. This was 1919, two years after the October revolution redefined Russia politically. Fear of the 'Red Menace' was rife in the American body politic, as it remained up to and throughout the Second World War and Cold War. This informed the latter half of 'The Street', but it's not the anti-communist stance as much as the xenophobia Lovecraft expresses that stands out as he projects the distrust of the 'red menace' on to the poor Russian immigrants who now inhabit the street.

And that, right there, is an irony that bypassed Lovecraft, much as its echoes by-pass too many people today. The Russian immigrants in Boston in 1919 were mostly, if not entirely, refugees from the October Revolution. People fleeing the same red menace which the story accuses them of being. If these Russians were Bolsheviks, they would not have fled Russia, after all, the Bolsheviks had won. While the USA did have communist agitators at the time, they were homegrown Marxists, not Russian immigrants. Russian immigrants were the ones who had taken the brunt of political upheavals in their motherland. What they sought in the USA was peace, work and a chance to rebuild their lives. In the 'The Street', however, Lovecraft has Russians planning a new revolution to bring down the United States from within. They fall foul of the street itself for the street has become entwined with the souls of all who have dwelt there from its humble beginnings, and has taken on their nature, their independence and the fighting American spirit of pride and patriotism. So, when the nation is threatened by these evil Bolsheviks, it rises up to defend its people, its nation, and collapses itself upon the Russians plotting in its cellars, killing them all. Which answers a question posed early in the narrative, can places and things have souls? Clearly, in the case of Lovecraft's street, they can and do, and it is the soul of, to Lovecraft's mind, a 'patriot...'

Fear of the unknown is often at the very heart of Lovecraft's fiction. Fear of unknown things in the darkness, like the beast in his earliest published story. Fear of alien intelligences watching us from out in the cosmos, fear of strange cults, ancient evils, strange ruins, and rats crawling in the walls. Xenophobia, however, is one fear his fiction could do without. Unfortunately, xenophobia is something very much part of Lovecraft's phycological make up, so it is no great surprise it surfaces in his stories - and it is that xenophobia which makes this an uneasy read. That aside the story is otherwise well worth a read, it is an interesting idea and an excellent exploration of the growth of a nation, but the final message within it is one humanity would do well to grow beyond, in my opinion at least.

THE SCORE: 2 OUT OF 6 LATTERLY UNCOMFORTABLE TENTACLES

MYTHOS CONNECTIONS: None.

LOVECRAFT TWATTRY: Xenophobia and racism run rampant.

SHOULD YOU READ IT: NO… Well, for the concept of a place with a soul witnessing its growth over the centuries perhaps, but otherwise no.

BLUFFERS FACT: Ironically, when the Boston police first threatened to strike, they were accused of being Bolsheviks by the Boston newspapers.

THE DOOM THAT CAME TO SARNATH

Thirteen is an ominous number. 'The Doom that came to Sarnath' is the thirteenth of Lovecraft's published works. This is perhaps appropriate for more reasons than one, as the story is about an impending doom befalling a city and is a tale of dark omens. It is also the real beginning of Lovecraft's Mythos stories in a way none of the previous ones are. A varied bunch those earlier stories may have been, but from here on in things get stranger. To have a Mythos, you need a Mythology to build it on and mythologies require myths, the story of Sarnath is Lovecraft's first great piece of myth writing.

Mythologies always have a few things in common, other that is, than the urban kind. They always refer to events that happened a long time ago, before written histories. They happened in some idealised other place, often now beyond reach. And they happened to earlier half remembered versions of the culture whose myths they are. 'The Doom that came to Sarnath' ticks all those boxes and is told as myths are told, in hints and partly remembered truths.

There is another thing that myths have in common, in that they are referenced throughout our culture. Just as a writer may make mention of Icarus to illustrate a character pushing his luck beyond the bounds of the expedient, or some witty cad might say of a popstar that she has 'a face that launched a thousand tweets...' or hiding their intentions may be accused of acting as a Trojan horse. Refencing a myth is so commonplace we often don't even notice we are doing it. Even in this modern age, the roots of mythology run deep.

Lovecraft was aware of this back in 1920 when he wrote 'The Doom that came to Sarnath', as it is at heart the beginnings of a fictional mythology with which to frame his stories. Unlike the earlier stories this tale is referenced repeatedly in his later work. Mentions of Sarnath and its occupants crop up directly in 'At the Mountains of Madness', 'The Nameless City', and 'The Quest of Iranon'. But more importantly the story also introduces the idea of the 'Old Ones' and 'Old Gods' which run as a common thread through so many later tales.

In short, it is the first tale that starts to tie Lovecraft's stories into a greater whole. Lovecraft, from here on in goes beyond simply telling isolated tales and starts what we would latterly call world building, or perhaps in his case would be more exactly called cosmos-building. Pre-1920 his stories are a loose collection of mostly unrelated creepy tales and while plenty of his stories post-'The Doom that came to Sarnath' still fit within that description, from here on in you can start to feel that behind it all Lovecraft has a bigger story to tell, a greater 'truth' for want of a better word. Mankind is not merely adrift in the uncaring cosmos, he is not alone, there are other things out there, and some of them are hungry...

The story sets itself somewhere in prehistory, long before the rise of Egypt, Sumerian and Babylon, near the very dawn of human civilisation. A time when, according to this story, we still shared the world with the last vestiges of the older races. Like all good myth, it makes no attempt to actually set itself in time, except in the vaguest of ways 'more than 10000 years ago...'

A race of men who will become known as the Mnar, but are still little more than wandering tribes, begin to found cities along the fertile river Ai, but some few travel further, craving fresh land and founding a final city on the shores of an isolated lake. Further around the shores of this lake lies a city of strange folk, folk that are not human in any way we would recognise. The men of Mnar do not take kindly to these others. They find their aspect unpleasing, which is a wonderful euphemism. In fact, the residents of this city are proto-deep ones, left behind by mankind's ascent to dominance. The city is named Id, its populous strange mist-dwelling humanoids with faces that are just a little 'fishy', who worship a giant lizard god called Bokrug, whose idol sits in the centre of their greatest temple. The men of Mnar unite in a common cause, killing the denizens of Id and stealing the idol. Then they make a point of celebrating this 'cleansing' every year afterwards with a huge festival. Presumably because when you've committed a genocide that's just what you do... At the first of these festivals, however, their high priest is struck with a strange affliction, writes the word 'DOOM' on the pedestal where sits the stolen idol of Bokrug, which then disappears, after which he dies.

As this is the recounting of a myth, we are then treated to a thousand years of the ascent of Sarnath which in time becomes the greatest of cities. This rise is written rich with description and a certain mythic foreboding. The rise to power is followed by a slow descent into decadence and as time passes only the priests remember that forewarning of 'DOOM'. Time passes and the many cities of the Mnar all pay homage to Sarnath, greatest of cities. So, in time men from all over the known world come for the festival of 'the raising of Id'.

And then… On the thousandth anniversary of the genocide, on the night when the festivities reach their height, a great mist comes up from the lake and engulfs the city of Sarnath, and there are things in the mist, things which want vengeance. The long foretold 'DOOM' had arrived…

This is, it has to be said, good myth. More importantly, it's good Lovecraft Myth. It sets up so many other tales and so many concepts that Lovecraft refers back to time and again in later stories. Without 'The Doom that Came to Sarnath' or something like it, it is hard to imagine where the wider mythos would have come from. It is the rock upon which the foundations of Lovecraft's cosmos are based. It's difficult to stress how important this story is to the mythos. It is the first of the rock on which Lovecraft built such tales as 'At the Mountains of Madness', 'Call of Cthulhu' and the rest. With it he established the 'Old Ones' - a nonhuman civilisation that pre-date humanity. The 'Old Gods' lurking in the darkness.

But the final twist is right at the end when he puts in modern man, examining the ruins of the past, and seeds the idea that there are some things best left undisturbed. Things that foolish and inquisitive men will someday awaken. It is a story that signifies all that is to come, that 'the stars will be right' someday and that which sleeps will awaken…

THE SCORE: 6 OUT OF 6 MYTHOLOGICAL KRAKENS TENTACLES REACHING OUT FROM THE DARKNESS

MYTHOS CONNECTIONS: Effectively the founding stone upon which all else is built

LOVECRAFT TWATTRY: None, unless you count mythological genocides

SHOULD YOU READ IT: Yes, preferably out loud in the voice of Russell Crowe

BLUFFERS FACT: Mike Mignola's 'Batman: The Doom That Came to Gotham' which combines Batman's world with various elements of the Cthulhu mythos, takes its name from 'The Doom that came to Sarnath'.

THE STATEMENT OF RANDOLPH CARTER

'The Statement of Randolph Carter' is a tale that leaves you with no more than a half-hearted um... because it is simple and straightforward and doesn't have any real depth to it. A run of the mill tale that never quite steps beyond itself. So, if it leaves you with anything, it's a mild sense of disappointment, a vague feeling it could have been something more than what it is (though at no point does it try all that hard to be so).

This is not to say there is anything wrong with it but it's a workaday pulp magazine story at best. The kind of story that could have some from any of the dozens of writers who were contributing to the east coast amateur press magazines at the same time as Lovecraft. Unlike Lovecraft the majority of those other writers are long forgotten. Unless someone delves through the archives of a collector it's unlikely their stories will ever be read again, because no one is doing reprints of authors no one remembers.

If this seems an overly harsh criticism, that's because it is. The problem is not the story. it's a rather neat little story, featuring a rather neat idea, that may well have been entirely original at the time.

The problem is that the story is being read by me and my 21st-century eyes. Jaded eyes that have read and seen too many stories that are just the same as this one.

So, let's take a step back and consider this story a moment or two with less jaded eyes. Let us consider the main element of this tale which is a witness statement from Randolph Carter recounting what he heard as he listened to all the really interesting stuff in this story happening to his friend on the other end of a telephone line. A portable field telephone line of a type which was used in the trenches in World War One. It's a technology which, while familiar to Lovecraft's readers in 1920, was still something rare and strange that they would not often have come across. Therefore, the idea of Randolph having listened to his friend fight for their life against some nameless horror at the other end of the wire would, to those readers, be a wild concept.

In the story, Randolph Carter is an antiquarian and one-time student of Miskatonic University. Randolph is a recurring character and in this, the first tale involving the character, he is the nice but somewhat dim sidekick, left outside at the mausoleum doors, watching the steps that lead down into the catacombs, talking to his compatriot Harley Warren down the field telephone as the other man wanders deeper and deeper into the unknown, trailing out the phone cable behind him. The character of Carter comes back in five later stories and goes through some changes in the later ones, but in this early tale he is in shock, recounting his story to the police who suspect him of murdering Warren or being otherwise involved in his disappearance. His tale is stuttering and disjointed but is ultimately the survivors' tale of a horror witnessed down a telephone line as the person on the other end is lost to some unknown terror that remains off stage.

It's a plot we have all seen a hundred times. It's the mid-season episode of every crime show that is just ticking over. It's a 'B' movie filler plot point. In fact, it's not a major stretch from the opening ten minutes of the movie Scream. In short, it's unoriginal at best, a cliché.

In the same way as every found footage movie is just a reiteration of 'The Blair Witch Project', whereas what made 'The Blair Witch Project' new and exciting when it was first released was that it was original. Yet to the next generation it is just another found footage movie…

And there is the crux of that half-hearted 'um'. 'The Statements of Randolph Carter' was, when it was written, an original idea. Now, however, to my modern readers eyes it's an idea that has been copied so many times it's the least original story I could imagine. It's difficult to separated how unoriginal it seems now, a hundred years after it was written, from how inventive and fresh it must have seemed at the time. Had I been writing this guide then, it would have scored much higher no doubt, but as its unlikely you're reading this in 1920's, unless a copy of this guide fell through a wormhole in the space time continuum to the 1800's and a rather dust moth-eaten copy surfaced in a secondhand bookshop, the score is reflective of my jaded 2020's eyes.

THE SCORE: 2 OUT OF 6 CREEPING TENTACLES IN THE DARKNESS OF THE CRYPT, BEGETTING THE DAYS WHEN THERE WERE SIX OF THEM AND THEY WERE FRESH AND NEW

MYTHOS CONNECTIONS: The first incarnation of Randolph Carter, of whom there is much to come.

LOVECRAFT TWATTRY: None

SHOULD YOU READ IT: Probably give it a miss, unless you have never indulged in 21st century culture

BLUFFERS FACT: The character of Randolph Carter is generally accepted as Lovecraft's alter ego. Carter shares many of Lovecraft's personal traits: He is an uncelebrated author, whose writings are seldom noticed. A melancholy figure, Carter is a quiet contemplative dreamer with a sensitive disposition, prone to fainting during times of emotional stress.

THE TERRIBLE OLD MAN

Among other things, I am a bit of an aficionado of the 'Future Shock'. For those that have never heard of them, they are short one-off stories in the British comic 2000AD, generally written by new, up and coming writers looking for their first break into comics. Luminaries of the craft like Neil Gaiman, Alan Moore and Grant Morrison all started there. Often, the strips themselves stay just that, as short one-shots. Sometimes though one of these short stories will become a springboard for characters and ideas that morph into long-running series. Perhaps the finest and most famous example of this is 'Comic Rocks-Terror Tube' which spawned 'Nemesis the Warlock'. Despite the actual character Nemesis not actually appearing in the original one-shot, except as the unseen driver of the 'Blitzspear'. While that was an atypical 'Future Shock' as it did not follow the standard formula, it is an excellent example of a bigger story coming out of something small. Of which the same can be said for Lovecraft's 'The Terrible Old Man'. A tale which follows the same simple formula as the average Future Shock. A simple formula that has been around forever.

The formula is to set the scene, introduce your protagonists and some form of goal, be it survival or revenge or whatever, then let the scene follow an expected course before a twist in the end.

To give an example from the pages of 2000AD: there is a rampaging horde of star barbarians on an endless righteous crusade of pillage and slaughter across the stars. They do this for generation after generation. Then millennia later the great star horde, who have long forgotten the purpose of the crusade, attack yet another planet in a backwater star system. This is the most peaceful heavenly place they have ever encountered and of course they shatter that world, wiping out the saintly inheritance. Only then do they discover the planet is their own home world, and its people their own who have over the generations found peace with their barbaric nature. The nature of universe is it seems curved. Travel far enough you always end up back home...

Protagonists Scene Goal Twist....

'The Terrible Old Man' follows the same formula. The protagonists are a gang of housebreakers staking out an old house on the outskirts of a small New-England village. They plan to break into the house of an old man who is shunned by the other village folk. It seems like easy pickings. There are some weird sounding stories about the old man, but the burglars are...

'of that new and heterogeneous alien stock which lies outside the charmed circle of New England life and traditions.'

As such they are not men to put much stock in village rumours, besides they are a rough lot used to taking care of themselves when the need arises.

You may detect a little of Lovecraft's habitual xenophobia in that description of the burglars, you're not the first to do so. The robbers are named Angelo Ricci, Joe Czanek and Manuel Silva. Names which point to them being new immigrants of Eastern European, or Italian stock, rather than New England Anglo Saxon/Dutch.

The three robbers' plan is for one to wait outside while the other two go in and 'interview' the old man about the treasure he is reputed by the villages to horde in his old house. So, there we have the setup, three thieves set to rob and threaten a helpless old man. Two go in the house and what happens to them in the house happens off stage while the third waits for their return with the engine running.

Protagonists, scene, goal...

And then the twist - the old man is not helpless, but a practitioner of dark arts. He appears in the doorway, eyes glowing yellow and all hell comes with him. The bodies of his would-be robbers are found the next day, miles away, mutilated and very, very dead...

It's a short story, following a formula of short stories and doing so in almost as few words as I have used to talk about it. It's not particularly notable or original in that. Foolish robbers discovering to their cost that a mark is not as easy or defenceless as they believe. It's more or less the plot of 'Home Alone' only with dark magic and slightly less vindictiveness from the 'victim' in the house...

What is notable, and the reason I talked about future shocks in the first place, is like 'Terror Tube' what comes in this story's wake. The small New-England village is called Kingsport and this appears in later stories as a somewhat larger town. It's visited by Nyarlathotep in 'The Dream-Quest of Unknown Kadath', Randolph Carter in 'The Silver Key', mentioned in Lovecraft's only full-length novel 'The Case of Charles Dexter Ward' and four other tales as well. The 'Terrible Old Man' himself reappears in 'The Strange High House in the Mist' though in that story he is far more a benevolent figure. So, while this story is formulaic and somewhat uninspired, what it leads to is something more.

THE SCORE: 3 OUT OF 6 TENTACLES, ALTHOUGH FAIRLY UN-REMARKABLE ONES.

MYTHOS CONNECTIONS: Both the setting of Kingsport and the 'terrible Old man' feature in future tales.

LOVECRAFT TWATTRY: Xenophobia, if only in passing.

SHOULD YOU READ IT: Maybe, if only as an example of the classic short story form.

BLUFFERS FACT: Providence Rhode Island these days has among many other things a large LGBTQ population and was recently given the title 'Best Lesbian Places to Live' It also had the first openly gay mayor of any state capital. I can't help wondering what a staunch old Republican like H.P. would have made of that, I suspect he would not have been pleased, and shame on him for that... Then again, he may have had a different reaction, due other factors, but we will come to them later, so moving on…

THE CATS OF ULTHAR

Cats have always walked between worlds, the real world and the mystical, the mortal and the spiritual, the land of the living and the land of the dead... Least ways this is a recurring theme through the mythologies of the ancient world. Bast, or Bastet, the Egyptian cat goddess is perhaps the most well-known, but she is far from alone. Humanity has always had an odd cultural relationship with the feline. Unlike their canine equivalents, cats are more house guests than pets. No one ever trained a cat to hunt alongside them, or to guard their homes, and the chances of the cat fetching your newspaper is minimal at best. Lovecraft was also a lover of cats, proving that everyone has some redeeming features to their personality.

'The Cats of Ulthar', perhaps inspired by his love of cats, is Lovecraft writing his own folklore, in much the same way as 'The Doom that came to Sarnath' was written as mythology. This is not, perhaps unsurprising given it is Lovecraft, folklore of the fairy-tale variety, at least, not the modern kind. It's folklore reminiscent of the dark roots behind the sanitised modern versions of fairy tales. Folklore of the type collected by the brothers Grimm from the backwoods of Germany in the early 1800s. Those original Grimm fairy tales were bloodier affairs, the 'happily ever afters' we are all so used to didn't feature heavily in them. In their 'Snow White', the queen died by being made to dance in red-hot iron shoes. The original 'Sleeping Beauty' is repeatably raped by the prince and is awakened not by true love's kiss but when one of the children she has borne the prince sucks the spinning wheel splinter from her hand. And the less said about 'Red Riding Hood' the better... Yet those are among the more pleasant examples. For 'the Cats of Ulthar', Lovecraft takes his cues from those original tales rather than the children's stories they became. 'Ulthar' is a piece of dark woods folklore, and yet somehow it has a charm all of its own.

While this Lovecraft tale was undoubtedly inspired by folklore, it was also inspired by Irish writer Lord Dunsany. Lovecraft was a Dunsany fanboy and 'The Cats of Ulthar' is written very much in imitation of the Irish writer's style.

The story is set in the village of Ulthar, a place where no one harms a cat, and certainly no one would ever be so foolish as to kill one. Because of this the village is something of a haven for felines, or to put it another way, overrun with the furballs. This amiability towards felines is not from a communal love of cats, however, but stems from bloody events in the village's past. Just like all good folklore, it all comes back to blood at some point.

The villains of the piece are an old couple with evil habits, who take a certain glee in tormenting and killing their neighbour's pets. The villagers know of the old couples vile habits, but they also fear them, for they have a dark nature, so dare not act against them. Instead, the villagers learn to keep their animals away from the old couple and their cottage. And so time, as it is known to do, passes.

Then one day a group of travellers pass through the village. Among these travellers is a simple-seeming, young orphan boy beloved of the people. He, however, speaks little and only to a small black kitten, which is his constant companion. Not knowing to avoid the old couple, the young boy is tempted over to their cottage with his kitten, and events take a predictable turn. The young boy has some power and unleashes a curse upon the old couple. Once the caravan leaves, the villages notice all their cats disappear for a time. And then, well the shedding of blood leads to more shedding of blood in a grisly and feline fashion.

It is far from a particularly complex tale, but folklore is seldom very complex, at least at first view. Lovecraft understood that about folklore, in much the way he understood how to write mythology. Folklore may seem simple at the outset, but it needs a darkness to it, a layer of shadow, of suggestion and possibility. 'The Cats of Ulthar' is a masterclass in how to write a dark fairy-tale. It also has a touch of morality to it, just to give it strength - bad things happen to the bad people. The guilty pay for their actions. While others live with the consequences. No one harms a cat in Ulthar, because should they ever be tempted to do so, they have only to look towards the ruin of the vile old couple's cottage on the edge of the village, and remember what little remains were found within…

Of all his own stories this was one of Lovecraft's favourites. I must admit to having much fondness for it myself, but then I have a fondness for dark folktales, cats and the odd whisper of blood in the wind.

THE SCORE: A FULL SET OF 6 TENTACLES, AS IN MY OPINION THIS IS ALMOST FLAWLESS AND QUITE WONDERFUL

MYTHOS CONNECTIONS: Ulthar and its feline problems are mentioned in passing in several other stories

LOVECRAFT TWATTRY: None, unless you're not a cat person, in which case, well cats....

SHOULD YOU READ IT: Yes, you should put this book down and read it now in fact and be nice to cats.

BLUFFERS FACT: Of all Lovecraft's tales this one is, in the opinion of most readers, the most Dunsian, but it is far from the only one inspired by the writings of Lord Dunsey, (whose real name was Edward Plunkett). There are elements of Lord Dunsey in most of Lovecraft's Dreamlands tales.

THE TREE

Some stories chime with my inner soul. They cut to the quick and speak to me in ways others never can. There are stories of Lovecraft's I like, there are stories that leave me ambivalent, there are stories I merely appreciate and there are those I hate. He is not unique in this; I feel this way about many writers. Occasionally, however, there are some stories that go beyond me just plain liking them, a story that cuts past all the rest. One that stays with me and wanders back across my mind days, weeks, or even years later. Stories I'll go back to again and again, be it the grand epic that is Stephens Kings 'Dark Tower' or smaller but perfect novels like Tolkien's 'The Hobbit' or Neil Gaiman's 'Neverwhere'. And sometimes it's just a short story that echoes within me and says something that, to me at least, is true - or at least a truth of a kind. Lovecraft's 'The Tree' is one of those stories that does it for me every time…

It is far from his most famous work, far from the strangest, it's arguably far from the best written. It's a tale that is frankly a little prosaic, and it certainly isn't horror, though it contains a few elements of horror in its makeup. It certainly lacks the eldritch grotesquery of some Lovecraft tales or the unsettling quality of others. It is actually nothing more than a study in human nature, human subtext, and the power of a lie, of concealing a truth even in its climax, that twists the context of the story in on itself. Indeed, the most powerful thing about how this story is told is just that, it is a lie, told to us by a narrator who does not understand the falsehood in his words. And because of this the reader has to come to their own revelation at the end of the tale. If someone reads this story and takes everything told to them at nothing but face value, then the ending doesn't even make sense. In short, it is a clever little tale that demands its readers are reading with their intellect engaged. Which is one of the reasons I hold it in such high regard.

'The Tree' is not unique in this, lots of fiction requires its readers to think about what they are reading and consider the subtext. But few writers, and still fewer tales, ever do this with the eloquence and somewhat contemptuous calculation that Lovecraft does with this story. It is, in that, a rare gem indeed. Demanding a cynicism of its reader, or perhaps just exploiting the cynic within them.

With the story, Lovecraft takes us back to ancient Greece and tells us, through his narrator, the story of two friends, Kalos and Musides. They are both masters of the art of sculpture, who though wildly different in personality and tastes, share a common bond. Both are lauded by all, and such is their friendship that neither would claim mastery of the other. They even share a home, and each calls the other brother.

Then, it comes to pass, that the Tyrant of Syracuse challenges Kalos and Musides to compete in the creation of "a wonder of nations and a goal of travellers". The tyrant's reasoning is simple enough; with two masters each strive against the other to create the greater work they cannot fail to produce masterpieces to grace his city. Which is indeed what they do.

The narrator tells us, however, that there are none of the usual traits of rivalry between them and their friendship remains as strong as ever. But even as they both strive to create the finest work, Kalos fall ill with a beguiling wasting sickness much, we are told, to the dismay of Musides who nurses him throughout his long illness, indeed will let no other doctor to his friend.

Kalos wastes away to the strange affliction and dies in time. His last request to his friend is to be buried in the garden of the house they have shared so long, with simple olive twigs near his head. Musides wants instead to make him an elaborate tomb, in part to ease his grief, we are told. But Musides follows his friend's wishes and Kalos is buried with the olive twigs in their garden. Then over time, a tree begins to grow above Kalos's grave. A strange and far from a normal tree.

We are told throughout the story of the great love between the two men, of how Musides becomes morose and strangely tempered as his friend wastes away. After his friend dies, Musides pours all his energy into in sculpture, determined to create his masterpiece, he claims, for the memory of his friend. He is, however, a changed man, of dark humours and has a great anger within him. Meanwhile, the strange tree grows as he works and that tree has an odd sinister aspect to its nature, that seems to scare Musides, though none can fathom why. The branches of that strange tree that grew from the grave of Kalos do seem to be ever reaching close to his studio though, ever closer as the end of the tale draws closer...

And that there is where the lie the narrator is telling us sits in plain sight, yet it remains hidden and dismissed throughout the tale. Which is why I love it so much. but I'll not spoil the lie by telling the truth of it here. It's a tale that needs to be read to be appreciated, in my opinion. Ironically, Lovecraft did not share my appreciation for this tale.

"If typed on good stock make excellent shelf-paper, but little else."

But then it is a tale which owes as much to its reader as its writer. It speaks to the cynic in me. Which make it fitting as it is set in ancient Greece... I cannot say whether you will enjoy it in the way I do (or love it as much as I do, in the case of this story) it is, as ever, all down to the reader's view of the world.

THE SCORE: A FULL SET OF 6 TENTACLES, THE FULL SQUID IN FACT... FOR ME IF NO ONE ELSE.

MYTHOS CONNECTIONS: None

LOVECRAFT TWATTRY: None

SHOULD YOU READ IT: Yes, though I cannot promise you will find it as wonderful as I

BLUFFERS FACT: The end of the story recalls the Latin aphorism that precedes the text: *Fata Viam Invenient,* 'fate will find a way'.

CELEPHAIS

As I explained in the introduction, this book came to be because of a challenge I set myself back in 2017 to read the complete works of H.P.Lovecraft and blog my thoughts and insights about each story in the order they were written. The plan was to do the whole series of blogs in a year. It took four. There were a lot of reasons it took four years to do the whole series, one of which was 'Celephais'.

I finished 'The Tree' and hit a wall because I knew 'Celephais' was the next story. It was a story I knew I had tried to read in the past and never gotten past a couple of pages, so I was a little lacking for enthusiasm to start with. I'd also just got hold of a copy of 'Fall Out 4', was in the middle of the first draft of the novel that was to become the first in the Hannibal Smyth books, and summer was on its way. In short, reading a story I already knew I didn't like held little incentive for me. So, I put off reading the story for a while, and then a while longer after that.

To be clear here, 'Celephais', is a tale much beloved by Lovecraft's fans the world over, but it leaves me cold. It has always left me cold. So, I had been dreading 'Celephais' since I started my Lovecraft project. It had been looming on the horizon since I first put together the list of stories in order and knew where it fell in the chronology. 'Celephais' was there leering at me even before I read 'The Tree', but if you're going to read them all, then you have to read them all, and that is all there is to it. So, read it I did and tried to put my thoughts together for blog.

Unfortunately, the page was determined to stay blank save for one word…

So, I left it a while, til the guilt at leaving the blog unwritten caught up with me, then I read 'Celephais' again. Yet, after the second reading I still only had the one word.

So, I left it a while longer, deciding I was probably in the wrong mood to write about 'Celephais'. Besides which I had Molerats and Super Mutants to kill, springs and tiny screws to rescue from fans, those bottle caps weren't going to collect themselves. I also had to get Hannibal Smyth to India at the behest of Old Iron Knickers' Ministry. I had beaches to walk on, cocktails to drink, music to listen to, and so much else to do.

Besides, I was sure when I finally went back to it in a better mindset

'Celephais' would inspire a few more words on my part...

Time past, as it is wont to do...

So then, eventually, I made myself read 'Celephais' again, or at least attempted to, though every time I did, I gave up a page or two into what is not even a particularly long tale. Eventually though, I summoned up the willpower to finish reading through yet again and wrote down my thoughts.

One word again, same word again...

Let's recap a moment, 'Celephais' is, as I said at the start, a story much loved by the Lovecraftian literati. It is clear that they see something within it that I do not. So, let's talk about the tale itself a moment.

'Celephais' takes its name from a city dreamed of by an English man who takes the name Kuranes in his dreams. He dreams of the place first as a child, then later in his mid-forties he starts to dream of it again. In his dreams knights take him on a quest through a medieval version of England. Eventually he becomes both king and god of his dream city. Whereupon his body in the real world washes up on the shores of Cornwall…

In many ways, it is almost the archetype of a Dreamlands tale as everything you expect to be in a Dreamlands tale is here. It is Dunsian in nature, full of strangeness and oddity, about a man seeking a world beyond the mundane and taking solace in his dreams of a far-off land and a strange city...

In fact, it is little different in context from 'The White Ship' or 'Polaris', the latter with which it shares many particular hallmarks. Both 'The White Ship' and 'Polaris' are stories I like, though 'Polaris' somewhat grudgingly. To an extent, however, therein lays the problem. Compared to 'Polaris', 'Celephais' reads like a story that's just been phoned in. A poor imitation of those earlier stories that lacks the originality that made them interesting reads. Perhaps read in a different order 'Polaris' would be the tale that felt stilted, a rehashing of ideas, and offering nothing new.

In short, 'Celephais' is best summed up by that one word I kept writing in my notes, an achingly Yorkshire word filled with derision. I know there are many who may disagree but I hope I have offered a little context for my review. I will expand on it a little at least and make the review three words, but no more.

'Celephais', it's twaddle...

THE SCORE: 1 OUT OF 6 TENTACLES, MAINLY FOR NOT BEING 'A REMINISCENCE OF DR SAMUAL JOHNSON' WHICH IS ABOUT THE BEST THING I CAN SAY ABOUT IT.

MYTHOS CONNECTIONS: Kuranes, is visited by Randolph Carter in 'The Dream Quest for Unknown Kadath,' who has dreamt part of the dream city to seem like the Cornwall where he grew up in the real world.

LOVECRAFT TWATTRY: None

SHOULD YOU READ IT: No, clearly, but others will doubtless disagree with me here.

BLUFFERS FACT: The village of Innsmouth that appears briefly in this story is an Innsmouth in England and not Innsmouth Massachusetts where 'The Shadow Over Innsmouth' is latter set. It is based on the actual fishing village of Fleetwood in Lancashire, rather than Newburyport MA on which the more famous Innsmouth is said to be based.

THE PICTURE IN THE HOUSE

Lovecraft's tales cover a broad and on occasion eclectic spectrum, but the best of them, for me, are the ones that inspire a visceral response deep in your gut. The ones that get under your skin, gnaw the back of your mind and invoke a little of the fear what waits in the darkness. 'The Picture in the House' does this in spades, as it lowly builds tension within both its narrator and the reader.

Published in 1921, it was the first of Lovecraft's tales to really root itself in the New England countryside of his imagination. While earlier tales were set in the region, it's with 'The Picture in the House' that New England itself becomes, in a wide sense, a character within the story. Lovecraft did this on purpose as is obvious in one of the early passages in the text.

'Searchers after horror haunt strange, far places. For them are the catacombs of Ptolemais, and the carven mausolea of the nightmare countries. They climb to the moonlit towers of ruined Rhine castles, and falter down black cobwebbed steps beneath the scattered stones of forgotten cities in Asia. The haunted wood and the desolate mountain are their shrines, and they linger around the sinister monoliths on uninhabited islands. But the true epicure of the terrible, to whom a new thrill of unutterable ghastliness is the chief end and justification of existence, esteem most of all the ancient, lonely farmhouses of backwoods New England; for there the dark elements of strength, solitude, grotesqueness, and ignorance combine to form the perfection of the hideous.'

This passage that really sets the tone for the whole story. Strange as it may seem to compare the backroad farmhouses of New England to Germanic castles and lost cities in Asia, it manages to convey a sense of dread about these places that seeps through the pages. It is the same kind of dread that 'Evil Dead' style cabins inspire in the woods, that moment of recognition when you know in the core of your being that something dark lies within those walls. It is a theme that Lovecraft returns to time and time again in his later fiction, gradually building his own grim New England landscape.

That actual picture in 'The Picture in the House' is an engraving in an old, rare, and thankfully entirely fictional book which is another of

Lovecraft's tomes of dark intent which he liberally sprinkled throughout his fiction. In this case it is an engraving from 'The Regnum Congo' a somewhat vile work on ritual cannibalism. The book is in the possession of the inhabitant of the old New England farmhouse, which our narrator takes refuge in when a storm comes upon him suddenly, in the mistaken belief it is uninhabited, and this is where the terror begins.

There are many echoes of classic gothic horror within this story, despite its New England setting. The pace of the story, the slow building up of tension while nothing overt is happening, the way you find yourself anticipating the grim darkness of the ending waiting for you, echoes much of Poe and the early chapters of Dracula and other works of that ilk.

The story draws you in, gets under your skin and sits there like an itch waiting to be scratched. Meanwhile the tension just keeps on growing and the story becomes all the more engrossing.

This then, is Lovecraft at his eerie, unsettling best.

The story is not universally praised, though for me it is seminal Lovecraft, right down to the carefully understated nature of the ending which lets the reader's imagination colour around the edges. It makes the story all the more brooding and chilling for what it doesn't say - but then the best horror is always the darkness of the unknown, given light by the reader's imagination... Less is more.

After taking so many strolls through the Dreamlands, getting back to pure horror when I came to this story was a welcome relief, and 'The Picture in the House' is most certainly that.

It may not be Lovecraft's best work, and indeed I may praise it too highly because I first read this just after the disappointment that is 'Celephais' But it's a tale that needs to be read, preferably on a dark stormy night, in a silent house with no one upstairs.

So, I have to ask you now, what caused that floorboard to creak?

THE SCORE: 5 OUT OF 6 GROPING SLITHERING TENTACLES COMING UP THROUGH THE FLOORBOARDS, DOWN THE STAIRS AND FROM BETWEEN THE WALLS...

MYTHOS CONNECTIONS: 'The Picture in the House' is the first tale to make mention of 'dear' old Arkham and the Miskatonic Valley, though only in fleeting reference. It lays the groundwork for what was to become 'Lovecraft country', as it is on occasion referred to (and was before the TV show used the same name).

LOVECRAFT TWATTRY: None

SHOULD YOU READ IT: Yes. On a dark night, alone, in a quiet house.

BLUFFERS FACT: In 'Cabin in the Woods' there is a reference to this tale in Joss Whedon's movie, in the visceral dread inspiring picture on the wall that hides the two-way mirror between rooms. 'Cabin in the Woods' is a movie littered with references to much of the horror genre so this should probably does not come as a surprise. The picture is also far from the only Lovecraft inspired aspect of the movie, but I digress...

THE TEMPLE

"He is calling! He is calling!"

The question of who is doing the calling, well that's one open to interpretation, but whoever it may be, they reside in an ancient temple submerged deep below the waves of the Atlantic... Of course, this being an H. P. Lovecraft tale, and involving a 'calling' from one that dwells in a temple deep below the waves, I would invite you to draw your own conclusions...

In actuality Lovecraft neglects to clarify what dwells within the temple, leaving it instead to the fevered imagination of his readers, who with the hindsight of the modern eye can easily make the leap to Howard's most famous creation, old squid face himself... However, this tale was written in 1920 and for all this is the 21st story, this was still the early days of Old Tentacle Hugger's career. The foundations of his mythology were still being laid, it would still be some six years until Lovecraft penned 'The Call of Cthulhu' so, in all likelihood, Big C had not even begun to form as an idea in the darker recesses of Howard's mind. At most this is a tale based upon the germ of an idea, the thing in the temple may have been many things, but Cthulhu it wasn't, not yet at any rate.

'The Temple' tells the story of the last few weeks in the life of Karl Heinrich Graf Von Altberg-Ehrenstein. The brutal, cruel and arrogant commander of a first world war Imperial German Navy U-Boat. Von Altberg is a man with little to recommend him, so finding sympathy with the main protagonist is difficult, not usually for Lovecraft's characters. The narrative opens with the sinking of a British Frigate, and Von Altberg ordering his crew to then sink the British lifeboats against the generally accepted rules of conduct for war at sea. As I say, the commander is far from a pleasant man, but by this irreconcilable act he is also the architect of his own demise. His actions set in motion a chain of events that lead to his U-Boat floundering at the bottom of the ocean, his crew dead and with him seeing strange lights through the port holes coming from 'The Temple' of the title, and feeling it is calling to him.

There is a lot going on in this tale, which is one of the criticisms thrown at it. Unlike much of Lovecraft's early fiction where there is a tendency to focus on a primary aspect of a tale and events, 'The Temple' wanders down many supernatural pathways. A strange piece of ivory is found on a body clinging to the side of the U-boat after the sinking of the British frigate. Dead sailors are seen swimming around the sub. The craft gets caught in strange currents dragging it ever southwards, then the craft loses power and all control and starts sinking slowly downwards. Some of the crew mutiny and are summarily executed by Von Altberg. Indeed, most of the crew are eventually killed by their captain for one reason or another, but not before they start to suffer from nightmares, see strange visions, hear strange noises and other things. As I said there is a lot going on in this story and it doesn't all quite gel as much as Lovecraft intended. All the while Von Altberg witnesses his junior officer Lieutenant Klenze (the one who took the strangely carved ivory figurine), descend slowly into madness as the U-boat itself descends to the ocean floor.

It is Klenze who issues those ominous words, "He is calling, he is calling." This happens just before Von Altberg helps the Lieutenant into an airlock, giving a final 'mercy' to the madman, or perhaps just to finally shut him up… All if which happens before the currents take the U-boat to its final destination.

Von Altberg discovers the sub has drifted, or been taken, to a ruined city on the ocean floor which he assumes (wrongly one would surmise, this being a Lovecraftian lost city of a cyclopean nature), to be the fabled Atlantis. In the midst of this city there lies 'The Temple' of the title, strange lights and all. Finally, the tale ends with Von Altberg about to walk out of the airlock in a diving suit, and make his way to the temple, the strange sounds and hallucinations having driven him to the end of the 'Iron Germanic Will' of which he is so proud. But not before he places his logs in an airtight bottle and releases them to the ocean currents.

I've some history with this tale, it always been one of my favourites, as much for its flaws as anything else. The criticisms of the tale, its lack of coherence and the many elements that swamp the reader, I understand and to an extent would agree with, but my take is that the narrative is written by a man on the very edge of his sanity. While Klenze falls to madness before Von Altberg, Altberg is not far behind. There is an interpretation of the tale which I have always liked, that Klenze and Von Altberg are one in the same. Von Altberg is watching himself go mad, and observing it dispassionately by projecting his own degrading sanity on to his junior officer… While that interpretation is perhaps a stretch beyond what Lovecraft intended and may be something we interpret as members of the 'Fight Club' generation, it does make the tale hang together better as well as answering some of the criticisms of the story.

All that said, while I'm fond of this story, I can also see the flaws, but I recommend it all the same. There is an ominousness to it. It speaks of more to come. It speaks of old gods in lost cities and the madness in the darkness which is waiting to consume us all. While the ideas at its core aren't fully formed, it lays the foundations for the mythos and the horrors to come. This story is Lovecraft feeling his way around the edges of everything that makes his writings what they are, and finally, it hints at what is to come, who is to come, what lies beneath the waves, the eater of minds, the edges of sanity and the void below.

"He is calling… he is calling!"

Indeed…

THE SCORE: 4 OUT OF 6 TENTACLES, GROPING UP FROM THE INKY DEPTHS…

MYTHOS CONNECTIONS: He has wings and a face full of tentacles, he sleeps in the depths, till the stars are right once more.

LOVECRAFT TWATTRY: There is a hint or two of adulation for the Teutonic which hints towards Aryanism, but there's nothing too obviously racist about it, and if we are fair here it fits well with the narrator's viewpoint as a German officer of 'old stock'.

SHOULD YOU READ IT: It is well worth the read, is flaws are obvious but minor

BLUFFERS FACT: One common theory among Lovecraft readers is that the temple is part of R'lyeh, the city spoken of in 'The Shadow over Innsmouth', though that tale was not written until the back end of 1931, eleven years later so this too requires quite a stretch of imaginative logic…

FACTS CONCERNING THE LATE ARTHUR JERMYN AND HIS FAMILY

As titles go, 'Facts Concerning the Late Arthur Jermyn and His Family.' is rather laborious - it also fails to give the slightest inkling of what the tale is about. Even for Lovecraft, a writer known for having occasionally vague titles, 'Facts Concerning the Late Arthur Jermyn and His Family.' stands out as both the longest and one of the vaguest titles he ever penned. It reads like a reporter's misplaced journalism, right before his editor took hold of him and explained how to write a headline…

This may well have been the reason the editor at 'Weird Tales' republished it in 1924 with the title 'The White Ape', against Lovecraft's wishes, three years after it originally appeared in 'The Wolverine' under its more onerous original title. Later reprints shortened the title to 'Arthur Jermyn' right up until 1986 when the full title was restored in a collection entitled 'Dagon and Other Macabre Tales' - all of which goes to show that an author might get his own way in the end, he just might have to be dead for fifty years before his preferred title finally gets restored.

Laborious is a word that many might ascribe to more than just the title of this story. Spanning several generations of the Jermyn family as well as their rather odd genealogy, it does have a long road to travel, and it's a tale with many detractors. Personally, however, am not among them. While this is not Lovecraft's finest work, there are a lot of quirks within it I enjoy (even have the odd chortle about), because with this story, while it may not be entirely deliberate Howard seems to be trying his hand at writing comedy. Tragic, rather depressing comedy, but comedy all the same. To understand why I say that you need look no further than the Jermyn family tree.

The roots of that tree belong to Sir Wade Jermyn, an explorer who spent years in Africa's dark interior, in particular, exploring the upper reaches of the Congo, because it's always the Congo…

After one extended trip he returns to England with a new, and decidedly odd, wife. Wade's wife, he told everyone, was the daughter of a Portuguese trader, though you don't get that much further into the tale before you realise that this may not be entirely true. It is his wife's strange heritage that accounts for the oddities of the Jermyn family tree from there on in. Mysteriously she almost exclusively stays in the family home, and Sir Wade brings all her meals to her himself. Not long after, the marriage produces an heir, Sir Wade and his wife return to Africa and are promptly never seen again.

The child, Sir Wade's son, Philip, is raised by relatives, but then despite the family's wealth he chooses to become, of all things, a sailor. Not the kind of sailor that stands on the poop deck, barking out orders, but the kind who run up and down the rigging for a living, something he is extremely accomplished at. After a few years on the sea, he further estranges his branch of the family tree from his wealthy cousins by marrying a gypsy girl, on whom he fathers a son. Then a year or so later, he jumps ship off the coast of Africa and disappears into the Congo.

Philip's and the gypsy girl's son, Robert, end up being raised by his father's cousins and makes a good marriage to a viscount's daughter. Which is remarkable for the son of a sailor and a gypsy. He becomes a scientist, which is of course a far more respectable profession for the progeny of a noble house, and in time he fathers three sons and then in early middle age he goes off to follow in his grandfather's footsteps and explore Africa himself. Somewhere along the way, he meets another explorer called Seaton who tells him of "a grey city of white apes ruled by a white god" much like one described in his grandfather's journals. Robert later kills Seaton and goes on a bloody rampage killing all three of his sons before being locked up in an asylum. That would have been the end of the family tree had not a year before his murder Nevil Jermyn, Sir Robert's middle son, fathered a child call Alfred on a 'dancing girl' who is never named.

The extended family raise the dancer's child, who in time becomes Sir Alfred, father of the Arthur of the title. Alfred grows to manhood, then scandalises the extended family once more by marrying a music-hall singer upon whom he fathers Arthur. Then, somewhat randomly, he runs off and joins the circus, becomes an animal trainer, and develops a strange, unexplained passion for a gorilla described as being of 'lighter colour than usual'. A couple of years go by then Sir Alfred suddenly goes into a rage, and attacks the gorilla, who naturally kills him.

Which brings us at last to Arthur, who inherits the title, the family pile in the country, and decides to take up the gentlemanly pursuit of poetry, then goes on to write a lot of bad poetry about trees. Arthur is described as looking a little odd. A description that applies to most of his family line since good old Sir Wade came back from Africa with his reclusive wife - remember her?

A few years pass and then a Belgian explorer sends word of a strange discovery he has made, of a mummy in the Congo which he believes is linked to Sir Wade. It seems for all his professed fame as an explorer, Sir Wade had for a while been a bit of a laughingstock. This derision stems from a claim he'd made that he had discovered a city populated by white apes in the interior of the Congo. This claim has been a bugbear of the family history for several generations. It's believed it was the resurfacing of that particular rumour that drove Sir Philip crazy three generations back.

As noble lineages go, the Jermyn's take some beating as a comic progression of inbred oddity. Though Lovecraft does not lend himself to the comic as a rule. The implication throughout this tale is that Sir Wade's wife was not actually entirely human and had been worshipped as a goddess by the strange tribe of city dwelling white apes that Sir Wade had discovered in the deepest backwaters of the Congo.

Some commentators point to all this as evidence of Lovecraft's obsession with his own lineage, in-breeding, mental issues related to his own rather 'close' family tree. His own parents both spent the last few years of their lives in mental institutions. It's not the only time Lovecraft draws from this particular well, 'The Shadow Over Innsmouth' and other tales are full of such themes. Personally, I think this reads more like Lovecraft laughing at the idea and playing with it for comic relief. He does this with all the subtlety of 'Carry on Screaming...' (which remains the best 'carry on film ever made). If anything, that laborious title should be 'Carry on Lovecraft', and in the film version I have no doubt at all Sid James would be the one playing Sir Wade...

So, there you go. Ridiculous, and probably not actually written for humour but it makes me smile and it's a tale to be read with a certain degree of mirth in mind. It's a dry kind of wit... Arid even. But it amuses me all the same.

THE SCORE: 4 OUT OF 6 SLIGHTLY RUBBERY AND CLEARLY FAKE TENTACLES

MYTHOS CONNECTIONS: None

LOVECRAFT TWATTRY: None

SHOULD YOU READ IT: Yes. It's a story that is easily ignored, it certainly not typical Lovecraft, it is, however, an entertaining farce.

BLUFFERS FACT: Old Tentacle Hugger was less than pleased with 'Weird Tales' for changing the name of the story, reportedly he wrote to the editor and complained, "If I ever entitled a story 'The White Ape', there would be no ape in it".

FROM BEYOND

You don't have to read much of 'From Beyond' to know you're in the middle of Lovecraft country. If ever a passage screamed Lovecraft, it is this one from the first page of the story…

"What do we know," he had said, "of the world and the universe about us? Our means of receiving impressions are absurdly few, and our notions of surrounding objects infinitely narrow. We see things only as we are constructed to see them, and can gain no idea of their absolute nature. With five feeble senses, we pretend to comprehend the boundlessly complex cosmos…"

'From Beyond' is one of those strange little stories which Lovecraft wrote early in his career, that didn't get published until he had reached the apex of his fame in the latter years when he'd reached an audience beyond the amateur press. While he never quite managed to earn a good living from his stories, he had at least gained a following keen to consume his work. Little wonder then that dusty manuscripts began to finally find their way to the printed page. Works like 'From Beyond' that had been passed over when he was a complete unknown now had a market, albeit fourteen years after it was written. However, it does beg the question, given the story was not good enough for the amateur press in 1920, is it really worth reading now? Every writer (and I speak from experience) has the odd dusty manuscript kicking about that should never see the light of day. With this in mind, when I came to this story my expectations were not high

Thankfully, it turned out 'From Beyond' was better than my expectations allowed, though not as much as I would have liked. It's also a tale that perhaps benefits from the passage of time. The frontiers of 21st century physics add a certain credence to words of the bard of Providence. We're told now that the universe consists of over 80% dark matter. Of which we know next to nothing, beyond the formulation that predicts its existence. Which is to say, there is far more stuff out there than we can actually observe…

This is not to claim that Lovecraft predicted dark matter all the way back in 1920 as he tapped away with incessant loathing at his typewriter.

I don't know why I always think of Lovecraft typing away with incessant loathing, it's just always the image that comes to mind. That of a self-hating flagellant whose fingers bleed a little with each vowel-less name he types with hateful resentment... but moving on.

In fairness, had Lovecraft predicted dark matter it would doubtless have been a far darker matter than the somewhat benign stuff physicist imagine. It is, however, moving beyond our mere human perceptions which this tale goes on to explore. As the narrator's 'friend' the somewhat oddly named Crawford Tillinghast explains...

'We shall see that at which dogs howl in the dark, and that at which cats prick up their ears after midnight. We shall see these things, and other things which no breathing creature has yet seen. We shall overleap time, space, and dimensions, and without bodily motion peer to the bottom of creation.'

Of course, this is Lovecraft, and once anyone starts talking about 'seeing these things' things predictably go downhill from there. Indeed, there is a wonderfully grotesque description of Crawford Tillinghast at the start of the tale, which suggests quite strongly that things have been going downhill in the sanity department for Crawford for quite a while. Which does make you wonder why the narrator was so keen to follow him up to his attic to see the strange machine that Crawford had spent the months perfecting... But then what else would the narrator of a Lovecraft story do when faced with a dark staircase, a decaying friend with sanity issues and a strange machine that allows you to see 'beyond our mortal senses'? And this is exactly what the machine does, and then some. Strange worlds open up around the narrator, strange worlds with strange things lurking all around us, just beyond our meagre senses...

From the off, this story is in predictable territory for Lovecraft readers. The servants are all dead, the scientist is clearly mad, the cosmos is unbound by mortal constraints and the narrator has clearly never read any Lovecraft...

As I said, the story was better than my expectations for a forgotten early manuscript but all the same it is not hard to see why the tale took fourteen years to be published. It opens up no fresh ground. Instead, it treads a well-worn pathway, one walked better by 'Beyond the Walls of Sleep' to think of the most obvious example. When compared to other Lovecraft tales of a similar nature it has a certain weakness - while they follow a similar path they have more gravel to them, if you will.

In comparison, this tale is just too straight forward, it moves from beginning to end with nothing that really makes it stand out from its fellows. Which is not to say its badly written, it just isn't really anything new, a rehash of better, more mature tales. It also lacks something. It just is, yet it could have been so much more. The premise opened many possibilities but then ignored them all and instead kept to the well-trodden path. If you have never read Lovecraft this is probably a far more interesting tale, but there is the crux when it comes down to it. I have read Lovecraft, and this tale while screaming Lovecraft, in the end only does that. Perhaps the best way to describe this story is to say its Lovecraft-lite.

THE SCORE: 3 OUT OF 6 SOMEWHAT PREDICTABLE TENTACLES

MYTHOS CONNECTIONS: Minor

LOVECRAFT TWATTRY: None

SHOULD YOU READ IT: There's no reason not to, except there's no real reason to do so either.

BLUFFERS FACT: While lots of Lovecraft's stories have inspired musicians, 'From Beyond' has inspired songs by more than you would imagine including stoner doom metal band Sleep, death metal band Massacre (who name a whole album after the story), heavy metal band Manilla Road, dark ambient band Nox Arcana, and a song by the delightfully named band, Ripping Corpses.

NYARLATHOTEP

Nyarlathotep . . . the crawling chaos . . .
I am the last . . .
I will tell the audient void. . .

Of the pantheon of Lovecraft's mythos, 'Nyarlathotep' is perhaps second only to Old Tentacle Face himself in his impact on popular culture. He is also the only old god that ever appears in human form, though that is but one of his forms, and in other tales Lovecraft went on to write 'Nyarlathotep' is referred to or appears in a myriad of ways. Often, he appears as a 'tall, swarthy man' who resembles an ancient Pharaoh of Egypt. But he also appears as, 'the black man' in 'The Dreams of the Witch House' and 'A bat-winged tentacled monster' in 'The Haunter of the Dark'. My favourite description of him is from 'The Rats in the Walls', where he is mentioned briefly in passing as the 'faceless god in the caverns of Earth's centre'.

It's this myriad of forms that makes him so attractive as an antagonist in both Lovecraft's own work and beyond. Nyarlathotep can walk among us, whereas the rest of the outer gods are utterly alien, exiled among the stars (or sleeping fitfully beneath the waves, in the case of Cthulhu). Nyarlathotep walks among us, sowing seeds of disorder - a crawling chaos indeed. A creature of a thousand faces and none. Servant of Azathoth, the messenger of the outer gods, a bringer of madness for madness' sake.

Little wonder he has so much appeal to other writers, not to mention computer game designers, role-playing gamers, musicians, filmmakers and much more besides. The impact of Nyarlathotep on popular culture is extensive by any measure. Which is a little strange for a creation that began back in 1920, as the centre of a short piece of prose published in 'The United Amateur' in the November of that year.

With Nyarlathotep having such a huge impact, and tendrils reaching so very far through the zeitgeist of popular, and importantly geek, culture, it is perhaps a little odd that I must admit until I reach 'Nyarlathotep' back when this book was still a series of blogs, I had never read the original story. I have previously read most of the other Lovecraft tales in which he makes an appearance. I have also come across him in so many other ways over the years, from Call of Cthulhu games, to novels and in pixels all over the place. But never in this first and original form. Which I will admit lent a certain degree of anticipation when working my way down the list of stories, gradually getting closer to the point where I needed to read it. 'Nyarlathotep' had been coming since day one. What is the saying about 'never meet your heroes…'? Would it apply here? Or should that be never meet your 'faceless god in the caverns of the Earth's centre'? I was, after all, just asking to be disappointed.

So then, what is 'Nyarlathotep' about when it comes down to it? The tale itself, rather than everything that came after it. Did it indeed disappoint? The answer to the latter question is no. The answer to the former… that is more a matter of interpretation. For what it is worth, what follows is mine, but it could be read in any number of ways… But my own view stems from this particular passage, early in the prose.

A sense of monstrous guilt was upon the land, and out of the abysses between the stars swept chill currents that made men shiver in dark and lonely places. There was a daemonic alteration in the sequence of the seasons—the autumn heat lingered fearsomely, and everyone felt that the world and perhaps the universe had passed from the control of known gods or forces to that of gods or forces which were unknown.

This is a tale of the end of times, or the end of one age and the beginning of another. A time, to steal a little from elsewhere in Lovecraft's writings, when 'The Stars are Right' or on the cusp of becoming so, and madness rules. A tale of a world where logic and science has had its veils of sanity stripped away and magic of the old, dark, sinister kind is seeping into the world once more, and its harbinger is Nyarlathotep, emerging from old Egypt and walking among us. Everywhere he goes he leaves madness behind. Opening the eyes of humanity to a cosmos it cannot even begin to comprehend.

There is a lurid quality to this tale. In many ways, this is Lovecraft at his most descriptive. Where in other tales he hints at things, in this he uses that description as a blunt instrument aimed at the senses of the reader. Yet it is a blunt instrument used with enviable precision.

A sickened, sensitive shadow writhing in hands that are not hands, and whirling blindly past ghastly midnights of rotting creation, corpses of dead worlds with sores that were cities, charnel winds that brush the pallid stars and make them flicker low. Beyond the worlds vague ghosts of monstrous things; half-seen columns of unsanctified temples that rest on nameless rocks beneath space and reach up to dizzy vacua above the spheres of light and darkness.

This is a masterpiece in creative writing. If you ever wish to know how to get under the skin of a reader, to raise a heartbeat and constantly build to your conclusion, this is the tale to study. It builds with a slow progression through only 1149 words from beginning to end but is relentless as it does so. Like a piece of well composed music progressing towards its crescendo in the final passages.

Maddening beating of drums, and thin, monotonous whine of blasphemous flutes from inconceivable, unlighted chambers beyond Time; the detestable pounding and piping whereunto dance slowly, awkwardly, and absurdly the gigantic, tenebrous ultimate gods—the blind, voiceless, mindless gargoyles whose soul is Nyarlathotep.

There is something of terror in this tale, something of horror, and something primal. A fireside tale told by the damned. A tale you can let seep into you and be drawn along with its rhythm. Read it and imagine you are sat around a campfire in the ruins of the old world and I defy anyone not to feel the chill of the east wind, and perhaps to fear those six tentacles that are creeping towards you through the darkness.

THE SCORE: 6 OUT OF 6 TENTACLES OF GROPING OBLIVION THAT WILL HOLD YOU IN THEIR GRASP

MYTHOS CONNECTIONS: Central to everything

LOVECRAFT TWATTRY: None.

SHOULD YOU READ IT: Yes, or treat yourself to a good audio reading of it.

BLUFFERS FACT: In Charles Stross' series 'The Laundry Files', a human avatar of Nyarlathotep under the name Fabian Everyman becomes UK's prime minister.
To be fair, we've had worse.

THE QUEST OF IRANON

Some tales are more interesting in the abstract than in the telling. Sad though that may be, 'The Quest of Iranon' is one such tale. While it's a pleasant enough read, it does not really have anything that grabs hold of you in the way you want a story to grip you. It meanders, rolling along without much impetus, to a conclusion which is just a little too predictable. It is one of Lovecraft's weaknesses. He has a habit of walking you along a crooked path through the forest to a destination you could see long before you arrive, yet insisting he follows the path all the way, rather than cut through the trees. Often though the journey is worth it. 'The Tree', for example, does much the same thing, but there is a tension to 'The Tree' which is lacking in 'The Quest of Iranon'. This is more a meander for the sake of meandering rather than with any great purpose, and when you get to the end you can't help wondering why you made the journey at all…

Lovecraft himself may well have thought much the same, he wrote it in early 1921 but it resided in the bottom drawer of his writing desk for a long time, forgotten and uncared for. Much in the way of 'From Beyond' this feels like Lovecraft-lite, and like 'From Beyond' this story did not find its way into print until a decade and a half after it was written. There is, however, something about 'The Quest of Iranon' that sets it apart from 'From Beyond'. Unlike the latter, Lovecraft was trying to do something different with this tale, indeed it was also the start of something which helped to set Lovecraft apart from his fellow pulp writers.

While covering Lovecraft's early works, I've often made mention of later works that refer back to them. It is a common theme, which helps link the stories with reoccurring characters and places, as well as events. Often it is the case that he mentions something in passing that later crops up in another tale or even becomes the seed for the whole of a new tale. In 'The Quest of Iranon', however, is the first occurrence of the reverse, with earlier tales being referred back to. For the first time, Lovecraft was beginning to build a mythos, creating a web of stories that link into each other to create a greater whole. Which also explains much about 'The Quest of Iranon' and why it meanders around: because it is a vehicle built to do so. Everything about this story is deliberate, and the effect is to tell a story that is in essence a travelogue of Lovecraft's own work. If anything, it's an experimental piece, playing around with the idea of turning his tales into a greater whole, a cycle of stories, rather than a series of one offs.

Lovecraft wrote primarily for the kind of pulp magazines that thrived on characters coming back in new stories. For example, Lovecraft's close friend Ron E Howard's 'Conan' stories built on a world with its own histories and ideas that carried common threads. Conan came back time and time again and his recurring stories gave the character 'cover' potential and helped to draw in readers.

Lovecraft's stories had a weakness in this; his stories were all one offs with only the barest narrative threads to linking any of them. As such, his tales were unlikely to feature on covers and were thought of as fillers by most publishers. Later in his career he might get his name in a covers writer's list, but he was not seen as a draw and usually, he wasn't listed on the covers of early pulp magazines. Finding ways to tie his tales together, from a purely commercial point of view, made sense. Readers like to feel a story is part of something bigger. Which is as true today as it was then. It's the reason trilogies and long sprawling series novels like 'A Song of Fire and Ice' (the Game of Thrones novels that predate the tv series) and 'The Wheel of Time' novels are so popular. Readers like to invest in characters and worlds. Lovecraft did not give his readers such an investment. Each tale was separate, unique, and had to be sold on its own merits.

So when writing 'The Quest of Iranon', Lovecraft was looking for ways to link his stories together and give his readers something more. Which is what he gave them as he hid Easter eggs in the text. All of which makes 'The Quest of Iranon' interesting in the abstract to me as a writer reading Lovecraft's work in the order it was written, rather than the order of publication.

Ironically, by the time the story was first published Lovecraft's fan base was not only used to these little references appearing in his work and the greater thread which moved through his stories, they expected it. The greater was more than the sum of its part. The oblique references to Lormar, the land in 'Polaris' and Iranon stating he had "...gazed on the marsh where Sarnath once stood," a reference to 'The Doom that Came to Sarnath', were the least of the connections you would expect in his stories. But when he wrote 'The Quest of Iranon' it was a new departure for Lovecraft as a writer. As such it's interesting as a fellow member of the craft, but it is a prosaic read for all of that.

The story in the end is a simple one about a golden-haired wanderer, telling tales about his past as a prince in the great city of Aira as he travels. Tales of a city no one else has heard of, but he claims, is full of wonder, which is surely a case of Lovecraft writing Lovecraft… His obsessions with lost and mythical cities runs as a thread through many tales. In this case, the tales of Aira are ones Iranon has told so often he cannot separate truth from fiction. Longing always to return, but somehow never doing a great deal about it until a lifelong friend passes from the world of the living. The 'Quest' for the dreaming spires of his lost city, on which he poetically waxes constantly, leads him finally to an old shepherd in a land long fallen to ruin. There the shepherd tells him a truth, one which if you do not suspect long before it is revealed you have not been reading closely. It is all very Lovecraft, the style, the verbiage, the use of ideas and the way it reads. But it's Lovecraft by rote, and much like 'From Beyond' it's a story from which you would expect more.

The most interesting thing about this tale is, in the end, when it was written. That it took so long to be published says much about Lovecraft's own opinion of it. It was the context of the experiment and what it represented that is the important aspect of this tale. If anything, it was Lovecraft becoming Lovecraft as we know him now. The weaving of threads between stories and the gossamer links that build the web of the greater whole are what make this tale stand out. But as a read in and of itself, it is disappointingly below average, and when it finally became ink in the pulps it's unlikely it even raised an eyebrow.

Putting that greater context on one side it rates a measly three tentacles, grasping to be part of the whole, and if I am honest, I think I am generous to give it three… If, however, I was rating on the tale's importance it would probably be a quintet of the little suckers. This is the point Lovecraft began to craft a universe of his own making, rather than just give glimpses without a greater whole. It is interesting to me that he wrote this just after 'Nyarlathotep'. Perhaps the masks of the faceless one guided him to a take this broader view of his tales. It's strangely discomforting to think so…

THE SCORE: 3 OUT OF 6 RATHER TREMULOUS TENTACLES

MYTHOS CONNECTIONS: Several links to earlier tales, while it has few wider implications going forward.

LOVECRAFT TWATTRY: Surprisingly none

SHOULD YOU READ IT: It's of passing interest only so, perhaps...

BLUFFERS FACT: This story takes place in the same world and era as 'Polaris', a prehistoric Earth around 24,000 BC.

THE MUSIC OF ERICH ZANN

Listen to them, the children of the night.
What beautiful music they make ~ Bram Stoker

Music and horror have always been linked. Watch any horror movie, with the music track off, and you will see what I mean. We are programmed somehow to feel a chill down our spine when discordant notes are played. The shower scene in psycho as the knife comes down. That strange theme that gets played whenever someone is about to die in a horrendous way in the Omen series. Listen to them without the pictures, and they will produce the same guttural reaction. The music from jaws, the music from the Exorcist, the music from Halloween, Friday 13th - take your pick. They all have discordant and visceral natures. So, it's unsurprising that a tale involving discordant music crops up in Lovecraft cannon. 'The Music of Erich Zann' is, however, a tale with so much more to it than just music. It's a tale that is discordant by its very nature.

The story has a seductive nature to it; it draws you in, in much the same way the protagonist is attracted to the music of the viola being played on the floor above him in his boarding house on the Rue d' Auseil. There is a clue in the name of the street. A couple of clues to be exact. First, there is the Rue part. Lovecraft was always drawn to the stories of Alexander Poe, who famously wrote of murders in the Rue Morgue. Yes, it is true that Rue is merely the French word for street, but it is no coincidence that Lovecraft chose to place this, his most Poe inspired work, in a French street. The second clue to the nature of the story is the second half of Rue d' Auseil.

While the name is fictional and not truly a French word, the closest you can come to it in French is Au Seuil, which is the French for portal. Which subtly hints about what is really going on in this tale, not least because when we join the story, we are told by the protagonist that he cannot find the Rue d' Auseil, or even the district in which it resides, on any map of the city. Also, he remembers staying at the boarding house for a few months and the events that took place but not how he came to live there in the first place. The description of the district and the Rue d' Auseil itself is hauntingly familiar, yet unerringly strange, there is a slightly 'off' quality to it. It is a part of a city he knew well, but is somehow out of key, discordant, or just plain wrong. An older part of town which had gone to seed. The kind of area you wander into late at night and feel as if you have stepped across a boundary into some other place. The inhabitants look strange to him, the street is not paved, even the smell of the place is strange. It's an idea of purgatory, a place between our world and the next.

I have a fondness for this idea of purgatory, though not in the Christian sense of the word. The idea of places existing that are slightly out of key with our reality, soft places that you can wander into if the conditions are right, and through them find your way somewhere else. Literature is full of them, from Stephen Kings 'thinys', C.S.Lewis's wardrobe, the mist marches in Moorcock's Von Bek novels and countless other examples including my own 'Passing Place'. From the description given by Lovecraft, Rue d' Auseil is almost certainly one of these soft places, a bridge between here and somewhere else.

In his boarding house at the top of the hill that forms the Rue d' Auseil, the protagonist can only see a great wall at the end of the street which blocks all views of what lies beyond. He is told the only place high enough to see beyond the wall is the garret at the top of the house, where resides the viola player Erich Zann. Our 'hero' hears Zann playing strange hauntingly discordant music into the early hours each night and he finds himself both repulsed and drawn to it in equal measure. In time he works up the courage to meet the man himself and ask him about his music. Whereupon he discovers the man is mute, and beyond his viola communicates only by carefully written notes. Zann also seems to be a haunted man, strangely drawn and nervous, yet he agrees to play for our 'hero' - and it is at this point things get really odd.

As Zann plays what interests our protagonist most is not the strange music coming from the viola but the strange counter point that comes from beyond the shuttered window. The only window on the Rue d' Auseil that looks out beyond the great wall. What he really wants to know is what lies beyond the wall. A vista of the city all lit up in the night? Or something else, something strange and wrong? And as Zann plays his singular instrument, its notes crying out in the night, a wind gets up and events go downhill fast.

Indeed, everything goes to hell, one way or another…

Perhaps it is the subject matter, but 'The Music of Erich Zann' sings to me, for want of other words. It has strong elements of Poe at his best, but while there is some imitation of Poe's style involved, Lovecraft make it his own. You can feel the darkness of the city at night, the strangeness of the street, the discordance of the music. The deep impending doom of the violist - this strange mute man so gripped with an unnamed terror eating at his soul. It is Lovecraft at close to his best and it makes me wonder how many tentacles you'd need to play the violin.

THE SCORE: 5 OUT OF 6 MUSICAL TENTACLES REACHING A CRESCENDO

MYTHOS CONNECTIONS: Several links to earlier tales, while it has few wider implications going forward.

LOVECRAFT TWATTRY: None.

SHOULD YOU READ IT: Yes, with a nice violin concerto playing in the background

BLUFFERS FACT: The tale of Erich Zann's discordant music has inspired more than one musician and while it doesn't really fall within my normal tastes, there is something seductive and beautiful about Alexey Voytenko's piece which shares the same title as the story. But then doesn't the devil always have all the best tunes…

EX OBLIVIONE

"There is nothing better than oblivion, since in oblivion there is no wish unfulfilled." ~ H.P. Lovecraft 'In defense of Dacon'

As a philosophical statement, let's be honest here, the above is a bit on the bleak side. Though no one ever accused our man Howard of having a sunny disposition. This particular tidbit comes from a nonfiction essay he wrote in defence of his fiction in 1921, which by coincidence was also when he wrote Ex Oblivione. A certain nihilism was evidently on his mind at the time.

The tale itself is as much a prose poem as a story. It tells of a man that is close to the end of his life, who dreams each night that he is walking through a city. There, each night he comes to an imposing wall with a gate within it. He knows somehow that should he pass beyond the gates that he will never return. Beyond that he knows little. The wise dream sage's that lay within the city offer different accounts of what lies beyond the gates. Some tell of immense wonders while others tell of horror and disappointment. Yet all speak of a drug which will unlock the gates. And so, despite not knowing what lies beyond the gates, the man decides he must find out for himself - even with the knowledge that to pass through the gates is to never return.

Some have occasionally equated the tale with Lovecraft's supposed obsession with suicide. They choose to ignore the hints within the text of that the man sufferers a wasting disease, choosing instead to interpret 'forever being freed from the pain of the real world' as Lovecraft speaking of human existence itself. It's not an entirely unreasonable idea, it has to be said; Lovecraft's struggles with depression and the struggles of his family with that old black dog are well documented. To believe he never contemplated suicide at any point in his life would seem naive. However, personally, I choose to believe it is no more than an exploration of what may lie beyond this mortal life. Though it has to be said, the view expressed within the tale has a certain grim absoluteness to it. Insomuch that it says that nothing lies beyond that final gate but the infinite void that is death. Just oblivion. Just nothingness. An end to everything...

So happy little tale this is not.

Despite this, it has an intrinsic beauty about it, which belies its nihilistic nature. For the narrator of the story, that oblivion would be a welcome wonder. A final release from everything - and the idea of that nothingness is, to him, preferable to life.

When this story was first published in the 'United Amateur', it was under the pseudonym Ward Phillips, perhaps because of the nihilistic nature of the piece, and a desire to separate it from Lovecraft's usual fiction. It's grim from the outset, beginning…

'When the last day's were upon me and the ugly trifles of existence began to drive me to madness like small drops of water that torturers let fall ceaselessly upon one spot of the victim's body. I loved the irradiate refuge of sleep'.

When a man's life equates to water torture is not difficult to conceive why oblivion would be a welcome release from his torment. Yet, it is perhaps the dark nature of this tale that holds a certain fascination for me. There have been times in my life when I have suffered from depression myself, which I have occasionally written about. Because of this, at a certain level, the idea of what lies beyond Lovecraft's gates has played upon my thoughts. I suspect most everyone has at some point. But then what lies beyond is after all part of the zeitgeist of the human condition. It is a theme that goes far beyond Lovecraft's writings; whole swathes of philosophy are focused upon it. While Howard Phillips has no greater insight than any of us, there is always a certain grim attraction to its contemplation. Particularly in our darker hours. If this tale does nothing else, it explores that theme with all of Lovecraft's dark passion for the subject. It draws you into its grasp, till oblivion seems a welcoming end in and of itself. Which is a neat trick to pull off when you as a reader are happy as a sand boy at the time… Due to that certain fascination, I have with what lies at the other side of those gates, if nothing more, it scores four groping tentacles of nihilistic doom. Though I recommend being of a sunny frame of mind before you delve into its grasp. Oblivion may be a compelling idea of what lies ahead of us all, but personally, I would prefer to remain oblivious of what really lies beyond those gates for some time to come…

THE SCORE: 4 OUT OF 6 GROPING TENTACLES OF NIHILISTIC DOOM

MYTHOS CONNECTIONS: None.

LOVECRAFT TWATTRY: None, but its only reasonable to point out the obvious trigger warning

SHOULD YOU READ IT: Yes… but with a certain cynicism.

BLUFFERS FACT: "Ex Oblivione"—that nothingness is preferable to life—was probably derived from Lovecraft's reading the philosopher Arthur Schopenhauer.

SWEET ERMENGARDE

Some collections of Lovecraft which claim to be complete utterly ignore 'Sweet Ermengarde', thus expunging it from their pages. There are reasons to do so, not necessarily good reasons, but reasons all the same. I know this because of the two 'complete' collections I own (and only one of them) includes the tale within its pages. Also, Lovecraftian scholars commonly discount the story, as it is not linked in any way to the mythos (and I suspect because it is not in any way pompous or worthy). You see, Lovecraft, that most serious, austere and priggish of writers, which 'scholars' of his work admire, 'lowered' himself when he wrote Sweet Ermengarde, to the level of a common parodist... For this horrendous crime, being funny and enjoying himself by taking the piss, gently, out of a particular kind of story, some of his scholars denigrate this story as not being 'Lovecraft'. Despite the relatively clear fact that he wrote it. Though I must add here, others among these 'scholars' hail it as a comic gem alongside 'A Reminiscence of Dr Samuel Johnson'.

Now before we go any further, let me deal with that comparison. If you have read this far you will know my opinion of 'A Reminiscence of Dr Samuel Johnson' is a bit of a mixed bag. It was the only story so far to get zero tentacles (though it did get four Johnsons) and as I said at the time, it's not what you'd expect from a writer of horror and delver of the dark places of the human psyche.

Which of course puts me in the same category as those Lovecraftian scholars who dismiss 'Sweet Ermengarde: Or The Heart Of A Country Girl' to give it its full title, for not been real Lovecraft... So, that's me hoisted by my own petard. Dismissing a tale because it's outside the writer's typical genre. I really should know better...

I have never believed that writers should stick to a single genre. This is not to say common traits don't run as threads through writers who write in different genres. I can tell a text is by Stephen King whether it's horror, sci-fi, or contemporary fiction about escaping from a prison by crawling through the shit pipe... But no one is about to dismiss 'Rita Hayworth' and the Shawshank Redemption' for not being horror, just because its writer is most renowned for horror staples like 'Carrie' and 'Christine'. Nor do they degrade his play at the fantasy western 'Lord of the Rings' style epic 'The Dark Tower' for not being 'Misery'. No one applies genre restrictions to Mr King. So why should we prescribe such restrictions on what is and isn't Lovecraftian fiction? Howard wrote 'Sweet Ermengarde' and just because it is not his normal work does not mean it should be dismissed by anyone. Including me… So, let us regard 'Sweet Ermengarde' as her suitors Squire Hardman, and handsome Jack Manly do in the tale, as a simple country girl who should be judged on her own merits, or at least those of her father's farm and his liquid crop of good moonshine…

If you have not guessed from the names of her suitors alone, 'Sweet Ermengarde' is not a work of subtle humour. Indeed, Lovecraft does his best to throttle a joke out of every opportunity, as this early passage describing his erstwhile heroine shows:

Ermengarde confessed to sixteen summers, and branded as mendacious all reports to the effect that she was thirty. She had large black eyes, a prominent Roman nose, light hair which was never dark at the roots except when the local drug store was short on supplies, and a beautiful but inexpensive complexion.

Subtle is not the word… This is humour with a bludgeon, and strangely enough, it reminds me of very early Prattchett. 'The Colour of Magic,' and 'The Light Fantastic', are both equally pun-laden and aggressive in their parody - unlike Pratchett's later more successful and subtler works that cast direct parody aside. Oddly enough Prattchett parodied Lovecraft in 'The Light Fantastic' with a great old one in an ancient dark, dank temple causing havoc for Rincewind and Twoflower.

'Ermengarde' also has much in common with some of P.G.Wodehouse's shorter fiction of whom Lovecraft was a contemporary and Prattchett a fan. Though both are better writers of humour than Lovecraft on the evidence of this tale, there is enough here to draw favourable comparisons to them all the same.

The target of Lovecraft's parody is a certain kind of novel, which follows a predictable plot; young innocent girl falls in love with a manly boy, while she is subject to the attentions of a lecherous miser who seeks her fortune. There is much spurning, rejection and double-dealing leading to fortunes being reversed and reversed again - while the motives of all become more spurious as time goes by. Until, that is, the young girl becomes more worldly, far less innocent and manipulates events to best suit herself. There is innuendo, puns and a plot which holds a certain amount of delightful silliness about it. A rags to riches story, albeit a parody of one, of the type read by an entirely different crowd to the weird tales audience Lovecraft normally wrote for.

Is this Lovecraft's best work, no, not by any margin. It did not find a market until some six years after his death and even then it was as a filler in a collection of his stories rather than a work in its own right. It stands out only because it is so different from his normal work, and perhaps had he found a market for this kind of tale in the early 1920's, he might have written more under the pseudonym 'Percy Simple'. There was a market for such comic tales, a market from which many writers were making a good living. Perhaps, however, the loss to the comedic pages of magazines like 'Punch' etc. is our gain. Had Lovecraft focused on tales like this he may have gotten closer to his goal of making a living from his writing than he did, but the horror genre would have been poorer for it, and as I said, he was on this evidence no Wodehouse.

THE SCORE: 0 OUT OF 6 TENTACLES, BUT A FEW SMILES

MYTHOS CONNECTIONS: None.

LOVECRAFT TWATTRY: None.

SHOULD YOU READ IT: If you're looking for horror no, but if you want a chuckle, sure.

BLUFFERS FACT: Sweet Ermengarde is also the name of a German Goth rock band, who have produced among other things a whole album of Lovecraft inspired goodness called Ex Oblivione. I am not sure if Lovecraft would have approved, and Percy Simple I suspect would approve even less, but no one ever claimed you have the right to censor what you inspire in others… Any more than editors should decide what can be included in a complete set of your works…

THE NAMELESS CITY

> *"That is not dead which can eternal lie,*
> *And with strange aeons, even death may die."*
> ~Abdul Alhazred

There can be few tales of tales more Lovecraftian than 'The Nameless City'. A tale rejected by 'Weird Tales' twice and then by a succession of other professional titles, before almost being published in a magazine called 'The Fantasy Fan' which managed to fold just after accepting the submission, before finally being published six months before Lovecraft's death in the ponderously titled 'Fanciful Tales of Time and Space' - a quarterly magazine of such high reputation that you have probably never heard of it until now.

The orthodox view taken by many Lovecraft scholars would have it that 'The Nameless City' is the first true mythos story Lovecraft wrote. I don't entirely agree with that orthodox view; there are hints, and suggestions aplenty in earlier works, 'The Temple', 'The Quest of Iranon', 'The Doom That Came To Sarnath' and others. Lovecraft had been finding his way to the streets of 'The Nameless City' for some time. Indeed, the latter of those examples crops up in this story, when our narrator is describing the lost city he has stumbled upon in the Arabian desert...

> *...and thought of Sarnath the Doomed, that stood in the land of Mnar when mankind was young, and of Ib, that was carven of grey stone before mankind existed...*

That orthodox view stems from this tale containing the first mention of everyone's favourite mad Arab, Abdul Alhazred. The writer of that 'dreadful' two line poem at the top of this entry. Dreadful in the literal sense, in that it encompasses dread and the doom that will come to all when the stars are right, the big bad who sleeps below the waves reawakens and the old gods crash through the dimensions we laughingly call 'reality'.

The mad beard tugging, teeth gnashing, doom merchant Arab, and that two line poem, returns in most of the major mythos stories to come, 'The Hound', 'The Festival', 'The Shadow out of Time', 'The Case of Charles Dexter Ward', 'The Dunwich Horror', 'The Whisperer in

Darkness', 'At the Mountains of Madness', 'The Dreams in the Witch House', 'The Thing on the Doorstep', and of course, 'The Call of Cthulhu'. All of which were written after, yet almost without exception published before, 'The Nameless City'. To say Abdul Alhazred has an important role in the Cthulhu mythos is somewhat redundant, so this first mention certainly adds strength to the orthodoxy.

The story was also a favourite of Lovecraft himself, perhaps because this is where so many threads in his earlier work come together to form a greater whole. However, while Lovecraft may have considered this a favourite, it is not without criticism. Lin Carter, who among other works wrote a number of stories based in and around the Cthulhu Mythos, said of it…

"a trivial exercise in Poe-esque gothica", "overwritten and over-dramatic".

Lin's pastiches are probably the largest body of Lovecraft inspired work built directly upon his mythos - and they have made a better living out of Lovecraft's creations than Lovecraft ever did himself. Lin calling this story Poe-esque is firmly in 'pot calling the kettle to confirm its colour' territory as Lin built his career the shoulders of other writers. His Lovecraftian tales are very much written in the style of Lovecraft, just as his Conan and Kull tales are written in the style of Robert E. Howard. While he went on to write a lot of interesting, fun, and well-written work that was entirely his own, in the style of Lin Cater, it is fair to say Lin was a master of the pastiche and hasn't a leg to stand on in accusing Lovecraft of borrowing from Poe. That said, however, Lin is well placed to hold an opinion on whether 'The Nameless City' is 'over written', having spent so much time writing in the style of Lovecraft and here Lin has a point, though I am loathe to agree entirely. 'The Nameless City' does have a certain 'over written' feel to it. Take this passage…

In the darkness there flashed before my mind fragments of my cherished treasury of daemonic lore; sentences from Alhazred the mad Arab, paragraphs from the apocryphal nightmares of Damascius, and infamous lines from the delirious Image du Monde of Gautier de Metz. I repeated queer extracts, and muttered of Afrasiab and the daemons that floated with him down the Oxus; later chanting over and over again a phrase from one of Lord Dunsany's tales…

In that one passage, Lovecraft drops more names than a desperate-for-attention starlet at a Hollywood party. Only the Mad Arab himself is entirely fictional.

There is also the matter of the tension that builds up steadily throughout, as Lovecraft stories are wont to do. But even for Lovecraft, the piling on of tension in this story makes 'The Temple' seem like a merry little jaunt in a submersible… Overwritten may not be entirely fair, as the tale sets out to build layer upon layer of fraught tensions as the narrator delves deeper and deeper into the nameless ruins of a city that predates all historical records, and, as he comes to suspect possibly predates mankind. The more he delves, the more disturbed and the more disturbing his story becomes.

For me the layered approach Lovecraft takes to the tale negates that 'over-dramatic' accusation. It is what it is, and what it is supposed to be. A deep dive into the past, through the dust of aeons, in a city built by a race alien to our understanding, a race of lizard creatures who may still survive in the depths of the ruins, waiting for a time to emerge once more…

I said at the start, few tales are as Lovecraftian as this, the same applies to the tale itself. This is for me is Lovecraft writing for Lovecraft. He did not write this with the view to sell it (though god knows he tried to do so.) He wrote it for himself, for the writer he wanted to be, telling the stories he wanted to tell. Which is why I suspect it was among his favourites; we are always proudest of our true born… If it is, as Lin carter claims, over written, it is overwritten on purpose. This is exactly what Lovecraft wished it to be. After all what is more Lovecraft than this passage towards the end of the tale…

Monstrous, unnatural, colossal, was the thing—too far beyond all the ideas of man to be believed except in the silent damnable small hours when one cannot sleep.

It is not perfect, but it is close to being the perfect Lovecraft tale.

THE SCORE: 5 OUT OF 6 TENTACLES, GROPING OUT FOR US ALL FROM THE DARK RECESSES OF ITS CREATOR'S MIND.

MYTHOS CONNECTIONS: A myriad of references, and one mad Arab.

LOVECRAFT TWATTRY: None.

SHOULD YOU READ IT: Yes, in all its 'overwritten' splendour.

BLUFFERS FACT: 'Fanciful Tales of Time and Space' in which this tale was first published ran for a whole one issue before it disappeared due to the amount it had cost to produce in the first place… it is now a very rare collector's item, so rare in fact that even a copy of the 1977 facsimile reproduction would cost you $40 from a rare book dealer. An original 1936 copy in reasonable condition went for $350 at auction in 2007, which is the most recent sale of one I can find. Lovecraft collectors, in particular, would pay a lot more than that now for a copy should you ever find one in an old attic somewhere.

THE OUTSIDER

Every writer will, on occasion, be influenced in style and subject by those whose writing he admires. That's why they are called influences. Sometimes this is deliberate, sometimes not so much, and on occasion a writer may not realise they have been influenced at all until they read the story back some time later. With that in mind, this is what Lovecraft himself said of 'The Outsider' in a letter a few years after he wrote this macabre and visceral little tale…

> *"It represents my literal though unconscious imitation of Poe at its very height."*

So, when I say this story reminded me of Poe, in much the same way 'The Music of Erich Zann' did, I'm in good company drawing that comparison. Certainly, in style, (and more than a little in content) old Edgar looms large, but the story also harkens back to earlier gothic fiction, most noticeably for me, Mary Shelley's grand opus, which it should be noted, undoubtedly influenced Poe. All the resonances of Frankenstein's monster are here, along with the trappings. A dark, crumbling castle, long abandoned and rotting, the loneliness and longing of a protagonist devoid of companionship, the isolation, despair, and - in the climax of the story - a poignant moment of self-awareness. The tale's protagonist knows nothing of his own history. His first memories are of being alone, wandering the halls of the half-ruined, darkness enshrouded castle. A castle that contains no reflective surfaces, all mirrors long destroyed, and the ever-present darkness shrouding others. He reads old books in the library by the light of spluttering candles and explores the endless dusty corridors and wonders who he is, and from whence he came. He almost imagines himself a ghost, or some other long-dead remnant of this forgotten place. All he knows of the world beyond the castle walls he learnt from books. While he seeks a way to pass beyond the barriers of the forest and the castle walls, long years pass. Longing for companionship in a well of loneliness, dwelling in the decaying darkness among the shadows, the rats, and the ruins. A lost soul embodied in its own futility.

You could only get more gothic than this if you overlaid a 'Sisters Of Mercy' soundtrack, got Peter Cushing to read it to you in a dark velvet smoking jacket and had Peter Lorre serve you with red wine in crystal goblets while you listened...

And the gothic themes continue throughout. When he finally leaves the castle, the protagonist stumbles upon another castle, one strangely familiar to him, yet one full of life. A great party is in full swing, all light and life and joy. The positive to his home's negative. But when he enters the castle his progression through the party is reminiscent to Deaths walking through 'The Masque of the Red Death'... All who see him flee before him, fear and loathing upon their faces. Then there is the final scene, the moment of reveal, which is a replaying of Frankenstein and the pond...

I like a good gothic tale, and that is what Lovecraft gives us with 'The Outsider'. Its heritage is obvious, but it is none the worse for that.

THE SCORE: A SOLID 4 OUT OF 6 TENTACLES, JUST IN CASE THAT SHAMBLING FIGURE COMING UP BEHIND ME HAS BEEN READING MY THOUGHTS ON 'CELEPHAIS' AND WANTS A QUIET WORD

MYTHOS CONNECTIONS: A brief connection to 'The Haunter in the Dark' towards the end of the tale.

LOVECRAFT TWATTRY: None.

SHOULD YOU READ IT: Yes, on a dark and stormy night.

BLUFFERS FACT: Just to be certain of this story's Gothic pretensions, Lovecraft opens the tale with an epigram is from Mary Shelley's contemporary, and close friend of her husband, Keats the romantic poet's 'The Eve of St. Agnes'.

> *That night the Baron dreamt of many a woe;*
> *And all his warrior-guests, with shade and form*
> *Of witch, and demon, and large coffin-worm,*
> *Were long be-nightmared.*
> —*Keats.*

And all you can say to that is turn up the volume on 'Temple of Love' and dig out the eyeliner

THE MOON BOG

If in doubt, the sunken ruins of a lost city are just where you go, at least if you're Old Tentacle Hugger. You have probably noticed that - and if you haven't then you're not really paying attention. Lost cities and ruined temples, the last vestiges of some forgotten culture, often built by some forgotten race, are Lovecraft's staple right back to the earliest of his stories like 'The Tomb'. As a plot device, it turns up everywhere in Lovecraft fiction, even his Dreamlands tales are littered with ancient cities and strange ruins, or echoes of them. So, it no surprise that this tale features a lost city, submerged beneath an Irish bog. 'The Moon Bog' is a bit of an oddity all the same. It was written not as a story to be read in a magazine but as a tale to told over dinner. Specifically, at a Hub Club gathering of amateur journalists in Boston on March 10, 1921.

The tale is set in Ireland primarily because the gathering it was written for had a St. Patrick's day theme to it, and Boston then, as it still is today, is a city of the Irish. Likewise, it has a sunken city in it because if you're Lovecraft and you're rattling something out in a hurry, the sunken ruins of a lost city is just where you go, and handily he had some nice Irish mythology to lean upon…

Ireland is a land of myths, even more so than England, not least because the wilds of Ireland took longer to tame. Also, handily for Lovecraft, Irish myths have never been as well mined as their British, Greek, Norse and European counterparts. Ireland has always been a land on the fringes, and its Celtic roots run deep. The ancient history of the emerald isle, as told by the cycle of texts known as 'Lebor Gabála Érenn' or 'The Book of Invasions' is a rich source of mythology - Christian myths layered on top of their older pagan counterparts. The Ireland of 'Lebor Gabála Érennt' is a rich deep vein of pre-history and prehistoric peoples. The Cessair, the Partholon, the Nemed, the Fir Bolg and the Tuatha De Danann, all, it tells us, resided upon the Isles before the Gaels arrive, but it was the Gaels who eventually formed the core of the Celtic peoples.

Throughout this mythology the peoples of Ireland fight battles and wars against other non-human invaders referred to as 'Fomorians', or as a literal translation would have it 'the undersea ones'. Though Fomorians are also described in other ways, they are the great monstrous race of Irish mythology. A rich vein that was happily mined by

2000AD writer Pat Mills for his Slaine stories. A retelling of 'Lebor Gabála Érenn' with the warped one battling the evils of Fomorians civilisation, and freeing the enslaved people of Ireland from the grip of that ancient alien race…

So that's Ireland for you, steeped in a mythology that almost begs for Lovecraft to use it. The Fomorians could not be more of a myth that harkens to 'Deep Ones' if it held up a sign saying 'scaley prehuman civilisation R'US'. So, combining his own mythos with this ancient Irish mythology should almost be a free pass for Old Tentacle Hugger. A gift that would keep on giving. An open goal that just requires a nudge to get the ball over the line…

Somehow with 'The Moon Bog' Lovecraft manages to miss this open goal…

Don't get me wrong, there is nothing bad about this story. For what it is, it is well executed. It's also as Lovecraft as it can be. But it feels stunted. It lacks a spark within it that would make it more than its whole. I would posit it suffers from its original intent as an orientation. In these days of audiobooks, we are used to listening to stories, but even now were you to write a tale for the sole purpose of it being read out to a crowd you would write it differently. The pattern of words and the use of language you need for what is ultimately an after-dinner speech is different. This is why scripts seldom make for good books…

The tale is simple enough, perhaps too simple. A wealthy American returning to the old country buys the estates of his forefathers. In the process he brings life and wealth back to an impoverished region, but he remains a stranger in an alien culture all the same. What he sees as an opportunity to create more wealth by the draining of the bog, causes uproar. But he dismisses the locals' objections as superstitious ignorance. Thus, he lays the ground for his own fate when folklore proves to have more substance than he was constitutionally brought up to believe. It's simple, and it's predictable, yet passages like the one below hint at so much more that Lovecraft could have made of this tale…

There my eyes dilated again with a wild wonder as great as if I had not just turned from a scene beyond the pale of Nature, for on the ghastly red-litten plain was moving a procession of beings in such a manner as none ever saw before, save in nightmares.

Which is where my real problems with 'The Moon Bog' lie. The story seems rushed, hacked together in short order, without Lovecraft's usual meticulous craft. It was written for an audience rather than a reader. It doesn't invite you into an intimate tryst and allow you to explore with trepidation its hidden harbours. Instead, it just lays out the story and tries to elicit the reaction of a crowd rather than you as an individual.

Also, Irish Folklore it is such a rich vein to be squandered in this story. Perhaps because I have a good grounding in Irish mythology, as well as Pat Mills' explorations of them in the pages of 2000AD with Slaine, but I cannot help but feel there is so much that could have been done here. A combination of Lovecraft's mythos and Irish myth would be deeply layered. There is a good story, a novella, or even a novel to be made of such a combination. But with 'The Moon Bog' Lovecraft fails to make the most of that, and in doing so wasted the opportunity to seed his own mythologies into 'real' Irish mythology. In the end it's a pallid little tale with little to recommend it.

THE SCORE: A DISAPPOINTING 2 OUT OF 6 TENTACLES, WHICH TO BORROW THE WORDS OF SLAINE MCROTH CAN 'KISS MY AXE...'

MYTHOS CONNECTIONS: Oh, but I wish there were...

LOVECRAFT TWATTRY: None.

SHOULD YOU READ IT: No. You could perhaps listen to it on audio and pretend you're at an amateur writers' conference in Boston in 1921, but I'm not sure why you would wish to do that either.

BLUFFERS FACT: Speaking of Slaine... One of his most famous antagonists The Lord Weird Slough Feg would be at home in many a Lovecraft tale.
The ancient, rotting leader of the Drunes and the original Horned God who refused to die when his seven-year reign was over. He ate the Time Worm's eggs to prolong his life and resides at the drune capital Carnac where he spends his time making cave paintings and creating a cult to bring back the old ones.

THE OTHER GODS

Pantheistic gods are cooler than monotheistic ones. I say this not to denigrate anyone's faith. Somethings are just cooler by nature...
The cigarette smoking teenage Marlon Brando in black leather in 'Rebel without a cause'. Leaning against a Harley Davidson answering the onerous question "What are you rebelling against?" with a sneer as he replies, "What have you got...?" is by its very nature cooler than Old Marlon in 'The Godfather' being the don and talking with a mouth full of cotton wool.
Thor, Odin, Loki and all, or Zeus, Ares, Aphrodite and the rest of the toga-wearers who make mortals their playthings, are cooler, than the big, bearded guy in the clouds who created everything, knows everything, and is everywhere. Giant wolves that are going to eat the world, serpents that encircle the earth, frost giants, magic hammers, minotaurs, showers of gold that seduce princesses, hydras and golden fleeces. War gods, thunder gods, love goddesses, gods of wine, muses, fates, feasting halls and homes on clouded mountain tops... is all a whole lot of cool.
A Church of England chapel on a Sunday morning with a dozen choir boys and an organist, not so much...
Cool does not imply good, Bonnie and Clyde were 'cool', Charles Manson was considered by some to be the height of 'cool' right up to the point 'the family' started killing people, Roman Polanski was 'cool', Phil Spector was 'cool'. Cool in not always a good thing...
Besides which while the CoE Monotheistic god may not be 'cool', at least he isn't going around unleashing the Kraken, or hurling lightning bolts at people... Not since the end of the Old Testament anyway...
And that's the thing about Pantheistic gods, they may be cool, but they're also a right set of bastards as a rule, and every pantheon also has its 'other gods'.
For all the fertility goddesses and protecting All-fathers, there's a Loki and a bunch of frost giants or titans. The monotheists have the Devil, who may or may not have all the best tunes. The pantheons have their 'other gods' and they tend towards the nasty side of chaos.
You may sacrifice a goat or seven to Zeus, but you make sure not to upset Hades or Hectate at the same time. No one might openly worship Hel, but they probably tried their best not to upset her just in case. All this mildly heretical preamble leads us to 'The Other Gods'. A

Lovecraft story that sits in the middle of all his works. It also links to a fair few other stories both earlier and later in his bibliography. Its two main characters come from that village of the cat lovers Ulthar. Barzai, the elder of the two, was the one who convinced the elders of the town of the wisdom of not killing felines. This may have had something to do with a particular goddess of Egyptian persuasion who is somewhat feline herself. Or more likely that Lovecraft stalwart who 'came out of Egypt', who is himself later linked to this tale in 'The Dream-Quest Unknown Kadath'. When 'Nyarlathptep' speaks to Randolph Carter in a sardonic fashion of the ill-fated expeditions of other impertinent god-seekers and relates how Barzai's hubris brought him to the baleful attention of the Other Gods who then "did what was to be expected". So, if you don't read Lovecraft in order, thanks for the spoiler there oh wearer of many masks...

The other main character is Barzai's assistant/ apprentice Alat, the son of an innkeeper in Ulthar who witnessed the weird rites of the cats on the night that the old Cotter and his wife are killed. He also turns up in 'The Dream-Quest Unknown Kadath', though by then he is 300 years old, has a beard you could hide a yak in and is running a temple of the elder gods. All of which makes a certain amount of sense as 'The Other Gods' also is where Lovecraft first makes mention of 'unknown Kadath in the cold waste where no man treads.'

In short, there is a lot going on in this story, it sets up a lot of what is to come and not with mere hints - as tended to happen before.

There also a whole lot of lore being slipped into the background that will come back later in Lovecraft's stores. Barzai the wise, for example, earned his moniker by reading such works as the Pnakotic Manuscripts (first mentioned way back in 'Polaris') and the Seven Cryptical Books of Hsan. Though reading forbidden ancient texts seems a very unwise thing to do in the Lovecraftian universe... These strange books crop up again in 'The Dream-Quest Unknown Kadath.' Kadath itself crops up in several stories, including 'Beyond the Mountains of Madness' and in 'Dunwich'. Despite being written in 1921, 'The Other Gods' still predates most of the tales it links to.

Barzai and Alat set out on a quest to look upon the faces of the gods of the earth. It is clearly more Barzai's quest than Alat's. Alat, one suspects, would far rather be at home in Ulthar, sipping warm tea and surrounded by cats... But given what he witnessed in 'The Cats of Ulthar' as a boy, perhaps trailing after a half-mad prophet to a forbidden mountain to look at the faces of the gods seemed a safer option to him... But nevertheless, Alat goes traipsing off with Barzai to the mountain most likely to play host to the gods' version of a high school reunion. You know the kind of thing; drinking, dancing, reminiscing about when you were all powerful and worshipped with human sacrifices before those pesky humans got all monotheistic on you...

The gods of the earth, old pantheons long forgotten, or at least only half-remembered, have been hiding out at the top of mountains for aeons. But those pesky humans keep climbing them and forcing the gods to change mountains because the last thing you want as a declining pantheon is people to see you in your under-crackers watching gameshows in your retirement village, figuratively speaking. Better by far that the humans still think of you as the cool rebel Brando, but once in a while, they like to go to the old corner and hang out for a while. Luckily the locals know well enough to keep away when the clouds start to form around the mountains. Barzai on the other hand...

Barzai scales the mountain, in true zealot style. Regardless of his own safety, or the safety of poor Alat who follows on behind. Alat is at least wise enough to hang back a little, while his mentor races ahead. Into the clouds goes Barzai, to see at last the faces of the gods... But when he gets there, he is not greeted by...

> *"The other gods! The other gods! The gods of the outer hells that guard the feeble gods of earth! ... Look away! ... Go back! ... Do not see! ... Do not see! ... The vengeance of the infinite abysses ... That cursed, that damnable pit ... Merciful gods of earth, I am falling into the sky!"*

Well, there you go, what do you expect when you try to sneak up on the good half of the pantheon. When you crash a high school reunion there's gonna be the bullies there as well as your high school sweetheart and that smart guy from chemistry... Where there be gods, there be the other gods, the twisted ones, the monsters...

There is a lot in this short tale, a lot that ties other stories together, and which lays the seed of things to come. But it is also a good old yarn, a nice bit of mythology, and has a whole lot of cool about it. You can see the ending coming, but that's beside the point. The strange behaviour of the gods, so beyond the comprehension of mortal man is matched only by the idiocy of the one who is so determined to look them in the face. While the only sane ones here are the villagers in the foothills of the mountain who point out the gross errors Barzai and

Alat are making.

THE SCORE: A COOL 5 OUT OF 6 SLITHERING TENTACLES OF ENCROACHING DOOM AS THIS TALE IS STEEPED IN LOVECRAFT'S LORE AND KNOWS EXACTLY WHAT IT IS DOING. BUT THEN I AM A SUCKER FOR PANTHEISTIC GODS, IT'S THE COOL LEATHER JACKETS I'M SURE…

MYTHOS CONNECTIONS: They are everywhere in this story

LOVECRAFT TWATTRY: None.

SHOULD YOU READ IT: Yes, but not before burning an offering to Thor

BLUFFERS FACT: If there is a moral to this story it is this: if someone is proclaimed as wise due to reading a few books no one else understands and then starts raving about climbing mountains to look upon the face of the gods, giving them a wide berth is probably safer for your health.
It's a good moral…

AZATHOTH

The novel that never was, about a deity never mentioned in the fragment that remains, 'Azathoth' is arguably Lovecraft's great lost work. If a copy of the complete word exists, it is only in the Library of Unwritten Books in the castle of Morpheus, and if that's the case the Liberian Lucian isn't of a mind to lend it out.
Despite not being mentioned in the story that bears his name 'Azathoth' is the biggest baddest deity of all the outer gods and he of whom 'Nyarlathotep' is merely the Herald. He makes appearances in several other works by Old Tentacle Hugger including 'The Dream-Quest of Unknown Kadath'. That novella, some Lovecraft scholars believe, follows the same ideas and the basic plot that Lovecraft had planned for this abortive attempt at a novel. Notes by Lovecraft on the manuscript would seem to point to this being the case.

A terrible pilgrimage to seek the knighted throne of the far daemon-sultan Azathoth. And... Weird Eastern tale in a 18th-century manner...

Which is not too far removed from the core plot of Kadath. But alas unless we manage to sneak past the gates of horn and ivory to enter Dream's Library we will never know. What we are left with is only the 500 words that were published posthumously.
While the story is unimportant in the grand scheme of things, the influence of 'Azathoth' himself on wider Lovecraftian culture is enormous. The star-spawn gets everywhere and creeps into many other stories, which isn't bad for what amounts in modern terms to the equivalent of a scrap-end of fiction littering a writer's hard drive. All writers have a lot of scrap-ends floating about, be it as ones and zeros or on bits of paper, as it would have been in Lovecraft's day, but few ever have the overall impact of 'Azathoth' on popular culture. Something akin to a world-sized monstrosity eating planets... Though it is the 'Azathoth' of other tales which has sunk him so deep into the collective Lovecraftian zeitgeist. Were I giving out tentacles for impact, then this tale would get 6 of the little suckers. But for the tale itself, it is a disappointing 1. If that seems harsh then I would say this: Lovecraft never sought publication for these words, it is an incomplete passage, even as a short story and perhaps it would have been better

left buried in his scrap ends pile. If it had been left buried 'Azathoth' would still be who he is and have his same place in the zeitgeist. Nothing is added here, it's a neat piece of creative writing, but beyond that, it is nothing at all.

You may have noticed I have said very little, if anything, about the story itself, and that's because there is very little you can say about it. It is only 500 words or so long after all and doesn't go anywhere much in the process, but as its public domain, here are those 500 words for you...

AZATHOTH BY H P LOVECRAFT

When age fell upon the world, and wonder went out of the minds of men; when grey cities reared to smoky skies tall towers grim and ugly, in whose shadow none might dream of the sun or of spring's flowering meads; when learning stripped earth of her mantle of beauty, and poets sang no more save of twisted phantoms seen with bleared and inward-looking eyes; when these things had come to pass, and childish hopes had gone away forever, there was a man who travelled out of life on a quest into the spaces whither the world's dreams had fled.

Of the name and abode of this man but little is written, for they were of the waking world only; yet it is said that both were obscure. It is enough to know that he dwelt in a city of high walls where sterile twilight reigned, and that he toiled all day among shadow and turmoil, coming home at evening to a room whose one window opened not on the fields and groves but on a dim court where other windows stared in dull despair. From that casement one might see only walls and windows, except sometimes when one leaned far out and peered aloft at the small stars that passed. And because mere walls and windows must soon drive to madness a man who dreams and reads much, the dweller in that room used night after night to lean out and peer aloft to glimpse some fragment of things beyond the waking world and the greyness of tall cities. After years he began to call the slow-sailing stars by name, and to follow them in fancy when they glided regretfully out of sight; till at length his vision opened to many secret vistas whose existence no common eye suspects. And one night a mighty gulf was bridged, and the dream-haunted skies swelled down to the lonely watcher's window to merge with the close air of his room and make him a part of their fabulous wonder.

There came to that room wild streams of violet midnight glittering with dust of gold; vortices of dust and fire, swirling out of the ultimate spaces and heavy with perfumes from beyond the worlds. Opiate oceans poured there, litten by suns that the eye may never behold and having in their whirlpools strange dolphins and sea-nymphs of unrememberable deeps. Noiseless infinity eddied around the dreamer and wafted him away without even touching the body that leaned stiffly from the lonely window; and for days not counted in men's calendars the tides of far spheres bare him gently to join the dreams for which he longed; the dreams that men have lost. And in the course of many cycles they tenderly left him sleeping on a green sunrise shore; a green shore fragrant with lotus-blossoms and starred by red camalotes.

And that's it…. Until the Sandman opens up his library and lets us read the novel that was never written…

THE SCORE: 1 OUT OF 6 PROBING OUT OF THE DARKNESS, THERE MAY HAVE BEEN MANY MORE TO COME BUT WE WILL NEVER KNOW.

MYTHOS CONNECTIONS: From the story itself, none.

LOVECRAFT TWATTRY: None.

SHOULD YOU READ IT: Well clearly, as you just have this question is redundant, but yes.

BLUFFERS FACT: The treaty of the Azures, (a fictional treaty between humanity and the Deep Ones in Charles Stross's Laundry novels.) stipulates, quite wisely…
> *Neither party shall summon Azathoth without prior consent from the other party…*

As summoning 'Azathoth' would, if the blind, idiot star god answered, spell the end of all life on earth. Or at the very least an explosion the equivalent of a small nuclear arsenal going off. The most worrying thing about that clause is that either side thought it was needed. Though personally, I suspect it was the Deep Ones who insisted upon it, having met a few members of humanity over the years. I can see why they would…

HERBERT WEST RE-ANIMATOR

Opinions are, as someone famous once vulgarly said, like arseholes, everyone body has one and they stink up the place when let loose... 'Herbert West – Re-Animator' is a tale that inspires many opinions. S.T. Joshi, who has carved out a career as a Lovecraft scholar, opinion on old 'Herbert' is summed up as:

"Herbert West– Re-Animator" is "universally acknowledged as Lovecraft's poorest work."

Which is somewhat damning, but also a relatively bold statement. For one thing, it's not 'Celephais' and not being 'Celephais' alone debunks that statement in my opinion. Yes, I am aware that I am a voice in the wilderness when it comes to my utter distaste for 'Celephais', but at the same time, I am not entirely alone in considering 'Celephais' to be a festering pile of twaddle. I also suspect I am not alone in disagreeing with Joshi on this subject because 'Re-Animator' may have its problems, but it is far from the poorest piece of Lovecraft's fiction. Indeed, quite a few people like it rather a lot...

S.T.Joshi is, however, in good company in his disparagement in one sense at least, as the Old Tentacle Hugger himself was far from happy with it. He reputably claimed he wrote it only for the $5 fee per instalment he received from 'Weird Tales'. He wasn't a fan of writing serials, detested the need for a cliffhanger at the end of an 'episode', and loathed doing a recap at the beginning of every instalment. None of this was his usual style and 'Re-Animator' was the only out and out serial he ever wrote. His later works in a longer format were often serialised, but they were serialised without the trappings of the serial. It's not an unjust criticism either as, when you read the story with modern eyes, those recaps and the hacked in buildups to 'cliff-hangers' are a little on the painful side. It's also fair to say it's not the kind of journey you expect when you read Lovecraft. It's far more pulp than any of his usual writings, there is little that could be considered literary art going on here and it all those cliffhangers and recaps get in the way of the usual slow creep towards impending doom that is oh so familiar with Lovecraft's work.

Putting aside the issues Old Tentacle Hugger had with this tale, it is worth mentioning that he was actually breaking new ground in horror with Herbert West. This was one of first widely published stories which framed the re-animated dead as mindless flesh-eating monsters. Effectively Herbert gave birth to a genre in this respect. As Bram Stoker's Dracula is to vampires, Lovecraft's Herbert West is to zombies. Without Herbert West there may never have been a 'Night of the Living Dead', 'Dawn of the Dead', 'Day of the Dead', 'Light Supper of the Dead'… George Romero owes Lovecraft a bit of a debt for his inspiration here. As does anyone sitting down to watch Rick Grimes have another bad day in 'The Walking Dead'. Ultimately for all the cultish following Lovecraft has through his tales of Cthulhu, Nyarlathotep, and Azathoth, the much-disparaged Herbert West has had the biggest and longest lasting impact on popular culture out of everything Lovecraft wrote. It's rather a shame, therefore, that he was less than proud of this creation…

Importantly, if you put aside that irritating recap at the beginning of every instalment, this is actually a good read, which is all you should really be measuring a story on. While far from his best, it's certainly not the worst. The pulpy nature of it adds to its appeal as well. I grew up on Saturday morning Flash Gordon serials, rerun on the BBC as cheap kids programming. There is an aspect of the serial format I genuinely enjoy - and I love a good B movie. While this story is, in effect, six short stories following a common narrative it is still something I'd been aching for when I first started reading through Lovecraft's work in order; a tale which has some story arc to it. It's the longest story up to this point in the list and because of that the characters have space to develop.

Lovecraft other long works were still unwritten in 1922 and at this stage in his career Lovecraft was still trying to find his audience. Doing this serial opened up the likes of 'Weird Tales' and other magazines to Lovecraft which until this story were a market he'd never had. After, Herbert Lovecraft's stories were much more in demand, and many earlier tales were first published after Herbert West. For all its faults this was his breakthrough piece and without his Re-Animator, we may never have heard of old tentacle face and the rest at all.

Yes, it's pulpy, and yes, it's not classic Lovecraft fare, but it's none the worse for that. While the Old Tentacle Hugger and his more devoted minions may look upon it with scorn, it has both an important place in the cannon and charms all of its own. There is something infinitely interesting in the way Herbert descends towards that 'mad' scientist tag as his story develops. Lovecraft does a great job of describing this slow decline towards insanity, edged with a cold logic that puts his work beyond mere concepts of morality. When we first meet him, he is messing about with mice in the lab trying to find a way to defeat death. By the end, he is less interested in restoring a semblance of a true life back to men as to animating dead tissue in the form of amputated limbs attached to bits of lizards and other macabre constructions. While the narrator, the Igor to his Doctor Frankenstein, steadily moves from a form of hero worship to terrorised victim, incapable of breaking away from his abuser. There is horror and humanity in this tale, the latter is something Lovecraft has often been accused of lacking.

There are however also a few elements the story could do without, the darker stuff like Lovecraft's unfortunate racism, which I would sooner edit out that the annoying recaps at the start of each episode.

Overall, though Re-Animator is just a fun story, its pulp qualities adding to its charm. Purist Lovecraftian scholars like Joshi may disapprove of it but it's fun to read. And in the end, isn't that the point of a story?

THE SCORE: A COOL 4 OUT OF 6 ZOMBIE TENTACLES REACHING OUT FOR BRAINS.

MYTHOS CONNECTIONS: Some minor connections to Miskatonic University and Arkham.

LOVECRAFT TWATTRY: Unfortunately, there is more than a little racism in this story, it's not entirely overt, but it is there.

SHOULD YOU READ IT: Yes, its light, its pulp, its frankly a tad ridiculous, but it is certainly entertaining

BLUFFERS FACT: Re-Animator is the most successful of all Lovecraft's tales when it comes to the film industry and other media. The story has a broader appeal than other Lovecraftian fiction. It doesn't have the issues that have caused so many other attempts to bring Lovecraft to the big screen to falter. It has a story that can be told on the simplest of levels which certainly does it no harm. It's a mad scientist makes monsters story after all. Both Hollywood mainstream and its 'B' movie studios have been using that basic idea for many decades. It also has all the tropes of a cut-price Frankenstein without the self-consciousness. 1985's Re-Animator was probably the most successful of several adaptations and managed to spawn two admittedly less successful sequels. Then there was the 'Herbert West: Re-Animator' Italian reboot movie in 2017, which oddly is the best of the four.

HYPNOS

"…Young with the youth that is outside time, and with beauteous bearded face, curved, smiling lips, Olympian brow, and dense locks waving and poppy-crowned."

As gods go in Lovecraft's fiction, the Greek god of sleep is probably one of the least disturbing. Lovecraft's elder gods are usually utterly terrifying after all. Tentacle-faced gigantic, winged beasts who consider humanity to be an all you can eat buffet laid out for breakfast once the stars are right. Gods whose visage (should you fully comprehend them) will cause your brains to start leaking out of your ears, tend to inspire a modicum of awe. A god of sleep seems a little mundane in comparison yet before we make any sweeping judgements let's consider sleep a moment. In the original Greek myths, Hypnos is the son of the night and darkness, a brother to death, who resides in Hades. Sleep is often described as the little death. Which is why old tentacle face lies in a sleep akin to death beneath the oceans. And where there is sleep, there are dreams - and dreams in Lovecraft's fictions have a nasty habit of being more than mere nightly meandering of a mind trying to bring order to the chaos of the day. So, let's not write of Hypnos just yet. After all the night is dark and full of terrors…

Fear of sleep is what haunts the narrator of this story - a fear that the narrator brings on himself. As so often with Lovecraft's stories, the narrator is unnamed. I occasionally wonder what fear of naming protagonists is called. But while we do not know his name, we do know he is a sculptor, a bit of a recluse and has been, for most of his life, friendless. This is until he meets a mysterious man at the railway station and with somewhat strange logic, he realises the stranger will be his friend the moment he opens his:

'immense, sunken, and widely luminous eyes'

Because let's face it, when you meet a mysterious stranger in a railway station with huge sunken eyes that glow, the first thing that crosses your mind is the word 'friend'… but hey, artists have always had a certain fluidity of sanity even outside of Lovecraft's fiction. What our sculptor sees in this stranger is 'knowledge he has always sought' reflected in those strange eyes. And so, he takes the stranger home with him and spends his days making sculptures of his new friend, while spending his nights...

'exploring worlds beyond human comprehension.'

He and the stranger together in their dreams seek to transcend into the unknown in order to rule the universe, through the excessive use of drugs... Artists, what can you say?

Eventually in these explorations of a shared dreamscape they come to a barrier they cannot cross and when they awaken once more the stranger warns the sculpture that from then on they must avoid sleep at all costs. Which can only be achieved through the excessive use of drugs... It's like the sixties all over again...

Or would have been if Lovecraft had been alive in the sixties and writing this story then. The sculptor would doubtless be a pop culture artist called Andy and spend his time hanging around with assorted Beatles. For a teetotaller Old Tentacle Hugger certainly wrote his share of drug fantasies. This is hardly the first time his narrators have been heavy users of powdery substances...

With the aid of drugs, the two men avoid sleep as much as possible, but when on occasion they succumb, they rapidly age in appearance and are plagued by nightmares which, in true Lovecraftian fashion, the narrator refuses to explain.

Eventually one night, the stranger falls into a deep sleep and becomes impossible to rouse. The narrator finally snaps, starts screaming wildly until he faints, and when he awakes, he is surrounded by his neighbours and the police. When he tries to explain and express his fear for the stranger, his neighbours insist he never had a friend staying with him, yet there in the centre of the room, is a statue of the stranger with the weird eyes. Engraved with the Greek word: ΥΠΝΟΣ. Which is Hypnos in the Greek alphabet.

So, there you go, the story is either the drug fuelled fantasy life of an artist, his obsession with a strange man that he equated to a lesser-known Greek gods... or a visitation of that lesser-known Greek god upon a mortal that ends in madness... A little sixties vibe written by someone who never lived to see the sixties.

In all honesty the only thing missing is a girl called Lucy hanging about on a cloud wearing nothing but a diamond studded tiara and Sergeant Pepper playing in the background...

There are those who speculate that the interactions between the two main characters in Hypnos, much like in his other Greek story, 'The Tree', are rooted in Lovecraft's repressed homosexual tendencies and his desire to be punished for them, rooted in his firm right-wing political affiliations and self-loathing.

In fairness, the signs are all there - the failure of his marriage to his cousin, his closeness to female relatives, bouts of depression, inherent misogyny and homophobia, while far from conclusive, do suggest repressed homosexuality may have been behind many of these issues. It is, however, speculation; no one knows the truth apart from Howard, who isn't in a position to speak on the matter, and ultimately is purely his own affair and no one else's business.

If this is the case, however, it would explain much of Lovecraft's character, and his somewhat predictable 1920's right-wing reactionary politics. As is so often the case, what he has been taught to despise within himself he learns to hate in others all the more. Which if true is very sad indeed, for if he had lived in more enlightened times, he may have had a far happier life.

But speculations on Lovecraft's sexuality aside, this in essence is a bit of an odd tale and one I am not very fond of, though I am not exactly sure why. I don't think the story has aged well, not because of anything internal to the story, but because the world has moved on. The narrator is not some strange junkie living a strange wild, life because we as a society have had the sixties, and the seventies, the eighties, the nineties… etc. Junkie artists are not unusual within our frame of reference, they don't inspire a sense of fascination when they have become a stereotype within the mainstream… The 1920's doubtless had plenty of junkie artists of its own, but they were just less run-of-the-mill, they retained a little alluring mystery to them that they just don't have for a modern reader. We are the 'Trainspotting' generation - even the actual sixties and LSD trip fiction seems a little tame in comparison to Irvine Welsh, dead babies on the ceiling and diving into the worst toilet in Scotland.

It's unfair of me I suspect, to expect a teetotaller from prohibition era Providence Rhode Island to match up in drug fantasies to the sixties, let alone the nineties. Normally I wouldn't compare fiction in such a way but with Hypnos I struggled not to. There is also the mild absurdity of the god of sleep telling someone not to sleep… Still, don't let me bring a downer on it all… Pop one of these and have pleasant dreams instead…

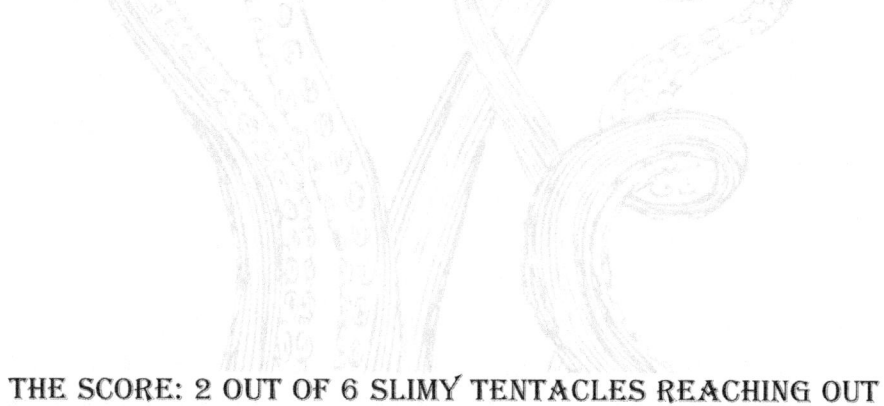

THE SCORE: 2 OUT OF 6 SLIMY TENTACLES REACHING OUT FROM THE PILLBOX.

MYTHOS CONNECTIONS: None of note

LOVECRAFT TWATTRY: Homophobia, for the reasons discussed above.

SHOULD YOU READ IT: Go read Irvine Welsh instead

BLUFFERS FACT: Hypnophobia, the fear of sleep, takes its name from the Greek god for whom this story is named.

WHAT THE MOON BRINGS

ales …the spectral summer when the moon shone down on the old garden where I wandered; the spectral summer of narcotic flowers and humid seas of foliage that bring wild and many-coloured dreams…

Lovecraft at his best is a master of lurid, weird description and verbose excess, sometimes he does this to such an extent you can read a whole story and find yourself wondering what the hell it was all about. It's one reason why we go back to Lovecraft so often and re-read the tales. It is also the reason that sometimes, mere fragments of a tale appear in his cannon of stories, as with the unfinished 'Azathoth'. Most of these fragments were not published in his lifetime but appeared posthumously when appetite for his stories caused those who managed his estate to dig through the equivalent of his old hard drives. It's not always the case, however, some of these short fragment tales were published before his death, 'What the Moon Brings' being a case in point - at least that is a view taken by many. Personally, I think it is a tale complete within itself, short though it may be. To call it a fragment somewhat belittles it…
Of the Dream Cycle tales, it is among my favourites, if not actually my favourite. Which may well be down to my dislike of the later Dream Cycle stories. I am not counting tales like 'The Cats of Ulthar' here, but those purely Dream Cycle stories that other tales are sometimes lumped in with.
I'm not going to say a great deal about this story because there are only so many times you can say, 'It's based upon a dream Lovecraft had…' or, 'For a teetotaller, the bard of Providence didn't half have some odd dreams…' or even 'Old Tentacle Hugger's been on the night nurse again…'. Occasionally you just have to go with it. It is, however, public domain, so, read it, indulge yourself for a few minutes in verbose descriptions and a strange ride through the subconscious of that lamentable genius, Old Tentacle Hugger, and his odd desire to be eaten by sea worms, from which you can draw your own conclusions…

WHAT THE MOON BRINGS BY H.P. LOVECRAFT

I hate the moon—I am afraid of it—for when it shines on certain scenes familiar and loved it sometimes makes them unfamiliar and hideous.

It was in the spectral summer when the moon shone down on the old garden where I wandered; the spectral summer of narcotic flowers and humid seas of foliage that bring wild and many-coloured dreams. And as I walked by the shallow crystal stream I saw unwonted ripples tipped with yellow light, as if those placid waters were drawn on in resistless currents to strange oceans that are not in the world. Silent and sparkling, bright and baleful, those moon-cursed waters hurried I knew not whither; whilst from the embowered banks white lotos blossoms fluttered one by one in the opiate night-wind and dropped despairingly into the stream, swirling away horribly under the arched, carven bridge, and staring back with the sinister resignation of calm, dead faces.

And as I ran along the shore, crushing sleeping flowers with heedless feet and maddened ever by the fear of unknown things and the lure of the dead faces, I saw that the garden had no end under that moon; for where by day the walls were, there stretched now only new vistas of trees and paths, flowers and shrubs, stone idols and pagodas, and bendings of the yellow-litten stream past grassy banks and under grotesque bridges of marble. And the lips of the dead lotos-faces whispered sadly, and bade me follow, nor did I cease my steps till the stream became a river, and joined amidst marshes of swaying reeds and beaches of gleaming sand the shore of a vast and nameless sea.

Upon that sea the hateful moon shone, and over its unvocal waves weird perfumes brooded. And as I saw therein the lotos-faces vanish, I longed for nets that I might capture them and learn from them the secrets which the moon had brought upon the night. But when the moon went over to the west and the still tide ebbed from the sullen shore, I saw in that light old spires that the waves almost uncovered, and white columns gay with festoons of green seaweed. And knowing that to this sunken place all the dead had come, I trembled and did not wish again to speak with the lotos-faces.

Yet when I saw afar out in the sea a black condor descend from the sky to seek rest on a vast reef, I would fain have questioned him, and asked him of those whom I had known when they were alive. This I would have asked him had he not been so far away, but he was very far, and could not be seen at all when he drew nigh that gigantic reef.

So I watched the tide go out under that sinking moon, and saw gleaming the spires, the towers, and the roofs of that dead, dripping city. And as I watched, my nostrils tried to close against the perfume-conquering stench of the world's dead; for truly, in this unplaced and forgotten spot had all the flesh of the churchyards gathered for puffy sea-worms to gnaw and glut upon.

Over those horrors the evil moon now hung very low, but the puffy worms of the sea need no moon to feed by. And as I watched the ripples that told of the writhing of worms beneath, I felt a new chill from afar out whither the condor had flown, as if my flesh had caught a horror before my eyes had seen it.

Nor had my flesh trembled without cause, for when I raised my eyes I saw that the waters had ebbed very low, shewing much of the vast reef whose rim I had seen before. And when I saw that this reef was but the black basalt crown of a shocking eikon whose monstrous forehead now shone in the dim moonlight and whose vile hooves must paw the hellish ooze miles below, I shrieked and shrieked lest the hidden face rise above the waters, and lest the hidden eyes look at me after the slinking away of that leering and treacherous yellow moon.

And to escape this relentless thing I plunged gladly and unhesitatingly into the stinking shallows where amidst weedy walls and sunken streets fat sea-worms feast upon the world's dead.

THE SCORE: 5 OUT OF 6 FIVE SLITHERING TENTACLES REACHING UP FROM THE SEAFLOOR AS THIS IS PERHAPS THE BEST DREAM SEQUENCE LOVECRAFT EVER WROTE.

MYTHOS CONNECTIONS: None.

LOVECRAFT TWATTRY: None.

SHOULD YOU READ IT: As you just have, it would be remiss of me at this point to say no, would it not?

BLUFFERS FACT: Lotos in Greek Mythology is a fruit that induces forgetfulness and a dreamy languor in those who eat it. Whether this is the reason for using Lovecraft's use of an archaic spelling of Lotus is open to conjecture.

THE HOUND

"From one of the crumbling gravestones–dated 1747–I chipped a small piece to carry away. It lies before me as I write–and ought to suggest some sort of horror story. I must place it beneath my pillow as I sleep…" H.P. Lovecraft

Just on the off chance, you had any doubts as to whether Howard Philip Lovecraft was a bit on the odd side, that quote is not from one of his stories. It is drawn from a letter Lovecraft sent to his friend Rheinhart Kleiner, after a visit to a Flatbush Reformed Church in Brooklyn NY which he spent looking at gravestones. This was in 1922, a few weeks before he wrote 'The Hound' a story which centres around a bit of gentle grave robbery by two young English men and the horrifying events that their thievery sets in motion.
There are two schools of thought on Lovecraft stealing bits of gravestones and sleeping on them. One would describe him by making a phrase out of the words 'mad frogs as a box of' arranged in a slightly different order. The other would suggest that Lovecraft's source of inspiration was no more than a tad eccentric. If you think it's perfectly normal behaviour then we should probably worry about you, or possibly you just wear a lot of black clothing, listen to 'The Sisters of Mercy' are into the whole 'dark' aesthetic and know all the words to 'This Corrosion'.
Personally, I wear a lot of black, grew up on the late 80's alternative music, dimly lit clubs, lots of hairspray and dark eyeshadow. Some of my favourite albums are 'Floodland', 'Nymphamine', and 'Some Girls Wander by Mistake' so I am not judging anyone here, not even Old Tentacle Hugger himself. That said, I can't remember ever stealing bits of gravestones and tucking them under my pillow no matter how much I was searching for inspiration… However, Lovecraft did and despite its rather eccentric (or just plain creepy) inspiration, 'The Hound' is both one of his more idiosyncratic 1920's tales, while also being one that could easily be set in modern times.
Here then is the thing, our usual unnamed narrator and his best friend, confidant and fellow despoiler of graves 'St' John are remarkably easy to relate to, for all their strange infatuations. Unlike many of Lovecraft's characters, who are generally firmly rooted in 1920 East Coast

American angst, these two have a far more modern angst about them. They are in love with, or at least fascinated by, the arcane and the mystical, but most of all death. Not for these things themselves but for the aesthetic of them. In short, for the look of the thing. If Lovecraft were writing this tale now, the sub-culture to which these characters aspire should be obvious. Because, well…The pair have built their own… 'Temple of Love' for the aesthetics of the night, the dark places, of death and the arcane, in the cellar of an old manor house out on a deserted stretch of moorland. In it, they keep relics and other things they collected between them, but only provided the aesthetics were right. If the moon was the right kind of luminous yellow on an autumn night, if the storm clouds were the right kind of ominous, if the left hand of a murderer was the left hand of a murderer buried in an unmarked grave at a crossroads, and not just some random left-handed murder buried within god's grace…

In case you have not guessed where I am going with this. St John and his friend are Goths… Or at least the archetypal portrait of goths that we are used to seeing in popular culture.

Before I go any further with this analogy, however, I need to point out real goths are happy, well-adjusted people, they laugh at cats on the internet, dance with joyous abandon, and - while they may have skull candle holders, ashtrays shaped like bats and love Tim Burton movies - they would also happily invite you to take part in their 'The Nightmare Before Christmas' singalongs. While the aesthetics of wearing black lace veils in a churchyard, looking moody in the twilight and pretending to avoid direct sunlight, may appeal to them, they don't as a rule go around despoiling graves. They are far more likely to want to go down the pub, sit around, and have a bit of a laugh with their friends. They are a happy people and they have the best Halloween parties…

But back to 'The Hound' and everything is going well for St John and his friend until they chose to despoil the wrong grave that lies in a small cemetery in the grounds of a Dutch Reform church in Holland. It is from this grave that the pair, having followed clues from an old text, take possession of a strange amulet with a stranger inscription. An inscription, they learn after some research, is taken from a certain book written by a certain mad Arab.

This is actually the first time this particular tome is mentioned in Lovecraft's stories, though it is not the first time Abdul Alhazred's name comes up. That the amulet bears an inscription taken from 'The

Necronomicon' would, you'd think, be enough of a warning not to play fast and loose with it - or would at least make you inclined to put the damn thing back where it came from and go join a monastery… But no, instead our two proto-Goths put it on a shelf in their basement shrine, and light a candle beneath it, because it seems like a good idea to draw attention to their new possession…

From this point on the story becomes predictable fare, as St John and friend begin a slow descent into fear and madness as strange occurrences start to take place. Fingers scraping on doors. Strange sounds in the night. The howls of some monstrous beastie that follows them. 'The Hound's' hunting of the pair and seeking retribution. St John is eaten alive by the beast, and the narrator endeavours to return the amulet to the grave in Holland. Guess how well that goes…

Lovecraft was not overly fond of this tale, dismissing it as "a dead dog" and "a piece of junk". I don't altogether share his opinion. Sure, it has some very obvious tropes, you know where it is going long before it gets there, and it lacks his normal slow brooding buildup. I'll also admit there is very little that stands out about it, apart from it being a tale that would be an easy one to set now, for all it's slight 'Gothexplotationess' which isn't a word but should be… Yet I've a certain affection for 'The Hound'. It is one of Lovecraft's easiest stories for anyone who has never read Lovecraft to jump in with. It's Lovecraft-lite in a way. Focusing on the story rather than his normal verboseness it's a gentle enjoyable read.

As for the proto-goths St John and his friend, well if they had just chilled out to The Cults, 'Love' Album rather than gone about digging up amulets in Dutch graveyards all would have been well…

THE SCORE: A COOL 4 OUT OF 6 EYESHADOW BLACK TENTACLES WITH OPAQUE CONTACT LENSES.

MYTHOS CONNECTIONS: Necronomicon, the mad Arab and the plateau of Leng are all mentioned

LOVECRAFT TWATTRY: Gothsploitation… but I'm not sure we can hold that against him

SHOULD YOU READ IT: Yes, while wearing black eyeshadow and listening to Robert Smith

BLUFFERS FACT: The reference to Leng is one of the first mentions of Lovecraft's imaginary plateau, before this story it had only appeared in 'Celephais'. This is not a reason to read 'Celephais', no such reason exists…

THE LURKING FEAR

Old Tentacle Hugger has inspired a lot of writers over the years. He's also inspired an awful lot of band names, enough to say there is definitely something about Lovecraft and musicians. Not that I can claim to be above the occasional musical reference as you may have noticed. With this in mind it would be remiss not to mention that if you google 'The Lurking Fear' the first things that pops up is not the Lovecraft story, but the Swedish death metal supergroup... Yes, supergroup. Formed by a group of death metal artists from influential and successful Swedish death metal bands, several of which I have even heard of... What is it about the Scandinavians and heavy metal? Must be the Viking in them...

The Lurking Fear are not, it has to be said, my usual cup of Earl Grey. While I appreciate death metal, I'd seldom listen to more than a couple of such cacophonous tracks in a row, but I can recognise good death metal when I hear it and The Lurking Fear are damn good death metal, so if it's in your ballpark give them a listen, I'd recommend the wonderfully Lovecraftian track 'The Starving Gods of Old'... But back to the 'literary' review...

With 'The Lurking Fear' Lovecraft is back up in the Catskill mountains - he has a real thing about the Catskills, or at least about the people living there. He is as unpleasant about the locals in this tale as he was in 'Beyond the Wall of Sleep'. Specifically, he refers to them as...

...a degenerate squatter population inhabiting pitiful hamlets on isolated slopes. Normal beings seldom visited the locality...

Normal, in this case one suspects means White New England Presbyterians. Lovecraft, as I have mentioned occasionally, but not as often as I might have done, was a man whose opinions on politics, race and gender don't sit well with me. I read him with my eyes wide open to his failings and a recognition that while 'he lived in a different time,' is no defence, it does require a little leeway. Suffice to say that Lovecraft's character's opinions about the people of the Catskill's are consistent enough whenever they crop up in his fiction that one can only suspect it reflects his own views very closely, and they are not pleasant opinions...

'The Lurking Fear' centres around an old mansion in the mountains which once belonged to rich Dutch immigrant. The Martense mansion is one of those places that abound in Lovecraft's fiction, an abandoned half ruin of which there are many foreboding local legends. Foreboding legends that, the locals at least believe, have more than a grain of truth about them, given recent events (which the narrator relates), including the massacre of a whole village one stormy night which led both the narrator and a flood of reporters to the region. It's odd that the narrator spends so much of this story belittling the humanity of the locals, (he is very fond of the word 'degenerate') while putting a great deal of weight on local's tales. He is, however, a man who describes himself as having a 'love of the grotesque and the terrible…' and claims to have 'made my career a series of quests for strange horrors in literature and in life'. So, he is a man used to listening to those he considers 'degenerate' when he wants something from them, but the isn't that always the way…

This is another tale that is separated into several parts, as it was originally published as a serial. Unlike the first of the serialised tales, 'Herbert West: Re-animator,' it doesn't suffer from recapping at the start of each episode, which is a blessing. It does, however, lack 'Re-animator's' quirky charm. More importantly, neither does it have the sense of progression you get in 'Herbert West'. In part that can be explained away because the story covers a shorter time span, 'Re-animator' covers a decade or more of Herbert's life, whereas the whole of 'The Lurking Fear' take place over the course of just a couple of months, but it is a poorer story for the lack of real progression in the character. Where 'Re-animator' charts Herbert West's descent into depravity and madness, which carries the story through its various threads, 'The Lurking Fear' feels more like a few short stories strategically nailed together with a common narrative to make a longer tale. There really is no reason you could not treat each of the four parts as separate tales if you wanted to, and it reads as if Lovecraft certainly did so when he wrote it…

The narrator manages to survive each episode, unlike whomever the 'hero' gets to tag along with him each time, who die off like red shirts on an away mission. Which is one of the problems; new characters are introduced as no more than fodder for the monster to kill, and you realise this very quickly because the author doesn't invest much in them either. By the third episode the redshirts don't even get names, just grizzly deaths at the hands of the monsters…

The monsters themselves are cave-dwelling mole-like bestial creatures that it's hinted are the degenerate descendants of the Martense family. They share a common genetic trait with the family in the oddity in their eye colour.

This is where this whole tale started to lose me. Unlike most Lovecraft, which both tries to explain itself or refuses to explain itself in equal measure, this story tries to do both and fails. But the final tipping point is when the narrator realises that the strange mounds of earth that are appearing around the mountains are 'molehills' and this is where my normally perfectly suspended sense of disbelief sinks without trace. Despite explaining too much with these 'molehills', Lovecraft utterly fails to explain what any of this has to do with the thunderstorms which crop up ominously in each part of the story.

This second serial style story fails to find its mark in all the ways that 'Herbert West' succeeded as far as I am concerned. So, Lovecraft himself was probably fonder of this one. It left me distinctly underwhelmed - in essence I was bored by it, perhaps because from a longer format I wanted more depth than this story held.

Someone somewhere probably loves this story, but that someone is not me.

THE SCORE: A COOL 2 OUT OF 6 SOMEWHAT FLACCID TENTACLES OF LITTLE INTEREST TO ANYONE

MYTHOS CONNECTIONS: Nothing so interesting here...

LOVECRAFT TWATTRY: Intellectual elitism and bigotry

SHOULD YOU READ IT: No, of course I could be wrong, but as you asked, God no.

BLUFFERS FACT: Back to Music, as well as Swedish Death metal's finest, Graham Plowman, was inspired two write a whole album of orchestral Lovecraft inspired music, one section of which is called 'The Lurking Fear'. So, if nothing else this story inspired music for all tastes... Remarkably I both like and recommend both...

THE RATS IN THE WALLS

The first Lovecraft story I ever read was 'The Rats in the Walls'. I always have, and will always, look upon it fondly despite its flaws. It always remains the tale I am most likely to recommend as a starting point to anyone who has never read the Old Tentacle Hugger's macabre scribblings. So, with that in mind, I cannot claim to be entirely unbiased on this one…

So let me get this out of the way first, no matter what else I say, I love 'The Rats in the Walls', it is a masterpiece of the grotesque, the disturbing and the chilling. If, as a writer, you want to write horror, if you want to send chills down the spines or your readers, if you want to know how to get under their skin, to make them feel the itch they cannot scratch, study this tale. It is the quintessential horror story, it is as good as it gets for insidious, nasty narratives about the worst of humanity's failings and the thoughts of a disturbed mind. It is, in a word, perfect…

Here's the thing, despite this book being a generally light-hearted look at Lovecraft and occasionally stumbling blindly into literary criticism, I don't really want to tell you all about 'The Rats in the Wall', because of all the Lovecraft stories, this is the one I most want people to read. So, before I go any further, I urge you to seek it out and give it a read…

Okay, so chances are that you haven't put this book down and gone and read 'The Rats in the Walls' but I'll pretend you have, and therefore I think having read it you'll agree it's perfect… So now let's talk about its many flaws.

When I originally read 'The Rats in the Walls' for the blog series that became this book, I couldn't help but feel I'd read it before. Okay, in my case I most certainly had read it before on several occasions, As I said, it's my favourite Lovecraft story, but that's not what I mean. There were people reading these stories in order along with me as I was doing the blogs (at least three people are apparently according to the emails I received which I found both gratifying and horrifying in equal measure) The story centres around an American who has gone out and bought back the old ancestral pile, and is the last remaining descendant of a scion of a family with a long history that fled to the United States a century ago to escape some dark events in that family's past… So, does that sound familiar yet? Further to this, the American has to bring in workers from far afield, as the locals of the region still tell black rumours of the old house up on the hill and the family who once lived there... If you're thinking you've heard this tale before that's not a surprise... While the house is repaired, the American also manages to glean more of his family history from the folklore and whispered tales of a few locals willing to talk to him. Not that most do, because of the shadowy history of his family and dark acts they committed over the centuries. Even fewer are willing to talk to him once he adopts his original family name rather than the Anglicized version he began life with... So, have you got it yet?

Basically, if you aren't sure, this is the plot from 'The Moon Bog' which was written a couple of years earlier and which I gave a measly 2 tentacles. It's not even the case that this story was written after but published before, with 'The Moon Bog' only coming to light when Lovecraft achieved a degree of popularity. 'The Moon Bog' was actually published two years before 'Rats', and this recycling of so many elements of the plot really is undefendable. That said, a good story stays a good story no matter how many times you retell it. Doctor Who has been saving mining colonies in outer space from the ancient evil freed by a cave-in for over fifty years. Every incarnation of Star Trek has a time loop story in it at least once a season. Every James Bond novel tells the same basic plot. Also, the problems with 'The Moon Bog' was never the plot itself. All the same, to read 'Rats' so soon after 'The Moon Bog' is somewhat jarring in its familiarity. Beyond one being set in Ireland and the other in Sussex, there really is hardly a sliver between them in the basics of the setting and background plot.

There are other problems too. Not least the name of the narrator's favourite cat. Let's just say it's a black cat and shares a name with the black Labrador in 'Dam Busters', it was, as they say, a different time. I am, generally speaking, against censorship. I am also absolutely against the diluting of an author's work to make them more acceptable to their audience. For the same reason I understand why Ray Bradbury was angry that 'Fahrenheit 451' was butchered to make it more acceptable to some America schools. But there is a case for some minor tampering to bring some works more in line with 21st-century sensibilities when it comes down to the name of the cat. Calling the cat 'Shadows' or 'Darkness' would leave it clear that it's a black cat we are talking about without detracting at all from the story.

What sets 'The Rats in the Walls' apart from the likes of 'The Moon Bog' is the intensity of the tale and the way it quietly and slowly builds up. It is also a window into the mind of madness, or possibly not, as the story is told from Delapore's (the narrator's) point of view exclusively. Is he really hearing the rats, or is it his fevered imagination? Is he slowly going mad, is this madness a family trait, is it just karma for naming his cat N*******-man…? The descent of Delapore's sanity is matched by the descent into the caverns below Exham Priory and the revealing of the ancient site's dark history. Yet what you chose to believe is the truth of the tale is left open-ended, all of which adds to its strength as a narrative. That and those wonderfully telling hints of links to the winder Lovecraft universe like the one below…

…the rats seem determined to lead me on even unto those grinning caverns of earth's centre where Nyarlathotep, the mad faceless god, howls blindly to the piping of two amorphous idiot flute-players…

I am not alone in thinking this is the perfect Lovecraft tale. Robert E. Howard, the creator of Conan the Barbarian among other characters, wrote to 'Weird Tales' praising 'Rats' after it was published. This letter was passed on to Lovecraft and became the start of a friendship that lasted for the rest of H.P.'s life. Lin Carter, who wrote a few Conan stories himself, called 'Rats' "one of the finest stories of Lovecraft's entire career. If you read one Lovecraft Tale in your life, then Rats is the one to read, as it achieves what Kingsley Amis described as 'a memorable nastiness'…" So, it's not just on my recommendation that you should read this one. You just should.

Finally, in keeping with another increasingly long-running theme in this book of, 'Lovecraft stories inspiring Metal bands,' American Power metal band 'Seven Kingdoms' wrote 'In The Walls' based on the tale. It's a surprisingly cheerful bit of speed metal. Also, it was at about this point in writing the original blog this book is based upon that I would have been surprised if I came to a story that hadn't inspired a heavy/death/goth/metal band of troubadours to pen a tune and suspected I would be disappointed when that happened.

THE SCORE: A WONDERFUL 6 OUT OF 6 TENTACLES THAT MAY ALSO INCLUDE A COUPLE MORE SNEAKING OUT BEHIND THOSE SIX.

MYTHOS CONNECTIONS: Minor, but they are hiding in the text in odd places

LOVECRAFT TWATTRY: Mainly just the name of the cat…

SHOULD YOU READ IT: YES!!!!! Sorry was I unclear, read it, read it now.

BLUFFERS FACT: As an alternative to reading this story, I can highly recommend the version you can find on You Tube read by the wonderfully dulcet tones of David McCallum (him of Sapphire and Steel, the Man from Uncle, NCIS and elsewhere fame). It's frankly fabulous.

THE UNNAMABLE

What is it about Randolph Carter and sitting around in graveyards? It never turns out well for him, you would think he would learn... At least this time he is in the pastel surroundings of New England rather than the middle of a swamp, because if you remember the last time we came across Mr Carter, one of the Old Tentacle Hugger's favourite and oft a tad 'autobiographical' characters, was in 'The Statement of Randolph Carter' of which I gave this somewhat damning summing up.

...simple and straightforward, without any real depth to it. A run-of-the-mill tale that never quite steps out beyond itself...

The same sadly can be said of 'The Unnamable'. Indeed, it is even more run-of-the-mill as, unlike 'Statement', it wasn't even breaking new ground at the time it was written. 'The Unnamable' is at its heart is no more than a fairly straightforward ghost story. It treads an oft-tread path that was no more original a hundred years ago than it is today, but let's not damn it for that. There are no new stories after all, as the argument goes, there are only seven basic plots, and so a tale is all in the telling and it is in the telling that this tale gets interesting.
There is in this story a certain measure of self-awareness from Lovecraft. There is a meta quality to the tale; the character of Carter is both narrator and Lovecraft himself. In the earliest parts of the story, Carter talks about his own writings and the criticisms that were thrown at him by his peers. Or as Carter puts it in the tale...

...my constant talk about "unnamable" and "unmentionable" things was a very puerile device, quite in keeping with my lowly standing as an author. I was too fond of ending my stories with sights or sounds which paralysed my heroes' faculties and left them without courage, words, or associations to tell what they had experienced...

To an extent, the whole story is a thumb in the eye to his critics with Carter's friend Joel Manton playing the role of 'devil's advocate' and foil to Carter spouting Lovecraft's own opinions on his style. Manton argues that nothing is unnamable because everything can be experienced through our senses, so ultimately everything can be perceived and therefore can be named. While Lovecraft, through Carter, argues the opposite and to illustrate his point refences a 'haunted' house of local legend near the Providence graveyard. He notes the stories of strange events and strange apparitions that abound in the New England town, and experiences he has had himself. Though Carter is dismissive of his ability to win over Manton with his arguments. Very dismissive as it happens with the glorious words on the...

...the futility of imaginative and metaphysical arguments against the complacency of an orthodox sun-dweller...

Anne Rice, eat your heart out.
All this is, of course, the set up for a somewhat predictable ending to a slightly predictable tale. It is the first part, with its discussion between the two principal characters about the relative nature of perception, the supernatural and the mundane, which is easily the most interesting aspect of the tale. Though in fairness the rest of the story is well written, even if the ending is telegraphed from the start. This is, after all, both a ghost story and Carter... sorry, Lovecraft... justifying his own style and his most well-known trope. Why would you expect 'The Unnamable' to be anything less than that when this whole tale is based on a discussion of his own style between him and his religiously orthodox friend Manton? If you cannot win out an argument in real life, why not have your alter ego at least win the argument in your fiction. Even if it is a win by default...
So, as I say, what is most interesting here is the conversation in the graveyard, all that comes after is just a bit too mundane.
As an aside...
There is a movie called 'The Unnamable' loosely based on this story, and a sequel to it called 'Unnamable 2: The statement of Randolph Carter' which is almost certainly not based on the story of the same name... It stars no one you have ever heard of and doesn't get the highest of ratings on IMDB, so it's fairly consistent with most Lovecraft inspired movies in that regard. I've never seen it, so can't really comment, but it is a 1980's horror and as the plot keywords that IMDB throws out first are breasts, blood splatter, violence and gore, it can be summed up as an average mid-budget 80's horror movie... If, like me, you like pokey mid-budget 80's horror you could perhaps try and dig it out at some point. I mean, how bad could it be...
Though having said that's as it's a mid-budget 80's splatter horror, it's

probably unnamable...

THE SCORE: A 3 OUT OF 6 TENTACLES THAT MAY HAVE TO GROW A COUPLE OF EXTRA PSEUDOPOD LIMBS.

MYTHOS CONNECTIONS: Minor, but they are hiding in the text in odd places.

LOVECRAFT TWATTRY: Mainly the name of the cat...

SHOULD YOU READ IT: Yes, it is worth a read, there is something very interesting about Lovecraft's retrospective on his own work, but perhaps that's the writer in me, or something about it that's just a little... unnamable...
(Yes, okay I use the same joke twice, what do you want from me?)

BLAGGERS FACT: Carter's friendship with Joel Manton was based on Lovecraft's real-life friendship and correspondence with the wonderfully improbably named Maurice W. Moe, who I really hope was referred to as Mo Mo by everyone, because that's how the universe should work.

THE FESTIVAL

> "Efficiunt Daemones, ut quae non sunt, sic tamen quasi sint, conspicienda hominibus exhibeant."
> —Lactantius.
>
> (Devils so work, that things which are not, appear to men as if they were real.)

The mildly ominous quote above preludes a Lovecraft tale that is more complex and stranger the further you delve into it. Yet, on the face of it, it follows a path well-trodden by Old Tentacle Hugger. The tale told in the first person, is entreated to us by a man who returns to his family's native home of Kingsport, New England. A fictional town which grew out of a small fishing community on the coast north of the fictional city of Arkham. The tale itself was inspired by a visit by Lovecraft to a real town called Marblehead on the coast of Massachusetts, in late 1922. What Lovecraft later had to say about that visit is interesting in itself…

It was the most powerful single emotional climax experienced during my nearly forty years of existence. In a flash all the past of New England–all the past of Old England–all the past of Anglo-Saxondom and the Western World–swept over me and identified me with the stupendous totality of all things in such a way as it never did before and never did again. That was the high tide of my life.

With a buildup like that inspiring a story, you would expect the story itself to be something special would you not? Yet on the face of it, this is a straightforward, 'other place' tale, in which the narrator finds himself in a Kingsport which is not quite the real Kingsport. Drawn there by a family myth and down into the deep caves below to witness an ancient rite, which, unsurprisingly, drives him a little over to the mad side of the spectrum. Leaving the reader with a tale told by a man of questionable sanity in which much is more alluded to than really told as, in true Lovecraft fashion, the narrator tells us…

…that no sound eye could ever wholly grasp, or sound brain ever wholly remember.

So there nothing very special here, its Lovecraft writing Lovecraft by the numbers to an extent…

And yet…

When you delve a little deeper and read it a little more carefully there is a lot more going on here. A great deal in fact if you're interested in the mythos around which much of Lovecraft's universe is constructed. The story has something else to it as well, it is more powerful than most of Lovecraft's earlier works, even if you're a little jaded by them having read your way through the first forty of his stories.

While it follows a path often trodden, its footsteps are surer and more grounded in Lovecraft's reality. This is in effect Lovecraft doing Lovecraft by the numbers perfectly… it's the right length, it has the right kind of ominousness to it, building slowly, drawing the reader in. You don't need to know what horrors are beheld by the narrator because by the time he beholds them you can picture them in your imagination yourself and nothing Lovecraft could have written would have been a match for your own imaginings… Which is the really a neat trick when it comes down to it. A trick other writer's occasionally make a mess of, but Lovecraft perfected at times - and this is one of these times.

As an aside, to illustrate my point, Lovecraft fan Stephen King, whose novels I love, wrote 'Needful Things', which should be among my favourite King novels. It is an exploration of some of the dark nature of humanity at its worst. All driven by a little shop that appears one day in a small town offering people their heart's desires, provided they are willing to do a little mischief in return… It's a wonderful novel right up to the end where the monster at the heart of everything that has torn the community of a sleepy little Maine town to shreds is revealed - and for me is the most disappointing of reveals. A nasty little goblin-like creature who giggles at everyone then runs away leaving the mayhem in its wake. It's disappointing because I had imagined so much more… If King had taken a leaf from Lovecraft's playbook and left that reveal hanging, my imagination would have filled in the blanks… For me it spoils the novel, but hey, that's only my opinion…

But let get back to 'The Festival' and what is going on underneath that makes this such an engrossing read. It's the things the narrator alludes to which cause you to read it back once more. The narrator, for example, is one of a people, a people who are possibly not entirely human. On the face of it, at first reading, he would seem to be talking of his people in the same way the descendants of European settlers talk about 'the old country'. Yet you start to realise, with little quirks of language, his 'people' are not Italians or from some eastern European principality

that ceased to exist in the previous century. His people, as is mentioned half in passing, came out of the sea many years ago... Out of, not across... Sure he could be talking about the evolutionary path of humanity from the first moments a few fish started to hang around on the shore and decided it would be a good idea to learn to breathe something less liquid. But you know he's not. His 'people' are similar to those of that other fictional seaport, Innsmouth, which Lovecraft wrote of in later years. The kind of people who have webbed toes and occasionally go swimming late at night to visit their relatives below...
Just as the descendants of early Italian Americans are somewhat more removed from the 'old country' than their forebears, so the narrator is more human than those of 'the people' in Kingsport. Yet at his core he knows he is still of 'the people' even if he is not entirely sure what that really means... Perhaps the web-toes are now just a little bit of extra skin and his eyes don't bulge out so noticeably, but inside he knows that this is more than simply a family trait... So, when an instinctive need to go back to the old town of his forebears, he does just that. Knowing intuitively and through some old family legends where he needs to go. 'Luckily' for him, the locals recognise him as one of their kin, and he is welcomed to the fold - if welcomed is the right word...
That book of 'ill-portent' the Necronomicon turns up in this tale too. Twice in fact, as the narrator comes across a copy with 'the people' and later when he finds himself in a hospital bed in Arkham, he is lent a copy once more. The latter lending is a trifle odd, as the hospital is a mental institution, which does beg the question of why a member of staff has a copy to lend him? Personally, anyone lending me a copy of an infamous book of dark legend I would give a wide birth... and in as fragile state of mind as the narrator no doubt is, one way or another, giving him that book as a bit of light night time reading seems downright peculiar...
This whole story is heavily steeped in Lovecraftian mythology. There is more within the text than I have eluded to here. But it was written in 1923, still early in Lovecraft's career. In many ways, it the most utterly mythos story to be written at that point. Which is a bit of an issue reading it now, as while originally it was a real tour-de-force for Lovecraft, it is now somewhat a forgotten cousin of 'Shadows Over Innsmouth', which was written 8 years later, and it doesn't fare entirely well in comparison - but that can be said for many stories.

THE SCORE: 4 OUT OF 6 SLITHERING SALTWATER TENTACLES, REACHING OUT OF THE DEPTHS OF THE SEA.

MYTHOS CONNECTIONS: So many

LOVECRAFT TWATTRY: None of note.

SHOULD YOU READ IT: Yes, for all those mythos connections, it's well worth a read, the only reason it doesn't score higher is it's not quite 'The Shadows over Innsmouth'.

BLAGGERS FACT: For the first time, however, Old Tentacle Hugger actually gives us a direct passage from the Mad Arab's opus…

…The nethermost caverns, are not for the fathoming of eyes that see; for their marvels are strange and terrific. Cursed the ground where dead thoughts live new and oddly bodied, and evil the mind that is held by no head. Wisely did Ibn Schacabao say, that happy is the tomb where no wizard hath lain, and happy the town at night whose wizards are all ashes. For it is of old rumour that the soul of the devil-bought hastes not from his charnel clay, but fats and instructs the very worm that gnaws; till out of corruption horrid life springs, and the dull scavengers of earth wax crafty to vex it and swell monstrous to plague it. Great holes secretly are digged where earth's pores ought to suffice, and things have learnt to walk that ought to crawl…

So, that's alright then, nothing to worry about there at all…

THE SHUNNED HOUSE

If there was a point in the original blog series that became this book when I considered packing it all in, it was when I go to 'The Shunned House'. As was the normal course of things, for the blog I read each story a couple of times at least. This story I struggled to get through once.
My hopes had not been high going into the story to start with, as I remembered trying to read it a couple of times over the years and never finishing it. But I hoped with fresh eyes and a willing determination I would solider on though it and perhaps find something to enjoy in the process...
So, I did, which brought me here. Now normally I explain what I think about a story and what the story brings to mind, I try to examine the text and come up with exciting things to say, and if that fails, I try to find things to say I find interesting about it. And that is where I came across a problem, because there is nothing I find interesting about 'The Shunned House'. My disparity fails against some popular opinions, among them, fellow author Robert Weinberg's who described 'The Shunned House' as:

> *'One of Lovecraft's best short novels.'*

It's not, at least in my opinion. It's not even the best of the worst of his 'short novels'. It is a dreadfully long, ponderous tale which would probably have worked much better as a short story. It would have been a good, entertaining read at a thousand words long - maybe two thousand words at the most would have been enough. The reason I say this is because a good ninety percent of this tale is exposition. Long, maladroit exposition on the history of a haunted house. In essence a 'haunt' tale is all this is, and that ninety percent exposition could have been removed and replaced with:

> *The house had a long dark history of strange occurrences, unexplained deaths and madness in the night...*

I am not saying that the story would be better for doing so, but believe me when I say I would have sooner read that line followed by the final events with a sprinkling of character backstory than crawl my way through the agonisingly slow, dry to the point of arid, relentless and glacial exposition that is the rest of the story.

Lovecraft has a habit of writing a lot of exposition. Sometimes this works in his favour, building character and depth to a story. 'The Rats in the Walls' is a fine example of this. But With 'The Shunned House' he goes into infinitesimal details that bring nothing to the story. Even that would not be a problem if the exposition itself weren't just so terminally dull. It just drones on like a slightly turgid uncle at a family gathering telling you about his foot fungus for several hours, while you really want to go talk to Tracy your second cousin thrice removed over at the bar who seems at least to have some life about her. Even if the best thing you can say about Tracy is she is unlikely to have a three-hour story about her foot fungus she feels the need to tell you.

So, my advice is you look at it like this, if you're a completest with a masochistic streak determined to read all of Lovecraft then fine, read 'The Shunned House' but don't say I did not warn you. Yes, this may just be my opinion, but it's also noticeable that there are no Scandinavian Death metal bands called 'The Shunned House'. No band under another name has recorded an album called 'The Shunned House', there is no low budget short movie made by fans of the story. There is no comic strip, no interesting artwork, no new genre or significant writer that I can find that has ever been inspired by this story, and believe me I looked in the vain hope of finding something to say about it other than, 'Festering old ones that spell doom to humanity, it's dull'

THE SCORE: 1 OUT OF 6 FLACCID, AND SOMEWHAT BEGRUDGED TENTACLE.

MYTHOS CONNECTIONS: None.

LOVECRAFT TWATTRY: None of note.

SHOULD YOU READ IT: No, just no.

BLUFFERS FACTS: This was to be Lovecraft's first printed book, rather than just being published in a magazine. Some 250 copies were printed, then never bound and never sold. My suspicion is whoever was funding this venture actually got around to reading it sometime between the printing and the binding, and decided to cut their losses.

THE HORROR AT RED HOOK

It was back in the 80's when I first came across the literary universe of H.P.Lovecraft, and I came across in it the way that most people of my generation did, in the form of the 'Call of Cthulhu' Role Playing Game. To be more specific, my first encounter with Lovecraft was in an RPG magazine called 'Imagine', and it took the form of a game scenario inspired by one of his stories. I could not tell you which story, in particular, inspired it, as I can't remember a great deal about it. I can just remember reading the scenario and thinking it all sounded both bizarre and wonderfully interesting. It was also completely at odds with the majority of 80's RPG fodder. Whatever 'Call of Cthulhu' was, it wasn't Dungeons and Dragons, Runequest or Travellers which were the big three RPGs at the time. This was a game of investigation, madness, dark atmosphere and a lurking sense of doom. It was in a word, different. Which is I suspect why CoC is still incredibly popular today when so many RPGs from the 80's boom fell by the wayside. CoC is also responsible in part for the resurgence of interest in Old Tentacle Hugger in the last thirty years. So, it is indirectly responsible for this book. Which leads me 'The Horror at Red Hook', because if ever a Lovecraft story read like the background to a CoC scenario it's this one. Which is also probably why it has been used for several over the years. It is quintessentially everything you could desire as a CoC player. A mystery set among the dank, dark streets of the Red Hook district of New York in 1920s. A place 'more people enter … than leave it on the landward side'. A mysterious cult is practising ancient rites in the cellars of dilapidated brownstones. There are kidnappings and disappearances, an eccentric scholar delving into old tomes and mixing with criminals and gangs. A police detective with a hobbyist's enthusiasm for the occult investigating. Events moving towards a climax, with tantalising hints of dark secrets. An innocent drawn into this world unknowingly as a sacrifice. Madness, dark events and the brooding suspicions abound, and then finally in the end…

… Red Hook—it is always the same. Suydam came and went; a terror gathered and faded; but the evil spirit of darkness and squalor broods on amongst the mongrels in the old brick houses, and prowling bands still parade on unknown errands past windows where lights and twisted

faces unaccountably appear and disappear. Age-old horror is a hydra with a thousand heads, and the cults of darkness are rooted in blasphemies deeper than the well of Democritus. The soul of the beast is omnipresent and triumphant, and Red Hook's legions of blear-eyed, pockmarked youths still chant and curse and howl as they file from abyss to abyss, none knows whence or whither, pushed on by blind laws of biology which they may never understand. As of old, more people enter Red Hook than leave it on the landward side, and there are already rumours of new canals running underground to certain centres of traffic in liquor and less mentionable things.

Yet despite this story being perfect for the roleplaying game Lovecraft's fiction spawned, the tale itself has many detractors. Not least of which is the Old Tentacle Hugger himself:

'Rather long and rambling, and I don't think it is very good'
~ H.P.Lovecraft

"A piece of literary vitriol" ~ Lin Carter

"Horrendously bad" ~ ST Joshi

But then Lovecraft and the rest of these critics never played 'Call of Cthulhu'… So, this may be the reason their views are not reflected by my own, and indeed the opinion of many others who came to Lovecraft through CoC. I suspect because this tale is exactly what you would expect to find in almost every CoC scenario. Which is also something of a problem, however, because what makes for a good game scenario does not necessarily make for a good short story. Yet 'The Horror at Red Hook' managed to be just that. It's a well-paced yarn that doesn't dwell too long on any aspect of itself. It suffers from none of the problems of 'The Shunned House' for example. It moves on at a steady but informed pace that lays the story out before you in its entirety without ever languishing in excessive exposition. So, for me the story remains foremost an interesting one, and while that opinion puts me at odds with the critics once more, at least it is in a positive way this time.
There is, however, another and far more damning criticism of 'The Horror at Red Hook' best expressed by Peter Cannon who says of it…

"Racism makes a poor premise for a horror story."

Which is unfortunately a very valid point; there isn't an argument I could put up against that view and I wouldn't even if I could think of one. Lovecraft was, as we know, a man whose racial politics were rooted firmly on the right in an era when the right was a fair step further to the right than in modern times. As a reader, as I take the view that he is a writer from a different time and social politics were very different. His views, abhorrent though they are, were far closer to the mainstream in the 1920s, so he is a reflection of the times and his education. Sadly, Lovecraft is not an outlier in terms of racism and misogyny when compared to the majority of the writers of his era. But even with that said, some tales are nastier than others and there is much to make the modern reader uncomfortable in 'The Horror at Red Hook'. A word or two here and there, his choice of descriptions, his use of illegal immigrants as the basis of his cult… Let's just say this Lovecraft story would be popular in the Trump White House if the resident was inclined to read…

Something to bear in mind as well is Lovecraft lived in New York when he wrote this story. It is an open secret that he wasn't fond of the city because, as he stated in a letter to C.A Smith talking of his inspiration for 'The Horror at Red Hook' he wrote of his dictates for the…

'Herds of evil-looking foreigners that one sees everywhere in New York'

Which is as openly xenophobic as it's possible to be. He uses illegal immigrants as the backbone of his cult in the story. In which he states they were 'rightly turned back at Ellis Island' before entering the US by less official routes and it doesn't get much better in this regard going forward. But if you can get past the racist elements of the story, it's a cracking tale. Certainly, the core of the tale has a lot of legs and some of the imagery around the scenes in the improvised temple below the Red Hook streets witnessed by Thomas Malone the 'hero' of the tale are astounding. There is much to love about this story.

There is also much that could be made from the core idea of ancient cults still existing beneath the radar of society, strange rites being practised and encouraged by an antiquarian in search of ancient power. It has echoes in more contemporary works like 'The Wicker Man'. It's far from a unique idea in Lovecraft either, it is the basis of the plot for 'The Festival' for example… but 'The Horror at Red Hook' is one of the best examples of the hidden cult idea in his work. It is also the kind of Lovecraft story which most inspired the RPG versions of his universe. The investigators slowly being drawn down into a world much darker and more terrifying than they ever imagined from the mundane facts they started with. An evil lying underneath society, waiting to consume them should they a misstep. Harbouring the knowledge that there is more going on than you can perceive and the things in the darkness bring madness with them if you look too closely...

Frankly, it's enough to make me reach for my dice...

So, as you may have gathered from that, I like this story quite a lot. Even if Old Tentacle Hugger himself disagreed with my opinion. So, I don't really want to explain too much of the story, as its one I would encourage you to read. It loses a point for the racism and comes with a definite warning about it, but it still gets five out of six little sucker-covered tentacle from me. Enjoy, but be warned, what awaits you, waits for you in the darkness below the streets...

THE SCORE: 5 OUT OF 6 TENTACLES REACHING UP FROM THE SEWERS.
(It would be six if not for the racism inherent within the story)

MYTHOS CONNECTIONS: Minor, some references to tombs that crop up elsewhere in his stories.

LOVECRAFT TWATTRY: As Peter Cannon said, 'Racism is a poor premise for a horror story' and there is way too much of it in this story.

SHOULD YOU READ IT: Yes, provided you can look past that one fairly major flaw, the story itself is excellent.

BLUFFERS FACTS: Robert Suydam, the academic in the story, lives in a 'lonely house, set back from Martense Street'. The Martense Family were the subterranean cannibals in Lovecraft's earlier story 'The Lurking Fear', who live in a location from which the river flows south to eventually emerge at Red Hook.

HE

New York, New York; the big apple, the land of dreams, where the canyon walls are made of concrete and glass, full of life and people of all creed and custom, the melting pot of the western world. Who couldn't love it…?

Well, Howard Phillips Lovecraft for one…

Old Tentacle Hugger hated New York and after a couple of years living there, he could not wait to run back to small-town Providence, Rhode Island where he was born raised and, in the fullness of time, died. His brief years in New York were as unhappy as his brief marriage, which was the reason he moved to New York in the first place. His matrimonial problems may have had much to do with how he felt about big city life, but never a man for self-analysis old H.P. blamed the city for his woes rather than himself, and just in case anyone was unsure of his opinion on the matter, in the first half of 'He' goes to great lengths to complain about New York as much as is humanly possible. If that's your idea of a good read, then good luck to you, but personally I dislike the thinly veiled wallowing in self-pity and NY hate fest that is the first half of this story. Suffice to say, H.P. never bought a 'I heart NY' T-shirt.

If, and I do mean if, you can drag yourself through that first half of 'He' then it is worth the pain. The second half of the story is more interesting and revolves around a meeting between the narrator and a strange individual on a park bench in Greenwich Village. The strange individual, the 'He' of this tale, is dressed as if he has just stepped out of the 18th century. 'He' offers to take the narrator on a tour of those parts of the city few know of - the back alleys and long forgotten courtyards boxed in on all sides, which you can only get to via the buildings containing them.

So, because it's exactly what you do when you're in a city you hate and a strange man, dressed out of time, comes up to you offering to take you down the back alleys, off the narrator goes, following his odd guide into the darkness between the buildings…

Yes… Alright… that does seem a stretch, but since when were Lovecraft's narrators entirely the sanest of people…

Eventually, 'He' takes the narrator to his house, a strange building that seems older than it should be, and there 'He' starts to tell the narrator his own tale. He claims that he is a man out of time, and he talks of a bargain he struck with the natives of the land, back when the land was still open hillsides and New York was still New Amsterdam… A bargain struck for secrets and rituals of power. A bargain he paid for in blood when, having got all he wished from the natives, he dispensed himself of his debt to them in the finest traditions of colonialism, with a little-poisoned rum…

'He' goes on to show the narrator visions of the past and the future, visions of a future for the city that so terrify the narrator his screams are literally enough to wake the dead. And as this being a Lovecraft tale of betrayal and dark powers gained from ancient tribal wisdom, the dead in this case have a bone or two to pick once awakened…

The second half of 'He' is wonderfully written, and wonderfully envisioned. It is one of the better short tales that Lovecraft ever wrote. It has pace, drama and a growing sense of unease about it that builds up momentum perfectly as it moves towards its climax. It has craft, it has guile, and it has an edge to it that Lovecraft occasionally lacks in some other tales of this era. Frankly, I love the second half of this tale, but the first half is awful…

My advice, therefore, is to skip the first half. And that first half is why this just gets three tentacles, each of them earned in the second half. It would have been six if I had not had to sit through the narrator's melancholy mopping around New York like a cut-price Emo wannabe with a personality bypass…

THE SCORE: 3 OUT OF 6 TENTACLES ALL APPEARING FROM ABOUT HALFWAY THROUGH

MYTHOS CONNECTIONS: None

LOVECRAFT TWATTRY: If you're a New Yorker, you probably don't want to read this

SHOULD YOU READ IT: The latter half yes, just skip the first half of the story entirely.

BLUFFERS FACTS: Sonia Greene, Lovecraft's wife, finically supported him while they lived in New York, after nine months she moved to Cleveland and left him in New York, while continuing to pay his living expenses. She never came back to either New York or Howard. She also once wrote that he 'performed satisfactorily as a lover,' which is damning with faint praise if ever I have seen it.

IN THE VAULT

Not for the first time, and not for the last, having read 'In the Vault' I find myself with little sympathy for the unfortunate main character in a Lovecraft short story. But let's face it, Lovecraft's characters often get what they deserve.

You might think that's harsh - who actually deserves to be driven to the point of madness by the scurrying of rats in the walls, or by listening too closely to the music of the wrong violin, or just because they are led down into the depths of subterranean tunnels below a crypt by their own morbid curiosity - you may ask… Well in some cases no, the characters don't deserve their fates, even the hateful among them. But there are some who, when push comes to shove, get off lightly all things considered.

One such character is George Birch, erstwhile undertaker for a small New England town by the name of Peck Valley.

George is not a pleasant man, he does an admittedly unpleasant job, but he also does it unpleasantly. He cuts corners in his trade, uses cheap coffins and has little or no respect for those left in his care. A ham-fisted man with light fingers when it suits him. He steals those little trinkets the dead are buried with, and if he has a spare coffin that's a little too small he'll make a body fit into it anyway to save himself the time and expense of making one the right size. After all, he reasons, it not going to matter to anyone that the six-foot town clerk is in a five-foot-five coffin. Just loop off a foot or so – literally - and he'll fit in there nicely, what with it being a closed casket and all.

So, as you can imagine, as a reader it's hard to find yourself overflowing with sympathy for George. That sympathy doesn't increase an awful lot when his sloth and general work-shy idleness leads him to find himself locked in a vault with seven coffins that he should have buried days before but had not quite gotten around to. If he had just oiled the lock and fixed the latch when he had first noticed, weeks before, that it was starting to stick… Well, everything that happens to him afterwards could be entirely avoided.

This whole story could be seen as a morality tale against the evils of laziness and callowness in general. Lovecraft puts a lot of work into establishing the character (or more accurately the lack of character) of George. Unlike some other Lovecraft characters, this is one you're supposed to despise, and on one level the story is entirely successful in that. As George tries to escape his self-made prison on the backs of those in his care - literally as he piles up their coffins - you're left with a certain anticipation of the comeuppance he has coming to him.

There is much of the grotesque to this story, not least the main character himself. It's grim, dark and nasty. Unfortunately, it is also a tad on the predictable side. Nothing about the ending is a shock, even though I don't doubt it was written with a shock ending in mind. Perhaps that is a reflection of my own jadedness. The twist at the end is just so, 'this is the twist at the end'... You can see it coming and I would be prepared to bet most people if asked, fifty words from the end to guess the final twist would have a fairly good stab at it, even if they didn't get it exactly right. The ending doesn't bite you, is all I am saying...

All that aside, if you reject the conventional wisdom that the reader must be able to identify with the main character and at the very least 'like' them, no matter how nasty they are, this is a fine example of how to write a character who no one will like and get away with it. Throughout reading this, I felt like a cheerleader to the story, I don't mean in a short shirt and pompom way (trust me no one wants that) but in that I was cheering on the end, looking forward to George getting what he deserved; the spiteful, idle, thieving, sloth of unpleasantness that he is...

It is, however, that cheerleading aspect that really kills this tale a little for me in the end. There is no real horror, or shock, or indeed anything disturbing about the story. It doesn't unsettle me or leave me wondering at the cosmos or make me thoughtful of the possibilities it throws up. It just is.

When I really like a Lovecraft story it is because its unsettling, because it makes me think, and sends me off on strange tangents. Instead 'In the Vault' is just a creepy little horror story the like of which I have read a hundred times by a hundred different writers. For all its grotesque nature and its hateful main character, it's just a bit too bland, a bit too run-of-the-mill and there isn't really anything much about it. Which is about as damning a thing as I can say of any Lovecraft story. Its well-written, reads well, but in the end, it is just nothing much, it doesn't even have something to be angry about, or disapprove of, or complain overly about... So, a couple of tentacles seems fair, but I find myself begrudging giving it that many for some reason, but then perhaps I am gravely wrong in this case...

THE SCORE: 2 OUT OF 6 MILDLY BEGRUDGED TENTACLES

MYTHOS CONNECTIONS: None.

LOVECRAFT TWATTRY: None.

SHOULD YOU READ IT: Not really, which is to say you can, but your life, nor even your day, will not be better for having done so.

BLUFFERS FACTS: The story was originally rejected by 'Weird Tales' in 1925 because, according to the editor at the time, Farnsworth Wright, "its extreme gruesomeness would not pass the Indiana censorship". I'd hate to think what Farnsworth would make of SAW…

THE DESCENDENT

One of the problems with a writer dying young, apart from the whole dying thing which let's face it probably puts a bit of a crimp in your day, is what happens to your legacy after you die. By legacy, I am talking specifically here about all those scraps and scrawls of half-finished works which are crammed into drawers and dusty box files around your study. Because a young writer, the young in general, never really consider the possibility of departing this mortal coil…

Well okay, yes they do, quite often in fact; it's the subject of a vast raft of youth culture, and sub-cultures, it's one of the reasons black eyeliner is always popular among youths of a certain mind-set… But unless you're actively contemplating taking the exit ramp, have a terminal illness or find yourself shipped off to a war zone, most of us under fifty never really contemplate the idea of actually just dying…

Why am I talking about this? Well, it's because personally, as a writer myself, I wouldn't want the unfinished products of my fevered mind to survive me, because they were unfinished, quite often they are unfinished for a reason. I have hard drives full of unfinished novels and scraps of this that and the other, half-baked ideas, random thoughts which amounted to nothing, and little side alleys of description which never led out to the main road. But just because I have never really considered what would happen to it when I die, though I suspect there would be little interest in it anyway, I have never really put any thought into what to do with it. Though as it's all up on my cloud, it will probably just dissipate away when someone stops paying the bill. I suspect I won't need to have the hard drives run over by a tractor to avoid anyone releasing my half-written works, unlike Terry Pratchett who had his hard drives destroyed publicly this way after his death.

In the case of H.P. Lovecraft, when he died relatively young, his old box files and folders were raided by those who 'wished to preserve his legacy' or if we are being more honest here, 'wanted to make money off it,' for every scrap and half written extract they could scrape together into something printable. If this was in line with Lovecraft's wishes, we will never know. It's true he did gift his papers away, but whether he did that with the intention that some of his small abstracts find print is somewhat questionable.

As for my own view on them, well 'Azathoth' is one such abstract, which I gave a solitary tentacle, as it is just 500 words of something which was intended to be much more, before it lay abandoned for years until Lovecraft died. I don't consider it worth reading because the author never intended it to be read. And this is not an 'it was the last thing he was writing when he died,' unfinished work. 'Azathoth' is just a scrap of an idea, which may have become his greatest work later in life had he lived, but it was a long-forgotten scrap he never got back to, and probably never intended to. So, I don't feel it has much business being out in the world, besides which from the notes found with it there is reason to suspect it was an early tinkering with the idea that became 'The Dreamquest for unknown Kadath' anyway.

Which brings me to 'The Descendant' which is another 'Azathoth', albeit a longer extract (three times longer at 1500 words). It is still only an extract, a possible idea, a fragment of a narrative that will never be complete. It was written a good ten years before he died, so it's a safe assumption he never intended to return to it. He may have reused some ideas from it, ideas we can't see because this narrative gives no real clue where he was going with it. But at a guess, he went there in a later story if his idea was worth pursuing, because nothing lays fallow at the back of a writer's mind for ten years without being used.

It's a shame we don't know more as it's an interesting fragment, and as a Yorkshireman myself I would have been interested to see where Lovecraft went with this tale of a noble house from my homeland, certainly, the little extract below is enticing.

Lord Northam, of whose ancient hereditary castle on the Yorkshire coast so many odd things were told; but when Williams tried to talk of the castle, and of its reputed Roman origin, he refused to admit that there was anything unusual about it. He even tittered shrilly when the subject of the supposed under crypts, hewn out of the solid crag that frowns on the North Sea, was brought up.

Which is fine right up to the word tittered. Tittered? No Yorkshireman ever tittered. I mean really, tittered? But as far as the story goes that just all there is to it. It's interesting in a vague kind of way, but it's interesting to me as a writer, not to me as a reader. It's a scrap of unpolished prose, even if you ignore 'tittered'. Lovecraft would have polished this to within an inch of its life before he published it, and I suspect 'tittered shrilly' would be one of the first things to go as it just sounds wrong. But we will never know. Which is kind of my point; why would Lovecraft want anyone to read a scrap of a first draft that was never fully realised?

So, to sum up, 'The Descendant' is of interest only to completists who want to read those small and incomplete twigs that reach out to Lovecraft's greater mythology, and those who write themselves in an abstract academic kind of way. What is there isn't of any real interest to readers and, in my opinion, it probably should never have been published at all. I suspect you can guess how many tentacles it gets… and I am being generous…

THE SCORE: 1 OUT OF 6 TENTACLES, WHICH IS GENEROUS.

MYTHOS CONNECTIONS: Mentions a nameless city in Araby… and that's about all.

LOVECRAFT TWATTRY: It's not his normal twattry, but stating a Yorkshireman would titter shrilly… well, it's unforgivable.

SHOULD YOU READ IT: There is no real reason to do so.

BLUFFERS FACTS: Lovecraft once wrote that he was "making a very careful study of London…in order to get background for tales involving richer antiquities than America can furnish." This story could well be a failed attempt to tap that rich vein.

COOL AIR

There are those who consider this macabre little tale the best of Lovecraft's New York stories. They are of course, in my opinion, wrong, which is probably not all that surprising to you having read this far. If there is one thing I learned in my time on this little project, it is that I almost always disagree with the commonly held opinions of both Lovecraft aficionados and his critics… For that matter, I often seem to disagree with the Old Tentacle Hugger's opinions of his own work. For me, 'Cool Air' holds that wonderful middle ground of being reasonably good, or at least not half bad and whatever other slightly damning faint praise you might happen to throw at it. It's not the crass unlovable 'He' that most critics seem to like, but it's not the wonderful 'The Horror at Red Hook' that every critic but me seems to despise.

When it comes to those 'New York Tales' I am very much at odds with everyone. So, exactly how much my opinion is worth is something you will have to decide for yourself. But if you want a nasty macabre story that's a little bit too predictable and, while being perfectly well written, doesn't really get under your skin so much as vaguely waft over it, then 'Cool Air' is just what you're looking for. Other than that, it's a bit, meh…

The narrator of the tale meets his upstairs neighbour, Dr Muñoz, a man with an obsession about air conditioning, who claims to need to keep the temperature as low as possible to preserve his life due to a rare disease. Meanwhile, New York in the summer is in the midst of a record-breaking heatwave… The days get hotter, and the air-conditioning units get ever bigger, nosier and something is going to give - either the weather breaks or the air con will…

And there you have the plot, more or less, which clearly has a degree of predictability about it. The narrator never offers us his name, but does tell us he is in New York doing 'some dreary and unprofitable magazine work', he isn't overly enamoured of the city and it's populous, and ends up living in a boarding house that, again in his words, 'disgusted much less than the others he had sampled'. Which, given Lovecraft's oft-mentioned distaste for the big city life of New York, suggests Old Tentacle Hugger did not look far for inspiration regarding his narrator. Not that there is anything awfully new about that, he may as well have called the narrator Randolph Carter and had done with it…

Considering this Not-Randolph ends up meeting his upstairs neighbour because of a strange chemical leak that starts dripping into his room, you have to wonder just how bad the other boarding houses were. Certainly, once noxious chemicals start dripping through the ceiling it's probably a good idea to look elsewhere. Yet even the landlady is strangely accepting of the upstairs tenant as well as his strange industrial cooling equipment, and through her the Not-Randolph meets Dr Munoz, a Spaniard who Not-Randolph describes as 'short but exquisitely proportioned, with a high-bred face of masterful though not arrogant expression' bearing 'a short iron-grey full beard, full, dark eyes, and an aquiline nose' as well as having a 'striking intelligence, superior blood and breeding' - and let's stop there for a moment…

Not for the first time, or I suspect the last, I found myself wondering when I read this particular section of this tale about a subtext which has occurred to me before. This Not-Randolph, like all the other Not-Randolph narrators, and indeed the ones he actually names (so often called Randolph…) seem to have a few traits in common. For example, they all seem drawn to older, more experienced men, and so many of them happen to be the Not-Randolph's uncles. These older, experienced men from the Not-Randolph's are drawn often because they can initiate them into dark, often forbidden rites and mysteries… This theme is almost a cliché in Lovecraft's tales. Lovecraft, who's writing is famously misogynistic, also suffered through a short, ill-fated marriage while in New York writing this story. The same Lovecraft who had a long, close friendship with a younger man called Robert Barlow in the later years of his life, One of several other close relationships with other young men throughout his life. While I'm not saying Lovecraft was of a homosexual bent… It's easy to read a whole lot of repressed sexuality into his stories and if he wasn't gay then he almost certainly leant a little in that direction.

Old Tentacle Hugger has a reputation, quite rightly, for right-wing views, xenophobia, racism and misogyny. I've made no bones about my own distaste at the influence those views have on his writing. However, if he was indeed repressing aspects of his sexuality, it would while not excusing, certainly explain some of those darker traits. He would not be the first, and I suspect not the last, to use deflection as a form of repression in this way. When you hate something about yourself, or society has impressed upon you that you should do so, projecting that hate elsewhere is a common human trait. Perhaps in more enlightened times, when we look back on themes in his writing with distaste, we should also try to look back on it with a little understanding as well - not that it forgives the more abhorrent influences on Lovecraft's fiction or his political beliefs. But it is still worth remembering that the America of the 1920/30s was a far more closeted time.

But back to 'Cool Air' and the latest of the Not-Randolph's wise old uncles who were able to initiate the Not-Randolph into strange rites and mysteries. In this case, the strange rites involve industrial coolants, bags of ice, bathtubs, strange hints and dark whisperings of prolonging life despite the lack of a few vital functions. Which drives us to an ending which is somewhat predictable, after all the plot is all about what will happen when the ice melts and Munoz's efforts to preserve himself finally fail. Something which is rather too obvious from the first and the friendship that develops between the two men is somewhat stilted, one-sided and not unlike the relationships the Not-Randolph's always seems to have with their various 'uncles' in so many of Lovecraft's tales. The junior partner fetches, carries and generally ends up doing everything the elder tells them to do, in an effort to please their 'uncle' and perhaps in doing so learn more about the great mysteries that they wish to partake of and observe...

So again, I'm not saying there is a sub-text here, but... sub-text.

Perhaps this is also why this all falls a little too flat for me. It's too much of a muchness with so many other tales. It draws on all those sub-textual lines and in doing so highlights just how much this follows one of Lovecraft's well-trodden pathways. But it lacks anything particularly new or different about it. It also seemed oddly passionless in places (despite the sub-text, it's all a bit of a cold fish - a description with a certain irony about it)... It's a story where the sub-text is more interesting than the text itself...

THE SCORE: 3 OUT OF 6 FROSTY TENTACLES

MYTHOS CONNECTIONS: None of note.

LOVECRAFT TWATTRY: More hate for New York but otherwise none.

SHOULD YOU READ IT: That would depend entirely on your desire to explore the subtext, but I would say no.

BLAGGER FACT: This tale has spawned many adaptations. Several short films, at least one (arguably two) full-length movies, radio plays, several comic book versions, a prog rock song by Glass Hammer, and it even managed to make the pages of Batman, in 'The Doom That Came to Gotham', with staple Bat-villain Mr Freeze more or less being portrayed as Dr Muñoz. So, what does that tell you, apart from the tale is far more popular than my 'Meh' would suggest, and that my opinion is not shared by everyone…

THE CALL OF CTHULHU

*"That is not dead which can eternal lie,
And with strange aeons even death may die."*

No story by H.P. Lovecraft has had a more pervasive impact on popular culture or done more to establish Old Tentacle Hugger as a major literary influence than 'The Call of Cthulhu'. As for the old star spawn itself, Cthulhu is without a doubt the most widely known of all Lovecraft's creations. Cthulhu is simply everywhere in modern popular culture.

Just how widespread Old Tentacle Face is can be demonstrated by a quick look around my front room at home, which for the sake of pretentiousness I'll call my study. I have in there a Cthulhu POP figure, a crocheted Cthulhu made by my friend Cal, a Cthulhu inspired piece of wall art (technically a page of the Necronomicon made by a Canadian artist, I have several), Cthulhu T-shirts occasionally hanging on the radiators to dry, any number of Cthulhu inspired books, Cthulhu inspired comic books, the Call of Cthulhu B/W movie on the shelf with other DVDs, Cthulhu inspired board games, Cthulhu inspired card games, Cthulhu Dice, Cthulhu badges, and several RGP game books for everything from The Call of Cthulhu, Cthulhu Dark Ages, Cthulhu Romans, Cthulhu in Space. And remember this is just in my study, I didn't bother looking for my Cthulhu cufflinks...

Old Tentacle Face is frankly everywhere in my house. Which is surprising because when it comes down to it, I'm not actually a collector of Cthulhu memorabilia, this is just stuff that has accumulated over the years... Even if you bear in mind that I am a habitual geek who has a fascination with such things, I still think it is safe to say that beyond just Geekdom itself, Cthulhu is everywhere in the modern cultural zeitgeist of western civilisation... So, with that in mind, this is a tale with a reputation to live up to.

The story itself is told in three parts, which begin with our narrator, Francis Wayland Thurston, who inherits the papers of a deceased wise old uncle... Stop me if you have heard that little nugget of plot before... Yes indeed, we are back in discovering strange rites and mysteries through the medium of a wise older man territory again... By now this should surprise no one.

The three parts of this tale are titled 'The Horror in Clay', 'The Tale of

Inspector Legrasse', and 'The Madness from the Sea'. In many ways, you could treat them as three different tales all closely linked by a central thread, with each story building on the threads of the previous one. Something which Lovecraft has on occasion failed to do with other long segmented works. But 'The Call of Cthulhu' is built on stronger foundations than anything he had tried before. Not only does it build on itself as you read it, it builds on the foundations of the best of his earlier tales and sits astride them, going all the way back to the earliest tales like 'Dagon'. Threads upon threads are in here. Cyclopean columns from the depths of the ocean, the ravings of everyone's favourite mad Arabian, the Necronomicon itself, all that otherwise tedious wandering about in the Dreamlands he is so fond of, all the mythos stories that came before build irrevocably towards 'The Call of Cthulhu'. It's with this story that Lovecraft as a writer really starts to come together, and while I am aware I have said similar things about other tales, this really is the point that Lovecraft starts to put the whole of his mythological jigsaw together.

As this is a tale in three parts and as the whole is 'The Call of Cthulhu' I am going to deal with all three separately because this tale deserves a closer look.

THE HORROR IN CLAY

As a read goes, this first part is slow, and it only really starts to build towards the back end. But it does give the reader a sense that something bigger has happened, something beyond the normal ken, and far beyond a simple ghost story. Which is the key to this story, both in this first part and as a whole. The idea that humanity is as nothing in the greater scheme of the cosmos, and there are things hidden from us that we should be grateful remain hidden. In the end, the opening paragraph of this story betrays the scope of it all, and with it the scope of what Lovecraft was attempting to convey in this story. And it is among the best opening paragraphs of anything Lovecraft ever wrote in my opinion… I defy anyone not to want to read on after reading this…

The most merciful thing in the world, I think, is the inability of the human mind to correlate all its contents. We live on a placid island of ignorance in the midst of black seas of infinity, and it was not meant that we should voyage far. The sciences, each straining in its own direction, have hitherto harmed us little; but some day the piecing together of dissociated knowledge will open up such terrifying vistas of reality, and of our frightful position therein, that we shall either go mad from the revelation or flee from the deadly light into the peace and safety of a new dark age.

The story begins with Francis Wayland Thurston sorting through the effects and papers of his deceased Grand-uncle George Gammell Angell, onetime Professor Emeritus of Semitic Languages at Brown University, Providence. His Uncle died in circumstances that were a little odd, though nothing seemed to be overtly untoward about his death, and the sorting of his old papers should have been a relatively dull if studious activity. Which it is, save for one box of papers, a set of papers filed under the strange heading "CTHULHU CULT". Within these papers are documented evidence that centres firstly around a young sculptor suffering from strange dreams and making an even stranger object: a bas-relief of an impossible, nightmarish creature. A creature with the head of an octopus, the wings of a dragon and the body of a man, surrounded by script in some unknown language.

The young artist was beset by these strange dreams between the last week of March and the first of April. These both lead to him to the Professor and 'inspired' him to make the Bas-relief. The professor, for reasons which come to light later, takes a great deal of interest in both the dreams and the relief, rather than kicking the young fool out the door. The young artist is not alone in suffering from strange dreams and odd compulsions. So, the professor has his interest spiked further when he discovers later that they seem to connect to other events around the world which occurred at the same period of time.

This first part, as is the nature of first parts, spends a lot of time laying the land and this part of the tale most closely matches the opinion expressed by Lovecraft himself about the story as a whole, which was:

"Rather middling—not as bad as the worst, but full of cheap and cumbrous touches".

While I'm no more inclined to agree with Lovecraft's opinion than I normally am, it does sum up this first part rather succinctly. It is a bit of a trawl, interesting certainly, occasionally hard going in places, but it does cover an impressive scope. While it tells the story of the artist and his compulsion to create his hateful little tablet, it also is full of hints and portents of something much bigger, indeed, global in its scope. It is the scope of the uncanny events going on which sets this story apart. For our artist is not alone; others around the world are taken be the strange madness, driven to create strange art and other oddities. It is these connections which cause the professor to dig deeper. His investigations lead him to discovers an obscure religious cult that seems oddly active, while inmates of asylums are unusually restless causing some concern among the medical community. These he has documented with a collection of strange and otherwise unrelated cuttings discovered among the professor's papers by Francis. As Francis delves deeper into what seems to be a strange obsession for an academic who specialises in ancient languages, for the first time he comes across that strange ominous name, Cthulhu… But it is not the first time the professor has come across it, which is what inspired his interest.

THE TALE OF INSPECTOR LEGRASSE

"Ph'nglui mglw'nafh Cthulhu R'lyeh wgah'nagl fhtagn."

The reason for the erstwhile Professor Angell's acute interest in the bas-relief that gave 'The Horror in Clay' its name harkens back to events entrusted to him some seventeen years prior at a meeting of the American Archaeological Society, when Inspector Legrasse of the New Orleans police came before the gathered alumni of that organisation bearing an ancient statue of a sinister providence…
The inspector tells the assembled great and good of American archaeology how he came by the statue, in the depths of the swamps below New Orleans, breaking up an occult ritual gathering but not before ten people were murdered to be the beat of tom-tom drums and strange chants in a language unknown to civilised man.

'Ph'nglui mglw'nafh Cthulhu R'lyeh wgah'nagl fhtagn.'

The policeman's tale is dark enough in the telling, but it gains added credence thanks to the observations of Professor Webb, one of Angell's colleagues, who had stumbled across a similar cult in Greenland years before, practising similar dark rites and chanting in that same dead language and the same words…

'Ph'nglui mglw'nafh Cthulhu R'lyeh wgah'nagl fhtagn.'

Professor Webb had bene unable to translate the words at the time. Legrasse, however, having heard that same chant in the swampland of Louisiana had managed to 'persuade' one of the arrested cultists to translate those words, insomuch as it was possible, into English…

'In his house at R'lyeh dead Cthulhu waits dreaming.'

All this excited Professor Angell, as with the events told in 'The Horror in the Clay' he now had evidence of events in New England, Greenland and the Louisiana swamps all tied to the same strange image. After his death, while examining his uncle's papers, it also starts to excite Francis and he begins to consider not just investigating his uncle's papers, but continuing his research. He also begins to suspect that his uncle's death was not entirely as innocent as it first appeared. Was his uncle killed by cultists of this Cthulhu entity? Could this cult really exist and have tendrils everywhere? What secrets lie behind all this? Francis starts to wonder. As does the reader.

It is those ominous secrets lying tantalisingly just out of reach that draws the reader along and make this story what it is. This second part is disjointed in places, but the further Francis' story goes into his own journey, the more he discovers, the more profound the mystery… The more horrifying the possibilities… Much of the heavy lifting of the story is in this second part. Trying to throw so many threads out to give the events a global nature could have been an easy way to ruin the story, yet it doesn't, Instead, it draws the reader further in and inspires a certain level of awe along the way, not just in the events themselves, but in Lovecraft's mastery of threading them all together.

This is myth building at its finest, this is not just a suggestion of a time before human histories narrow scope but something darker and more fleshed out than in any earlier tale by Old Tentacle Hugger…The middle third of a tale is normally the toughest cookie, but this builds on the first and sets up the third masterfully.

"That is not dead which can eternal lie,
And with strange aeons even death may die."

THE MADNESS AT SEA

MYSTERY DERELICT FOUND AT SEA
Vigilant Arrives With Helpless Armed New Zealand Yacht in Tow.
One Survivor and Dead Man Found Aboard.
Tale of Desperate Battle and Deaths at Sea.
Rescued Seaman Refuses
Particulars of Strange Experience.
Odd Idol Found in His Possession.
Inquiry to Follow.

In the final part of 'The Call of Cthulhu' Lovecraft steps it up a notch. It's here the world first got to 'see' Old Tentacle Face himself, the demi-god, old-one, dragon winged, octopus-headed, giant, late sleeper himself. The monstrous creation that has surpassed all the others Lovecraft dreamt up as a counterculture phenomenon. Old Tentacle Face is everywhere in geek culture, and it all started here...

But cultural impact of the tale aside, the tale itself, like the first two parts of the tale, is a bit of a letdown - but perhaps that is because the expectations are so high. If there is one Lovecraft tale you want to drag you in and then leap off the page at you it is surely this one. But that's a small complaint and one that readers of Lovecraft will get past easily enough.

In this third part, Francis continues to relay second-hand events he learned of after first rooting them out in his dead uncle's files. But at least in this he is not just repeating second-hand accounts his uncle discovered. Instead, he goes to visit the source itself, the last survivor of the encounter at sea the cutting referred to. That survivor, a Norwegian seaman, tells the real tale, a tale of cultist pirates warning the yacht off and being ignored by his captain. Of the mysterious island they stumbled over where no island should be. Of how, much like the island in 'Dagon' which Lovecraft wrote so many years before, it seemed to be part of the sea floor pushed up to the surface for a time. He goes on to tell of an ancient temple on the island, a structure that made no sense with its strange non-Euclidean geometry, and strange lights emanating from it (harkening back to 'The Temple'). Struck with fear, the crew fled the island and the ship being pursued by a cyclopean creature that resembled a strange little statue one crewman had found near the temple - a Cthulhu idol, just like the one Inspector Lagasse had found amid the cultists in Louisiana years before. The same creature depicted on the bas-relief.

More by luck than judgement, the Norwegian survived the encounter when all other hands did not... Afterwards he fled back to Norway and pledged to never return to sea. He is more than a little insane and dies soon after Francis visits him.

Finally, Francis returns home to America and writes all he knows, but the last entry in his story is written as he realises, "I know too much, and the cult still lives."

As a tale within a tale, within a tale, this story is the best of it. Much like the other parts, it is the stories within that make the tale as a whole great. The final ending of the tale as a whole, with the narrator waiting for death at the hands of cultists, that he is sure his investigations will bring down on him is bleak and cold. But it should be bleak and cold. For once Lovecraft's tone is perfect here. But as a part of the whole, this story is not quite as good as it should be. I can't place why but it is just a feeling I have, an itch at the back of my mind perhaps...

Summary of the whole story

There is, it has to be said, something of the grand scale here when you take on the whole of 'The Call of Cthulhu'. This is a tale in three parts, and each part is not quite as good as it could be. But, when you consider the story as a whole, it is so much more than the sum of its parts.

THE SCORE: ALL THE TENTACLES OUT OF MANY, AND THEN SOME MORE.

MYTHOS CONNECTIONS: It is the culmination of all Lovecraft's early mythos work, with connections everywhere.

LOVECRAFT TWATTRY: In the second part there is the shadow of racism in the ways the cultists are described. Though it is not overt in nature.

SHOULD YOU READ IT: Clearly, as this is the seminal work.

BLUFFERS FACT: The statue discovered by inspector Legrasse, perhaps unsurprisingly, inspired one of the most popular types of Lovecraft collectables; several hundred different versions of it have been created over the years by various artists. Which is a wonderfully odd fact when you think about it. The Statue in the story was found in the possession of an ancient cult practising foul rites in the worship of the great old one represented in this strange piece of cunningly carved soapstone. Now representations of this fictional statue of a fictional god-like being reside on mantlepieces and in display cabinets around the world. The fictional cult of Cthulhu has far and away been surpassed by the cult the fiction created…
What's that old chestnut about the power of belief shaping the gods, and the power of gods stemming from belief… In moments of whimsy, it is a strangely worrying thought that so many Cthulhu 'worshipers' look up at the craven image of the one who awaits the stars being right… with that in mind I think I should move my statue to a more respectful part of the mantlepiece because you never know…

PICKMAN'S MODEL

Whatever your opinion on the literary merits of the tentacle loving stenographer of old Providence town, it is hard to ignore the sheer influence his works have had on the wider fictional and creative worlds. It is an influence that is not restricted to his more famous works alone. Some of his less well-known works have also had an influence far beyond what you would expect for a writer who in his own time was little known, published in relatively obscure periodicals and often only the amateur press.

This is something I have given mentioned to before in this vainglorious quest to read his collected works. Take 'Sweet Ermengarde', for example, a little known 'comic' tale that managed to inspire the name of a German goth metal band, one of many bands who have taken inspiration for their names or music from Lovecraft's more obscure fiction. But it's not just musicians and writers, video game designers have likewise trawled Lovecraft's back catalogue for inspiration, which brings me to how I first encountered Richard Pickman, the Bostonian painter who is the main character in 'Pickman's Model', in the tunnels beneath a nuclear wasteland.

Some explanation may be in order. While I was aware there was a Lovecraft story called 'Pickman's Model' it's one of the ones I had never gotten around to reading until I started the blog quest that became this book. So, while aware of the name of the story I knew little about it when, while playing 'Fallout 4', I started stumbling across murder victims who seemed to have been posed in strange ways after the fact in the nuclear blasted wastelands around Boston. A closer examination of these bodies (it being a computer game, and me being a magpie of a player) revealed little calling cards from the 'artist' Richard Pickman. I never made the connection to the Lovecraft story until later when a sub quest took me to the Pickman house, which is a macabre house of horrors, piles of corpses having been posed by Pickman to act as models for his paintings. Pickman in this incarnation is both artist and serial killer, and as such is one of the most viscerally repellent characters in a game set in a post-nuclear future full of super mutants, crazed gangs and killer androids. Not bad for a character from a run-of-the-mill little tale that never quite pulls off what its writer was trying to achieve.

Lovecraft's story follows a slightly different path to the 'Fallout 4' incarnation of Pickman, but one which is no less horrific in its inception. Lovecraft's Pickman is not a serial killer painting his crimes, though that might have made for a better story. Instead, this Pickman is an artist who is thrown out of the Boston Art Club and shunned by fellow artists due to the horrific, albeit brilliantly painted, art he creates. Pickman later disappears but not before the narrator of this tale, an old friend of Pickman's goes to visit him and witnesses his latest creation. A huge life size painting of a cannibalistic humanoid, with red eyes and slightly canine features. It is only later, after Pickman leaves him alone in the room, and stars shooting in the cellar (he comes back and claims he was shooting rats) that the narrator finds what he first takes to be a preliminary sketch for this huge painting. Afterwards when he looks more closely, he realises it's actually a photograph. Whatever Pickman shot in the cellar was his model, and as to why Pickman later disappeared, the narrator suspects he sought out more models for his art, and the models were less than accommodating.

This isn't the strongest piece of Lovecraft fiction, partly because of the way it is written. In a departure for his normal style the story is told by the narrator in a conversational manner to the reader who is effectively the one listening to the story. It's a style that requires a degree more emotion in the narrator, to make the story seem more like a natural conversation. Lovecraft pulls this off quite well, but it feels stilted in places and as a style it doesn't quite seem to fit. But at the same time this is far from the weakest story he ever wrote, it's a middling little tale. As occasionally seems the case with Lovecraft's stories what it inspired is so much more than the subject of that inspiration.

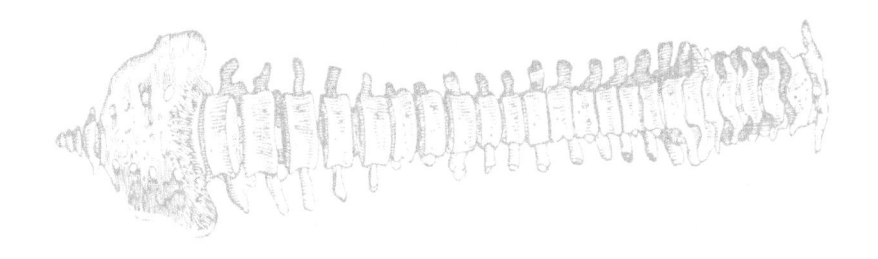

THE SCORE: 3 OUT OF 6 ARTISTICALLY DRAWN TENTACLES.

MYTHOS CONNECTIONS: None.

LOVECRAFT TWATTRY: None.

SHOULD YOU READ IT: Read it, don't read it, it's hard to recommend or not.

BLUFFERS FACT: Prince Street, Henchman Street, Charter Street and Greenough Lane are all actual streets in Boston's North End, and all appear in the story, but the location of Pickman's studio is left slightly vague. All these streets do however appear in the 'Fallout 4' version of Boston, and Pickman's studio is right in the middle of them. I don't recommend visiting it until you're 10 level at least and have a good supply of stim-packs.

THE SILVER KEY

Randolph Carter, where have we read that name before…?
More to the point where will we read it again?
Randolph first turned up in 'The Statement of Randolph Carter' about which there were a few good things to say. While it certainly didn't score highly in the slithering tentacles stakes, a lowly two in fact, it did have a certain charm and it was ground-breaking in its own odd little way. Since then, Randolph has popped back only once by name, ironically that was in 'The Unnamable'. Other stories with unnamed narrators are, however, often laid at Randolph's door, unsurprisingly as Randolph is Lovecraft's most autobiographical character. He also looms large stories yet to come, notably 'The Dream-Quest of Unknown Kadath'.

While it would be nice to think each of these stories is treated individually, the original incarnation of this book was a blog in which I was reading the stories in order and when I got to this story 'The Dream-Quest for Unknown Kadath' was definitely looming (having read it previously it is a novella I can't pretend I was looking forward to reading again) and 'The Silver Key' is to an extent a sequel to that novella, despite being written before. So, to be more exacting 'The Dream-Quest for Unknown Kadath' is a prequel to this story.

This makes certain aspects of the plot confusing, at least if you have read 'The Dream-Quest for Unknown Kadath' beforehand, because unlike the other Randolph Cater stories, this one directly alludes to its yet to be written prequel. Which wasn't written until several months later, though it is safe to assume Lovecraft had at least a working draft of that later story before he finished this one. But let me put that all to one side and explain the 'plot' of 'The Silver Key'.

In this story we find Randolph Carter around the age of 30 coming to the realisation he has lost the key to the gate of dreams - something that troubles him because he prefers his nightly dreams of fantastic places and beings to prosaic real life. Randolph also believes his dreams reveal truths to him regarding the purpose of humanity and the universe. So, no god complex here or anything…

As he gets older, Randolph finds that the real world and the scientific ideas of man have eroded his ability to dream as he once did, but while he accepts this and the mundane beliefs of the everyday, waking world, he is uncertain which is truer: the worlds of his dreams or the real world. In order to try and answer this question, as the world of dreams seems closed to him, he focuses on the real world and takes several ultimately unsatisfying philosophical stances. Eventually he becomes discouraged with the real world and withdraws from it, going into seclusion.

Once Randolph withdraws form the world, tantalising hints of the magical enter his dreams again, though he is still unable to dream of the strange cities he remembers from his youth - this return of the dreamworlds he remembers so vividly leave him wanting more. During one of these dreams, his long-dead grandfather tells him of a silver key in his attic. In the real world he goes looking for this key, finds it, then he takes it with him as he goes to visit his boyhood home in the backwoods of Massachusetts. Once there, he finds once again a mysterious cave that he used to play in as a child. Then, somehow, the key enables him to return to his childhood as a ten-year-old boy, and his adult self disappears from his own time.

Then at the end of the story we are told how Randolph's relatives noticed from the age of ten he started to somehow glimpse events in the future.

Finally, the narrator (who is or isn't Randolph) tells us he expects to meet Randolph (or possibly himself) soon in a dream of his own, "in a certain dream-city we both used to haunt", where Randolph now reigns as king. There the narrator hopes to look at Randolph's key, whose symbols will impart to him the mysteries of the cosmos.

So, as I said, it's all a little confused… Not least because the narrator may or may not be Randolph himself, hoping to meet his dream self where he reigns as a king in a city that never was. And there you go, there also is my problem with this whole story. There are plenty of people who find the all the ideas behind this story interesting. Indeed, I'm one of them. Just take the idea of a man returning to his youth and living his life again while retaining the knowledge of his own future… So many possibilities and/or bad teen movies to be had there. The idea that dreams and reality are just two sides of the same coin, one no more real than the other, equally has so much scope. What is reality but our perception of it after all…? If you dream vividly enough, who is to say that the dream is not the real world and the real world nothing but a dream?

The problem is that while Lovecraft has so many great ideas in this story, he somehow manages to make them all fall flat in the process. In essence, for me at least, they just don't work in this story. Ultimately there is too much here, too many layers hammered on top of each other and then they are written as dry as the empty quarter. So dry that lost cities could have been drowned in sand, forgotten to history and the dream world alike.

As a collection of ideas, this tale is astounding. In execution, it's torrid.

THE SCORE: 1 OUT OF 6 DESICCATED TENTACLES.

MYTHOS CONNECTIONS: Many Dreamland connections, in particular with 'The Dream-Quest for Unknown Kadath'.

LOVECRAFT TWATTRY: Despite being awash with his own cleverness throughout, none of note.

SHOULD YOU READ IT: I'm not saying don't read it, really I'm not, but if you do read it, for the love of all thing scaley don't blame me…

BLUFFERS FACT: The Editor of 'Weird Tales', Farnsworth Wright originally rejected 'The Silver Key' in 1927. A year later he relented and published it, though went on to regret doing so because, as he later told Lovecraft in a letter, the story was 'violently disliked' by the magazine's readers. Just what led him to choose those exact words, we will never know, but it does suggest 'Weird Tales' readers were a discerning bunch.

THE STRANGE HIGH HOUSE IN THE MIST

With this tale we go back to fair old Kingsport, an odd little town on the New England coast that Old Tentacle Hugger first brought to our attention in 'The Terrible Old Man', who, coincidently turns up at the beginning of this tale. Indeed, it is he who points out, to the story's narrator, the strange house residing on the northern cliff overlooking the town. That old house is one about which the residents of Kingsport tell many a strange tale. Tales that contradict themselves often it seems, but one thing is made clear to the narrator, no resident of Kingsport ever considers making their way up to the old house that overlooks the Miskatonic bay, where the river that flows through Arkham empties out into the sea.

With such warnings it should come as no surprise that this story is narrated by a philosopher who when visiting Kingsport, despite the wisdom of the locals, decides he should try to find a path that leads up to this strange imposing place.

Let's face it, who hasn't thought to themselves, 'oh look an odd-looking house in the middle of nowhere. Clearly that's the one 'The Terrible Old Man' I just met told me I should avoid. The same place everyone else who lives in this town tells me they would never go to. I think I shall go there…'

After all, what could go wrong…

As tropes go the narrator's decision to visit the house on the cliff is right up there with deciding to stay in a rundown little cabin in the backwoods. That one the strange old guy in the last gas station twenty miles back said you should avoid. Oh, look your cell has lost signal…

Is that a hillbilly over there?

The one with the beard you could lose a badger in? Yes, that's him the one sharpening his axe…

But let us be fair a moment, Lovecraft was writing long before 'The Evil Dead', and the hundreds of other movies that sunk that little trope into our collective zeitgeist. All the same while my sympathy is a devil to find for our philosophising narrator and his impulsive desire to visit the imposing house perched on the cliff edge, there is more to this tale than the slasher movie in the woods it brings to mind as you read it. For a start it is far spookier than any run-of-the-mill predictable slasher movie. The occupant of that strange house is more mystic than murderer. Once his visitor has negotiated the foggy paths that lead up to the house, he tells him many strange things. The narrator is told of old gods, of speaking to the mists and the mystery of the sea. Impossible things are told of and then as the story starts to slip into 'Beyond the Walls of Sleep' territory, there comes a knocking at the door, the door that hangs out over the cliff edge, over the abyss - and the odd bearded man who lives in this even odder house is not entirely pleased to welcome the one who knocks…

And then the story gets so much more interesting and downright weird…

This is a story that cries out to be read. All the more so, perhaps, as it comes at a time when many of these stories were increasingly dry to the point of Gobi Desert arid. With the exception of 'Call of Cthulhu' and 'The Horror at Red Hook' most of Lovecraft's output at this point in his life was mediocre fare at best and had been since 'The Rats in the Walls'. This story, however, has that missing something. The edge of Lovecraft's earlier tales. It even manages to do something akin to those increasingly tedious Dreamlands stories without sending the reader to sleep.

THE SCORE: 5 OUT OF 6 SLITHERING TENTACLES COMING OUT OF THE MISTS BEYOND THE OMINOUS PORTAL.

MYTHOS CONNECTIONS: Kingsport and 'The Terrible Old Man', as well as the resident of the house mentioning many places, and gods that link to other works.

LOVECRAFT TWATTRY: None.

SHOULD YOU READ IT: It is one of Lovecraft's most readable stories, so, yes.

BLUFFERS FACT: Lovecraft was surprisingly well paid for this little story, receiving $55 from 'Weird Tales' when it was published. This was a surprisingly large amount, particularly as they originally rejected the story two years before.

THE DREAM-QUEST OF UNKNOWN KADATH

When I reviewed 'The Silver Key', a couple of stories ago, I said that I was not looking forward to this novella. I'd read it before, years ago, and was feeling less than inspired about reading it again. As I was reading these stories in order, that is entirely true, but I had to read it, and at the time I put it off quite a while and the Lovecraft blog stuttered for a while. Eventually though I did read it, remarkably it was a more rewarding experience than I expected.
'The Dream-quest of Unknown Kadath' is a true novella. The first true novella Lovecraft wrote. We get to it here after almost fifty short stories of various qualities from the wonderful to the torrid, via fragments which should never have been published, a couple of serials (one fabulously entertaining, one best forgotten), and one novelette - the less said about which the better, in my opinion. It has been a long road to finally reach the first true actual novella, a story long enough to be a book all to itself. Not quite novel length it's true, but still an actual novella…
It is also a novella much loved, much applauded and highly rated among Lovecraft aficionados which features one of Old Tentacle Hugger's most-loved characters, Randolph 'Bloody' Carter. But putting my own petulant annoyance with Randolph to one side, the novella is also the pinnacle of the sequence of Lovecraft stories often referred to as 'The Dreamlands' tales, with which I have a love-hate relationship. So, let's face it, this could go either way…
If by this point, you're waiting for my verdict with bated breath (not that I can imagine why you would be) then you're going to have to put up with a minor diversion first, because, yes, I am going to talk about something else first. I am sure you will be shocked by this, as when do I ever go wondering off track rather than talking about the subject at hand? I know, unforgivable isn't it… But bear with me, it's worth it, I promise you, it will all make sense in the end…
Probably.
Now, my favourite New England writer has a habit of linking all his works together, which is something I have always found fascinating. You can read one of his stories and if you don't know his other works, you'll just read a passage and not notice the delicious link it to another

story as you skim past it. Take the story of a convict, with the power to suck illness out of people like sucking out so much poison. As he is walked to his execution through the yard, for a crime he never actually committed, he looks up to the sky and sees constellations that don't exist in our universe but do in the universe of another set of stories by the same author. This is done with such lightness of touch you'd never notice it unless you remembered a gunslinger in a desert looking up on those same stars in a novel written twenty years before the one you're reading.

Sorry, you may be confused, but if it helps my favourite New England writer, is from Maine, not Rhode Island and for the moment, I am talking about Stephen King, not H.P. Lovecraft.

If you have never read 'The Dark Tower' novels, this may also confuse you, because the references to 'The Dark Tower', that are scattered throughout just about every other novel King has ever written are references you only spot if you know what you're reading. They are, however, there all the same, in almost every novel (save perhaps his earliest ones before he started to write 'The Dark Tower' novels). In some novels 'The Dark Tower's' mythology and lore, form the whole backdrop, such as 'From a Buick 8' a novel about an extended family of state troopers, but which features a car which is also a portal that was, for a time, used by creatures from 'The Dark Tower' novels to move from another universe into ours. That is just a random example, however, the point is that King's novels interweave to form a greater whole and 'The Dark Tower' stands in the middle of that weave, the edifice at the centre of the web, and this, for me at least, is what sets King apart from most writers. Indeed, it is something I try to emulate myself with my own work and 'The Passing Place'.

But let's get back to 'The Dream-Quest of Unknown Kadath' and the reason for that little diversion. King, I know, read Lovecraft. It's reasonable to say there is more than a little Lovecraft influence in many of the stories King writes. But if you're looking for Lovecraft's greatest influence on King's work it is probably this novella, not so much because of the tale itself, but because of what Lovecraft set out to achieve with it. When Lovecraft wrote 'The Dream-Quest of Unknown Kadath' he wrote his 'Dark Tower', in that it sits right bang smack in the middle of everything he'd written up to that point - and I do mean everything. So, to fully appreciate this novella you really have to have read a whole lot of Lovecraft first. Which is ironic considering with King's 'The Dark Tower' it works the other way round in many respects.

In 'The Dream-Quest of Unknown Kadath' you will find references to, among others, 'The Cats of Ulthar', 'The White Ship', 'The Doom That Came To Sarnath', 'The Statement Of Randolph Carter', 'Celephais', 'Nyarlathotep', 'Azathoth', 'The Other Gods', 'The Silver Key', 'The Unnameable', 'Beyond The Wall of Sleep', and a whole host more, those are just the more obviously connected ones. Indeed, there is more 'Nyarlathotep' in this novella than in the story 'Nyarlathotep' itself, and indeed all the other times the many faced one turns up.

The story itself is a journey tale, which is to say it is long and winding. The journey of our old friend, and occasional bloody irritant, Randolph Carter, which takes him weaving his way through Lovecraft's universe. This is the joy of the novella; more than the writing, more than the tale itself, it is the journey and what you stumble over along the way that makes it fun to read. But, as I say, you have to have read all that earlier Lovecraft in order to appreciate that journey. The plot is… well let's just say there is a lot of plot but none of it is really the point. The point is the journey, not the end, and to ruin the ending now would seem foolish. Of course, this is a journey through the dreamlands, and at the end of such a journey, Carter is always going to wake up. But that's not quite how this ends, or quite what is going on. This may be Carter's dream, but it is much more than a dream, it is more a journey through Carter's subconscious and (as Carter is autobiographical in most respects) through Lovecraft's subconscious, through all his strange and wonderful imagination. Just remember the cats are important, be good to the cats and they might just save you…

I am not the biggest fan of the Dreamlands sequence, and far from a fan of Randolph 'bloody' Carter. Though that said, some of those Dreamlands stories are among my favourites so I am not sure my opinion can be trusted. I can, however, honestly say I really enjoyed 'The Dream-Quest of Unknown Kadath'. Far more than the first time I read it several years ago at a time when I had not read much Lovecraft. Which is why I think you have to love Lovecraft or at least to be well read of Old Tentacle Hugger's work to truly appreciate the novella. But if you have read those other tales, then it is something of a masterpiece, for all it not quite being on the scale of a certain Tower in which resides a Crimson King…

THE SCORE: 5 OUT OF 6 TENTACLES, THAT WOULD BE SIX, BUT SERIOUSLY RANDOLPH 'BLOODY' CARTER...

MYTHOS CONNECTIONS: So very, very many, basically everything written up to this point, and much that comes after.

LOVECRAFT TWATTRY: A surprising lack of it.

SHOULD YOU READ IT: Yes, provided you read as much of the earlier stories as possible first.

BLUFFERS FACT: Lovecraft took from many influences when writing this story (some are obvious, Lord Dunsany for example), but one odd influence often cited is the Wizard of Oz, because in both stories the main character chooses in the end to return home.

THE CASE OF CHARLES DEXTER WARD

'The Case of Charles Dexter Ward,' is Lovecraft's only full novel, a fact which may lead you to think it is his grand opus... Sadly it is not. What it is, is a long hard trawl through a Lovecraft story that had it been a mere ten thousand word long might have been quite fun. I say this in the full knowledge I am being slightly disingenuous. I vaguely recall enjoying the novel a great deal the first time I read it, some twenty years ago. Taste develop and change over time. What you like in one decade of your life you're not necessarily going to enjoy in the next. But there must have been something about this novel back then that sat well with me.

I suspect the main reason for these opposing opinions is that in those bygone days of youth I did not find 'The Case Of Charles Dexter Ward' a thankless trawl of a novel which drags itself along like a man who just lost a leg to a threshing machine trying to get to the phone in the farmhouse. The reason being that back then I'd not read everything else Lovecraft had written up to this point in his life. Having done so, I've acquired a different perspective.

It's a bit of a shame that I did not enjoy the read this time around, because as an introduction to Lovecraft's style of storytelling 'The Case of Charles Dexter Ward' is almost perfect. Lovecraft's style suits this novel down to the ground, except by having read everything else he has written it's that style which became my biggest hurdle with the novel. This reads like one of his short stories, but is a short story that goes on into eternity...

Style is not the only issue, there is also a small matter of the plot. Or to be more exact, knowing exactly where the story was going after the first ten pages. Now it is true I had read the novel before, albeit a long time back, but even if I had not, I suspect I could have taken a stab at the plot of this novel, and the big reveal ending, after the first few pages. Most any reader could, because, while in fairness in places the setup is complex, at times it is tracing paper thin.

Young Charles Ward becomes obsessed with a mysterious ancestor who 'dabbled' shall we say, in the dark arts and in the course of his research he becomes steadily odder. Which is all good apart from one bit of description early on which gives the whole game away. Indeed,

sells you tickets to the big blockbuster, while telling you Bruce Willis's character was dead all the time…
It's this line, though paraphrased just a little

'Ward's madness was strange, he seemed to know details of antiquity that were impossible for a man to know yet understood almost nothing of modern life…'

Which is 'here's the game, take it' even if you have not read much Lovecraft, but if you have read the sublime 'The Shadow out of Time', or the irritating 'The Thing on the Doorstep' (both of which were written later in Lovecraft's life) or 'Polaris' and 'Beyond the Walls of Sleep' (written years before) you can see what's coming. As you read further, everything you read just confirms what you expect from that point on. Ward has grown old in his skin and, while lucid, speaks in archaic terms and language, because Ward is no longer Ward.
There is a lot in the novel, ancient magic, witch trials, a whole lot of Lovecraft's Mythos lore, zombies or some other undead, strange paintings and souls that don't quite stay where they should. But the whole story is so drawn out that any gems buried in the text are lost within it. There are few actual surprises and fewer shocks and before long it all feels a bit too mundane. Perhaps that's the greatest problem with the novel. There is nothing new here, no big idea, it's just Lovecraft let loose in the long form with an idea better suited to a short story. An idea he has used several times to better effect in tighter short fiction that doesn't let you get bored with the central idea or give it away long before you get close to the end.
As I said this is all a tad disingenuous of me, I had read the novel before, even if I didn't remember it well. But having read all of Lovecraft's back catalogue believe me when I say he could have written this as a far better short story than it ever is a novel. Which is not to say I would not recommend 'The Case of Charles Dexter Ward' to someone new to Lovecraft, but there are a whole host of better stories I would recommend first.
'The Case of Charles Dexter Ward' does, however, mark a watershed of sorts. While the novel was not published in Lovecraft's lifetime, and was first published in an abridged form by some wise editor of 'Weird Tales', it was written around the time Lovecraft started to gain popularity and build up his own little cult of readers. It was also written just before Lovecraft's golden late period, when he wrote his most

consistently well received work. 'Dunwich Horror', 'At the Mountains of Madness', 'The Shadow over Innsmouth', 'The Colour out of Space' and more were all to come. While my opinions on the late period stories vary, they more than anything are what anchored Lovecraft in the popular zeitgeist, and without them all the earlier stories, even Old Tentacle Face, may have been long forgotten literary footnotes. While 'The Case of Charles Dexter Ward' would doubtless have never been published at all.

THE SCORE: 4 NOT ENTIRELY DESERVED TENTACLES OUT OF 6, MOSTLY FOR THE MEMORY OF WHAT AN INTERESTING NOVEL IT SEEMED THE FIRST TIME AROUND, ALL THOSE YEARS AGO.

MYTHOS CONNECTIONS: They are, as you would expect, many buried within this tomb, they take some digging out however.

LOVECRAFT TWATTRY: Reader beware…

SHOULD YOU READ IT: Even after everything I have said? Probably.

BLUFFERS FACT: At just over 50,000 words this is a short novel by today's standards, only just scraping into the definition, rather than being labelled a novella. However back in the early 1900s this was a quite a respectable length for a genre fiction novel. HG Wells' 'The Time Machine' is only 32,149, and Ray Bradbury's 'Fahrenheit 451' rocks in at 46,118.
Length is, however, no guarantee of quality and I would take those two short novels any time…

THE COLOUR OUT OF SPACE

It was a scene from a vision of Fuseli, and over all the rest reigned that riot of luminous amorphousness, that alien and undimensioned rainbow of cryptic poison from the well—seething, feeling, lapping, reaching, scintillating, straining, and malignly bubbling in its cosmic and unrecognisable chromaticism.

Now there is a sentence with a life of its own.
No one could accuse Lovecraft of underselling the strangeness of the lifeform that falls to earth in a quiet rural backwater of New England in 'The Colour out of Space'. This is life, if that's the correct word, but, to quote McCoy, 'not as we know it', not as we know it, at all.
This is the essence to this whole story. Life is undoubtedly out there in the cosmos, the universe is just too vast for that to be otherwise, but life as we know it? Nice, simple, understandable, carbon-based life? Well, there is probably little doubt too, as it is no more unlikely. However, life as we don't know it, life that did not evolve from the same roots of the tree as we did is almost a certainty. Indeed, not to put too fine a point on it, humanity can't be entirely certain there isn't life on our own little mud-ball that isn't actually life as we know it. Frankly, if your search for life is based on the premise that it must be carbon-based, you have already narrowed the scope of your definition and that in itself is the first mistake. But if we can't even trust our definition of life, even on our own planet, then how could we rule out the possibility of life out there in the endless beyond not conforming to that definition.
And if it doesn't? If something falls to earth that isn't just an alien with an extending neck, light up finger, and a strong desire to 'phone home'? Not a carbon-based, understandable kind of alien that, while beyond our experience, is not beyond our comprehension? What if it is something utterly alien to us not on a cellular level, or on a DNA level, or even on the level of amino acids and the basic building blocks of everything we understand as alive in our narrow, carbon-based way? What then?
You can call Lovecraft a lot of things, and over the course of reading his complete works and writing this book god knows I have, but by the late 1920s (1927 in this case) he was writing not only some of his best fiction but also some of the most insightful science fiction around.

'The Colour out of Space' is certainly both of those things. All the more so when you consider that science at the time had yet to really get to grips with cellular life and DNA. To say no one was writing stories quite like this back in the 1920s is an understatement because while it was written almost a century ago it still feels current and on the cusp of scientific understanding and how we comprehend the universe.

Besides being ahead of its time 'The Colour out of Space' was also, far more than even 'The Call of Cthulhu' a breakout story for Old Tentacle Hugger. It was one of his first stories to receive broad praise and to be re-published beyond the confines of 'Amazing Stories' and its fellow pulp magazines. After its first appearance in 'Amazing Stories' it was picked for the annual 'The Best American Short Stories' anthology, a rare accolade for any science fiction story.

Ostensibly, this is the story of a Boston surveyor visiting a remote rural area known locally as 'Blasted Heath'. He is there investigating rumours that centre around how the area came to be abandoned and spurned by the locals, after a meteorite strikes the earth in the region. It is what he discovers as he investigates that makes this story so compelling. Lovecraft, who let's face it was a bit of a strange bod at times, excels in his writing when it comes to describing the weird and uncanny. The description of the heath and its strange flora and fauna is a case in point. There are plants that glow a little in the dark that yield fruits that ripen sour and are inedible. Livestock turns grey and dies off. Well water becomes tainted and a series of strange events follow the meteor crashing to earth forty years before the story is set. This story is a masterpiece of strangeness. Something alien is about in this remote part of New England, something so alien it is beyond comprehension. But it's not just livestock and plants being made a little strange; the Gardner family who work the land are a little strange too, and sanity is wearing a little thin. And even forty years after the meteor crashed to earth it's still there, dormant, perhaps waiting… Though if it's waiting for something, who cares even to guess what that might be, and what may happen when its waiting is done…

Of all Lovecraft's tales, aspects of this one are among both the strangest and yet the most readable. There is a reason it remains so well loved today, as I said it still seems a modern tale, where other Lovecraft stories have dated or become fractured by time. This story could be written and set today with little of substance changed and it would still seem as vital, oddly possible and frightening with the possibilities it provokes. Life, as we know it out there in the cosmos, may come down here one day, and if we are lucky it will only be that, life as we know it…

THE SCORE: ALL THE TENTACLES OUT OF MANY.

MYTHOS CONNECTIONS: Surprisingly, none.

LOVECRAFT TWATTRY: None, save Lovecraft's usual elitism with regards to those who live in a rural setting.

SHOULD YOU READ IT: This story has my unhesitating recommendation, if you're looking for a story that will make you lay awake with thoughtful if rather chilling possibilities floating around your mind…

BLUFFERS FACT: The fact that the name of the story is 'Colour' not 'Color' is an oddity, Lovecraft wrote exclusively in American English, sans 'U' so this suggests a definite choice on his part with the title. The spelling was a subtle way to inject a little of the alien into the title, just to throw his mostly American audience a tad off kilter right from the get-go.
Richard Stanley's 2019 movie based on the story and staring Nicholas Cage, removed the 'U', which as I'm British, I feel is something of a shame.

THE VERY OLD FOLK

'Malitia vetus—malitia vetus est . . . venit . . . tandem venit . . .'

Or for those of you without a working grasp of Latin… Or google to hand…

'Wickedness of old—it is wickedness of old…happened…happened at last…'

Those are the last words of dying Roman officer at the end of 'The Very Old Folk', a tale that even by Old Tentacle Hugger's standards is not particularly inviting to the casual reader. Indeed, I would go so far as to say this is a tale for the serious Lovecraft reader only, the type of reader who wants to read everything he ever wrote regardless of if even Lovecraft himself would want you to do so… Which in the case of this story its fairly certain he would not want you to do.
I say this because Lovecraft did not write this story for 'Weird Tales' or 'Amazing Stories' (the latter of which he had just fallen out with anyway in a dispute about the money for 'The Colour out of Space') nor even 'The American Amateur Press'. H.P. didn't write this story for publication at all, or even as a story as such. The tale was taken from a letter he wrote in 1927 to Donald Wandrei. It found its way into print after Lovecraft's death because in 1939 the same Donald Wandrei was the co-founder of Arkham House Publishing.
Wandrei and August Derleth, set up Arkham House with the supposed intention of preserving and publishing Lovecraft's best work. This may have been their primary motivation, but they also needed to make money to keep their vanity-by-proxy project afloat, so they desperately needed 'new' stories to bulk out their portfolio while they acquired the rights to the bulk of Lovecraft's previously published work. 'The Very Old Folk' was among several 'lost' stories they unearthed for this reason - and it was they who came up with the title. Thus, it found its way into one of their earliest collections of Lovecraft's stories.
The world owes a debt to Wandrei, without him making the case for 'The Call of Cthulhu' to 'Weird Tales' editor Farnsworth Wright, that particular story may never have been published. Wandrei was a writer himself, and at the time more successful than Lovecraft, so had some

pull with 'Weird Tales'. Similarly, without Arkham House there is every chance Lovecraft's stories would have slipped away to obscurity after his death. Certainly, throughout the 50s, 60s and 70s they were the ones keeping Lovecraft's work and the work of many other pulp writers both in print and in the zeitgeist. They are also, regrettably in some cases, responsible for some of the more obscure and often more forgettable pieces of Lovecraft's bibliography coming to print. 'The Very Old Folk' falls neatly into that inauspicious band. Though it's not terrible by any means and contains hints and snippets of Lovecraft's broader mythos, it's also utterly bland and difficult to love. Not least because of all the Romans... More to the point the endless Roman names that are scattered throughout the story, which just become painful to read... (which is ironic considering he wrote 'Ibid' not long after, which is also has Romans in it, with names that are anything but painful).

The story itself is a narration of a dream which more than likely was one Lovecraft had himself, and wrote about in his letter to Wandrei, (just how much editing took place to make it an actual story is an open question). In the dream, the narrator is a Roman soldier in the north of a Spanish province and he is dealing with the strange goings-on of the hill-folk who live in the mountains. The hill-folk surprisingly don't take prisoners for sacrifice on their Sabbath. The lack of a raid makes the townsfolk afraid because they didn't have anyone kidnapped, and so they urge the Romans mount a punitive expedition into the mountains. Yes, that's right, because the local hill tribe decide not to kidnap a victim for sacrifice, as expected, they must be hunted down by the Romans...

I know, just go with it will you....

So, the Romans march up into the hills, and at that point bad things start happening...

There is nothing wrong with this story, apart from that strange piece of the internal logic, but it's just not particularly engaging or all that interesting. There is no resolution, not even a Lovecraft-style resolution, just the mildly ominous Latin above followed by a paragraph of what amounts to 'and then I woke up'. It's not Lovecraft at his best, nor is it Lovecraft at his worst. It's not a story at all. This at best is just Lovecraft playing with ideas, dying, and a friend then publishing his scrawled notes, with a little editing along the way... What it amounts to is:

Romans go up the hill for spurious reasons, Romans see things that scare the crap out of them, Romans run away... pretentious Latin... then I woke up... the end...

By this point in Lovecraft's career, he was not only capable of better, but he was also writing better consistently. If he wrote this with any intent to make something publishable out of it, I doubt somehow this was the story he intended to tell in the end. So read it, don't read it, forget its existence, or try and analyse the hell out of it to find something in there worth the time and effort involved (trust me, many have). For the most part there isn't anything here that the Lovecraftian world couldn't have lived perfectly well without. It gets a couple of tentacles because I don't hate it, but at the same time, that's because it doesn't hold enough interest for me to be bothered to have much of an opinion on it at all...

THE SCORE: 2 OUT OF 6 OVERLY PRETENTIOUS TENTACLES

MYTHOS CONNECTIONS: None.

LOVECRAFT TWATTRY: None. Except that he shared this 'dream' with anyone in the first place.

SHOULD YOU READ IT: Probably not.

BLUFFERS FACT: Arkham House did not just keep Lovecraft and a few other 20s/30s pulp magazine writers, it also launched the careers of among others, Fritz Lieber, Greg Bear and Ray Bradbury by giving them their first publishing contacts.

THE HISTORY OF THE NECRONOMICON

The history of the Necronomicon is not a story as such, but a brief faux-academic treatise on the history of the most famous book Old Tentacle Hugger ever dreamed up. He never wrote it, for reasons that are perhaps obvious (what with the requirement for human skin to bind it with and everything), but he employed it as a device and a MacGuffin in many of his tales. This is then, in effect, a piece of background material he wrote for his own fiction, which like many things, he probably never intended for publication. And oddly enough that's exactly what it reads like, background material, which would not be out of place in a 'Call of Cthulhu' RPG sourcebook… It's interesting stuff, and rich in detail, but not a story, and can't be read as such…. However, it is also public domain and not particularly long, so rather than talk about it, I have reprinted it entirely here, for you to have a read yourself…

THE HISTORY OF THE NECRONOMICON
BY H. P. LOVECRAFT

Original title Al Azif—azif being the word used by Arabs to designate that nocturnal sound (made by insects) suppos'd to be the howling of daemons.
Composed by Abdul Alhazred, a mad poet of Sanaá, in Yemen, who is said to have flourished during the period of the Ommiade caliphs, circa 700 A.D. He visited the ruins of Babylon and the subterranean secrets of Memphis and spent ten years alone in the great southern desert of Arabia—the Roba el Khaliyeh or "Empty Space" of the ancients—and "Dahna" or "Crimson" desert of the modern Arabs, which is held to be inhabited by protective evil spirits and monsters of death. Of this desert many strange and unbelievable marvels are told by those who pretend to have penetrated it. In his last years Alhazred dwelt in Damascus, where the Necronomicon (Al Azif) was written,

and of his final death or disappearance (738 A.D.) many terrible and conflicting things are told. He is said by Ebn Khallikan (12th cent. biographer) to have been seized by an invisible monster in broad daylight and devoured horribly before a large number of fright-frozen witnesses. Of his madness many things are told. He claimed to have seen fabulous Irem, or City of Pillars, and to have found beneath the ruins of a certain nameless desert town the shocking annals and secrets of a race older than mankind. He was only an indifferent Moslem, worshipping unknown entities whom he called Yog-Sothoth and Cthulhu.

In A.D. 950 the Azif, which had gained a considerable tho' surreptitious circulation amongst the philosophers of the age, was secretly translated into Greek by Theodorus Philetas of Constantinople under the title Necronomicon. For a century it impelled certain experimenters to terrible attempts, when it was suppressed and burnt by the patriarch Michael. After this it is only heard of furtively, but (1228) Olaus Wormius made a Latin translation later in the Middle Ages, and the Latin text was printed twice—once in the fifteenth century in black-letter (evidently in Germany) and once in the seventeenth (prob. Spanish)—both editions being without identifying marks, and located as to time and place by internal typographical evidence only. The work both Latin and Greek was banned by Pope Gregory IX in 1232, shortly after its Latin translation, which called attention to it. The Arabic original was lost as early as Wormius' time, as indicated by his prefatory note; and no sight of the Greek copy—which was printed in Italy between 1500 and 1550—has been reported since the burning of a certain Salem man's library in 1692. An English translation made by Dr. Dee was never printed and exists only in fragments recovered from the original manuscript. Of the Latin texts now existing one (15th cent.) is known to be in the British Museum under lock and key, while another (17th cent.) is in the Bibliothèque Nationale at Paris. A seventeenth-century edition is in the Widener Library at Harvard, and in the library of Miskatonic University at Arkham. Also in the library of the University of Buenos Ayres. Numerous other copies probably exist in secret, and a fifteenth-century one is persistently rumoured to form part of the collection of a celebrated American millionaire. A still vaguer rumour credits the preservation of a sixteenth-century Greek text in the Salem family of Pickman; but if it was so preserved, it vanished with the artist R.U. Pickman, who disappeared early in 1926. The book is rigidly suppressed by the authorities of most countries, and by all branches of organised ecclesiasticism. Reading leads to terrible

consequences. It was from rumours of this book (of which relatively few of the general public know) that R.W. Chambers is said to have derived the idea of his early novel The King in Yellow.
Chronology
Al Azif written circa 730 A.D. at Damascus by Abdul Alhazred
Tr. to Greek 950 A.D. as Necronomicon by Theodorus Philetas
Burnt by Patriarch Michael 1050 (i.e., Greek text). Arabic text now lost.
Olaus translates Gr. to Latin 1228
1232 Latin ed. (and Gr.) suppr. by Pope Gregory IX
14... Black-letter printed edition (Germany)
15... Gr. text printed in Italy
16... Spanish reprint of Latin text

So, there you go. As a story, well, it's not a story.

As source material and a window into Lovecraft's writing and the world-building he indulged in behind his stories, the weaving of real historical figures in with fictional ones, and the whole believable make-believe of it all, (the use of Elizabeth I's arcanist in chief, Dr Dee and the pope most famous for making a horse a cardinal for example), I personally find fascinating.

**THE SCORE: 5 OUT OF 6 TENTACLES
(EVEN THOUGH IT'S NOT A STORY)**

MYTHOS CONNECTIONS: Clearly...

LOVECRAFT TWATTRY: None.

SHOULD YOU READ IT: You just have but read it again by all means.

BLUFFERS FACT: This is proof that at its very best, Lovecraft's work makes for great roleplaying game background material... Or perhaps Lovecraft saw glimpses of the future of his work involving the rolling of d10s and sanity saves and decided to write his own background material...
Who knows, interesting it remains all the same...

THE DUNWICH HORROR

'The Dunwich Horror' was one of those stories that it took me some time to get around to when this book was an ongoing blog series. It sat in my to-do list for about six months after I posted 'The Necronomicon'. You might imagine it took me so long to get around to writing about it because I didn't like the story, which is not entirely incorrect, but is not the whole truth either. The whole truth was that I was busy doing the final draft of a novel at the time and kept 'forgetting' to do the post, but then 'The Dunwich Horror' is sadly easy to 'forget'. Not least because there is so damn much of it, or rather there isn't, but it feels like there is.

At a little over 16675 words, it's long for a short story. Partly because Old Tentacle Hugger drags the story out for all it is worth, and then a bit more. This is not to say the length of the story is an issue, the issues I have with it are more to do with the style of Lovecraft's writing in this story and the way he sets about building tension upon... well basically nothing.

Lovecraft at his best builds stories that are not unlike climbing a staircase. Each step raises the stakes a little more, each building tension on the previous step as you climb the stairs to a shadowy unlit landing where you just know something deeply wrong is awaiting you, some dark malignant force...

Quite often, when you reach the top of the stairs you find the landing empty, or that it leads to another flight of stairs... Lovecraft's best short stories all do this. They build to a climax in slow steady steps that take the reader ever closer and with each step a little higher, a little further into the shadow, a little more tense, a little more afraid of what they will find at the end of the climb.

'The Dunwich Horror' doesn't do this. For most of the story it just plods along vaguely hinting at a general vague sort of wrongness but failing to really build on itself. The scope of the story seems too wide for a short story. In it, Lovecraft charts the strange Whateley family's history over a number of years. Firstly, the sinister patriarch who is rumoured to have dabbled in dark rites and forbidden magics. Then there is his strangely fey daughter, oft seen wandering around the countryside, who has a reputation for being a few hens short of a hen house, before she dies suspiciously (but not before giving birth to a son who is also somewhat strange and sinister).

Old Man Whatley then seems to spend much of his time making odd changes to his house, while his neighbours make much comment about the number of cows in the family's small herd. This is because the farmers who regularly sell the cows to Old Man Whatley have noticed the family's herd never seems to get any bigger, as such they are worried about the cows and the possibility that they may be getting eaten… or something.

Yes, I know that's a tad flippant, but I find that as a tension raising device cows apparently been eaten mysteriously leaves something to be desired… It's not as if the farmers keep finding half ravaged bovine corpses or anything. The extra cows the Whatleys keep buying just aren't there.

A few years after the fey daughter of Old Whatley dies, the old man joins her in the grave and the farm falls to Wilbur Whatley, the grandson. Now Wilbur is an oddity - if all the farmers weren't obsessed with vanishing cows they may have taken more note of his odd genetics. Wilbur, it seems grew up rather quickly, a tad too quickly. At fourteen he is a full-grown man, beard and all.

With his grandfather dead, Wilbur who clearly knows something of his strange heritage, decides to go off to Arkham and the Miskatonic University, in order to 'borrow' the university's copy of The Necronomicon. As his borrowing involves breaking and entering this causes a bit of a ruckus and ends up with Wilbur being mauled by a dog and dying… At which point his odd deformities come to light, just before his body melts away.

This brings the actual 'heroes' of the story to the fore, Professors Armitage, Rice, and Morgan, who trundle off to Dunwich just in time for us to meet the final member of the Whatley family. The member of the family that hadn't been mentioned up to this point, merely alluded to. It also brings us neatly to the one really good line in the whole story, for Wilbur's twin brother we are told…

"looked more like the father than Wilbur did"

Which is to say he is a giant monstrosity who has been walled up inside the farmhouse, which has over the years been hollowed out to the point where it is no more than an empty shell, which his bloated form fills entirely. Until, that is, Wilbur goes to Arkham, in search of a means to control his twin (and presumably because his supply of cows has dried up). So, the twin goes on a rampage across the Dunwich countryside...

Except, that line, "looked more like the father than Wilbur did' doesn't entirely ring true because the giant monstrosity that is Wilbur's twin is also invisible...

The three professors manage to kill the twin, through use of a magic power that makes it visible, and a spell Armitage knows that destroys it once he can see it. But not before it screams for help form its father, Yog-Sothoth, an ancient deity that Old Man Whatley had 'wedded' to his daughter (which explains her madness before her end.)

The father chooses not to save his spawn, for which we should be thankful.

All of which is, to be fair, interesting to an extent and if it had been shorter, said rather less about the cows, and Lovecraft had built a little tension into the story it could have been so much better.

It is certainly one of the stories central to the mythos, and worth a read if you never have. Perhaps it is just because it is one of the more famous stories, I find it disappointing, and always have. This is far from the first time I have read it, but I always feel it lacks the tension and drama of 'The Call of Cthulhu', or 'The Mountains of Madness', nor does it have the wit of 'Herbert West: Reanimator' or the sheer strange allure of some of the better shorts. It fails at that most crucial of things: it never makes me want to read more.

THE SCORE: 3 OUT OF 6 TENTACLES.
Though it should perhaps get a 4 or even a 5 and yes, I realise that sounds odd after all I have just said but I suspect for me it gets a low score as much because I came to it jaded, knew the tale, and have never overly cared for it.

MYTHOS CONNECTIONS: Many, so in those terms at least it's a must read.

LOVECRAFT TWATTRY: None.

SHOULD YOU READ IT: You just have but read it again by all means.

BLUFFERS FACT: There are lots of people who love 'The Dunwich Horror'. It's certainly one of the most renown of Lovecraft stories, it has been the title story for several collections and there have been film versions, in this case a 1970s horror of true 1970s mid budget horror style (so somewhere between dreadful and awesome depending on your view of old horror movies), several comic book versions, audio productions, even a stage play. So, what do I know?

IBID

Parody is an art form.
The product of wit and witticism portrayed with po-faced sincerity. Truly great parody extends its subject matter from a simple premise outwards towards the increasingly ridiculous, does so with slow methodical steps so that each little absurdity seems only a small step further than the last and it's not until you reach the end that you look back and see just how far down a twisted road towards the ridiculous you have strayed. The end of a good parody should be a place so far down that road from the beginning that were it first muted without the preamble it would be dismissed as laughable in all the wrong ways, yet the journey you have taken to get to the end make it entirely believable in the context of the tale told.
The problem with parody is sometimes people don't realise the absurd is part of the joke. Sometimes this disconnect can be disastrous; I have a character in the Hannibal books who Hannibal (the narrator) first meets dressed as a maid, she is however 'not the maid'. Throughout the rest of the book she is referred to as 'Not the maid', but that description lengthens to increasingly ridiculous dimensions until eventually she is 'I think we have established by not she is most definitely not in any way the maid'. Most people realise this is a bit of parody and are generally amused by it, it's one of the aspects of the first Hannibal novel that almost always gets commented on positively when I talk to readers, because people like a bit of parody. Occasionally though I have come across readers who just don't get the joke...
That, in a nutshell, is the problem with parody, sometimes a reader just doesn't get the joke. Sometimes that is simply because they don't realise parody is what they're reading, which in fairness is not a bad mark of good parody. To be able to portray the ridiculous in a way that it presents itself as plausible is the aim after all. But as a writer, when someone misses the point, it can be disheartening...
So, to Ibid, which is a parody, in which Lovecraft parodies academia and academic papers - and as a parody it is eminently successful. It starts of as a piece of snarky commentary on a student's fundamental error about a Roman writer called Ibid. Throughout Lovecraft plays with the idea of ridiculous Roman names somewhat as you can see in the passage below (in case you were wondering why I mentioned

Hannibal's 'not a maid…')

His full name—long and pompous according to the custom of an age which had lost the trinomial simplicity of classic Roman nomenclature—is stated by Von Schweinkopf3 to have been Caius Anicius Magnus Furius Camillus Æmilianus Cornelius Valerius Pompeius Julius Ibidus; though Littlewit rejects Æmilianus and adds Claudius Decius Junianus; whilst Bêtenoir differs radically, giving the full name as Magnus Furius Camillus Aurelius Antoninus Flavius Anicius Petronius Valentinianus Aegidus Ibidus.

What starts out as a complaint about students lack of academic zeal becomes the life story of a Roman writer, and then of that writer's body after he dies, then just his skull which has the words 'Ibidus Rhoritos Romanus' inscribed upon it at some point in a 1600 year journey through the Royal courts of Europe, sainthood and several curious misadventures until it ends up in a prairie dog barrow in - of all places - Milwaukee where it is worshiped by the rodents as an envoy of the gods in the world above…
All of this, even the dark rites of the worshiping prairie dogs is presented throughout as a serious academic paper, with footnotes, while the slow slide from the plausible to the utterly ridiculous is perfectly paced. For what Lovecraft tried to do, this is as near perfect as it could be, the only downside is, it's a parody of an academic paper, it reads like an academic paper, and even knowing the joke, it is still very dry, so very, very dry.
I would love to give this six tentacles, and really I should, because it is exactly what it sets out to be and a perfect piece of parody, but frankly it's also dull in the way all academic papers are to an extent dull. Which while I know that is the point of the piece, it doesn't make it any more fun to read. So, it gets a four, but don't let that dissuade you if you can read the arid with a wry smile, because as parody, it is a master class.

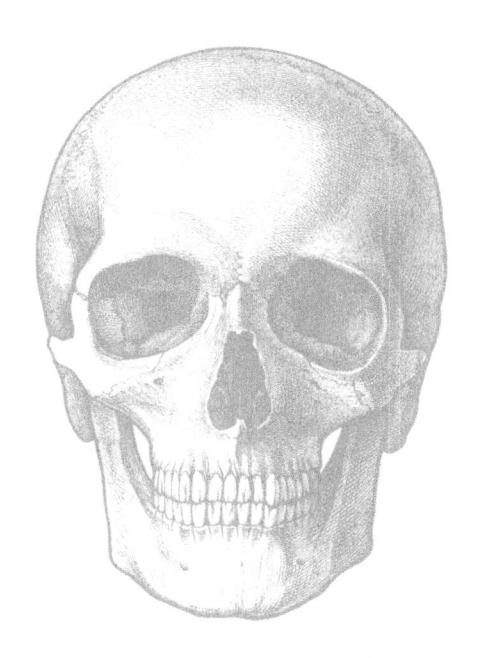

THE SCORE: 4 OUT OF 6 TENTACLES, OR 6 IF YOU LOVE A BIT OF ADMITTEDLY VERY DRY HUMOUR.

MYTHOS CONNECTIONS: None.

LOVECRAFT TWATTRY: None.

SHOULD YOU READ IT: Yes.

BLUFFERS FACT: Jokes about Roman names have always been something of a soft spot of mine, and the fact Lovecraft got away with presenting this as a straight faced piece of dry academia…

'Anicius magnus Furius Camillus'
(Ancient magus of furious calamity)

Well, it made me smile, even if my pig-Latin translations are a bit rough around the edges. If that amuses you, there are other jokes among those names above if you can figure them out.

THE WHISPERER IN THE DARKNESS

As an early unexpected spring warm snap creates a flood of meltwater from the Vermont mountains and local newspapers report strange things seen floating in bulging rivers, Albert N. Wilmarth, an instructor of literature at Miskatonic University becomes embroiled in a controversy regarding the reality and significance of the sightings. Wilmarth at first sides with the sceptics, blaming hysteria fed by old Vermont legends about monsters living in uninhabited hills. Then he receives a letter from the ponderously named Henry Wentworth Akeley who lives in an isolated farmhouse deep in the hills, who claims to have proof of the creatures' existence. So, Wilmarth sets off into the backwaters of Vermont to investigate.

This is the set up for 'The Whisperer in the Darkness'. As set ups go, this is a familiar one, a sceptic academic, the remote countryside, the ponderous names, a dark truth waiting to be revealed… This is Lovecraft 101 and draws a lot on the similar set up of 'The Dunwich Horror'. It's also longer than 'Dunwich', which itself was ponderously long for a short story. 'The Whisperer in the Darkness' is a full novella running to 26,000 words, which should be no surprise as this was the time Lovecraft wrote much of his longer fictions. Like 'Dunwich', this story suffers from the laborious style Lovecraft had adopted by this point in his writing career. It's a story that ten years before would have run to half this length, while losing nothing. As a result, it feels slow and methodical, though it does have that trademark relentless incremental build-up of all Lovecraft's horror. The trouble is that while this technique works so well in short fiction, it struggles to hold the interest of the reader in longer works when the plot is entirely linear.

When it came to reading this story for the blog, it took me seven months to get around to because every time I have picked up my bumper books of tentacle hugging goodness to read the story, I lasted about a third of its length before deciding to go read something else. While I don't generally have a problem with Lovecraft's style, I lose patience for it when reading this story. Unlike most of his longer fiction 'At the Mountains of Madness', 'The Call of Cthulhu', etc. this story is not cut down into acts that make it more palatable to the reader.

This is something of a shame, as there is a lot about this story that's good. Not least of which is Lovecraft more or less invented yet another sci-fi/horror trope with the brain a jar which is ultimately revealed. There are also innumerable links to his wider mythos, as well as Lovecraft's own brand of fanboyness in this particular passage.

I found myself faced by names and terms that I had heard elsewhere in the most hideous of connections—Yuggoth, Great Cthulhu, Tsathoggua, Yog-Sothoth, R'lyeh, Nyarlathotep, Azathoth, Hastur, Yian, Leng, the Lake of Hali, Bethmoora, the Yellow Sign, L'mur-Kathulos, Bran, and the Magnum Innominandum...

While you will doubtless recognise the mythos references in that passage, there are also refences to the writings of Lord Dunsany and Robert E Howard buried within that list. The story also contains some of Lovecraft's most creative otherworldly horror. Plutonian fungi with strange alien technologies, mind swaps and other weird and wonderful inventive creations.

Here though lies the problem for me, all of that fabulously interesting stuff is tied down by what a dull relentless trawl is the text itself. I find it so languid and morose I just find it hard to enjoy reading it - and always have - and if you do drag yourself through the rest of it, the ending has a predictable reveal that any reader can see coming a mile away, (if that is, they manage to read all the way to the end).

All that said, regardless of my opinion, plenty of people like this story, though few would claim it's one of Lovecraft's best, and in fairness it's far from his worst. I even agree with that assessment to an extent, but mainly because his worst is bloody terrible as a rule. This isn't terrible, it's just not very interesting despite having all the elements it needs to be a great story. Had it been tightened up and been shorter it could have been so much better, but perhaps that's just me, I am as ever just a talking head, or perhaps in this case a brain in a jar.

THE SCORE: 3 OUT OF 6 SOMEWHAT BEGRUDGING TENTACLES

MYTHOS CONNECTIONS: Many woven within the story.

LOVECRAFT TWATTRY: None.

SHOULD YOU READ IT: If you want to read the complete works, you need to read this one, if you want to read just the important mythos stories, then you should probably also read this one, but if you want to be entertained, I'd give it a miss.

BLUFFERS FACT: In the list of names above, after Lovecraft's own mythos and those of other writers the last one 'Magnum Innominandum' is a skilfully crafted joke of sorts. The Latin translates as 'The Great Not-to-be-named'. Admittedly as jokes go its dry to the point of arid, but it's a joke none the less.

AT THE MOUNTAINS OF MADNESS

It's fair to say that of all Lovecraft's stories 'The Call of Cthulhu' has had the greatest cultural impact in the zeitgeist, but in terms of overall impact and inspiration 'At the Mountains of Madness' probably tips the scales. The story has an influence that spreads further and deeper than any other Lovecraft tale. The long trek across Antarctica and back down through the pre-human history of the planet has been inspiring both writers and film makers for nearly a century now. Echoes of the ideas and images within this long novella appear in John Carpenters 'The Thing', and the 'Alien' movies, (in particular but not exclusively, 'Alien vs Predator'), Alan Moore's 'Heart of Ice' and others. Several sequels to the novella have been written by various writers, as well as adaptations of the original story in film, graphic novels and even a musical. It's a story that has gripped the imagination because its core idea, that alien civilizations existed on earth hundreds of millions of years before humanity's rise to dominance, is a beguiling one. As is the idea that dangerous remnants of those civilizations could still exists in far flung parts of the world, not quite dead, and far from benign...

As ever, because Old Tentacle Hugger knows no other way, the story is slowly narrated and builds in layer upon layer towards its ultimate climactic discovery. Unlike 'The Whisperer in the Darkness' and some others, however, despite its length the story builds towards that climax in stages which draw the reader into the story and onward.

There are several stages to the novella, which is recounted by geologist William Dyer, one of only two survivors of an ill-fated expedition to Antarctica composed of scholars from Miskatonic University. The expedition's aim, among other things, was to drill for rock samples, determine the age of ice sheets and other such scientific endeavours - and we are told it is the largest of its kind ever sent to earth's most remote continent.

Things start to get strange when an advance party, led by Professor Lake, discover the frozen remains of various prehistoric life forms deep under the ice. Reports of these discoveries reach Dyer at base camp via radio, with Lake's reports becoming steadily wilder as his team examine their finds, until suddenly contact is lost with the advance team as a blizzard sets in and it is never re-established. Eventually Dyer and Danforth, one of his graduate students, fly to the advance camp in the hope of re-establishing contact, assuming nothing more sinister that simple equipment failure to be the cause. What they find, however, is a blood bath. Both men and sled dogs have been brutally murdered - some showing signs of dissection. After they take a tally of the corpses only one man is unaccounted for, and Dyer suspects him to be responsible for the murders as it seems the only logical conclusion.

What they do find, is Lake's notes and the strange six-sided mounds of ice from which the bizarre specimens were extracted, the best preserved of which have vanished. Reading the notes, they discover the advance team found evidence of structures in the mountains where no human structures could be. Dyer and Danforth decide between them to fly on to these structures and investigate further, partly in the hope of locating the missing man, partly out of scientific curiosity. What they find there defies reason. The remains of a lost civilisation. A civilization of elder things that must have existed millions of years in the past. They naturally investigate the structures and as they go deeper within them, they come across murals that tell of the history of that long-vanished civilization, its rise and decline, across a million years of history.

It's at this point that things get really bad; they realise the city is waking up, that the remains found by Lake were hibernating creatures rather than corpses as Lake had assumed, and it was these creatures which destroyed the camp and killed Lake's team. These elder things then returned to their ancient city only to fall victim to something even worse that has been reawakened by their presence, the Shoggoth's. Bio-engineered slave creatures, who performed the function as the workers of the elder thing's civilization. As slaves, even formless gelatinous blobs, are wont to do, eventually the Shoggoth's rebelled against their masters. Possibly one shoggoth absorbed a lot of multi-coloured rocks and pulsed 'let my people go', or perhaps one forward thinking elder thing was called Abe, who can say? At any rate the shoggoth's being as they are virtually indestructible gelatinous blobs, were ultimately successful in their rebellion, and then went into hibernation, because bio-engineered slave races may well rebel but as their very existence was brought about to follow orders, once they weren't getting orders anymore, they got stuck in neutral for a few million years till someone woke them up… And of course, lastly, there are the giant blind albino penguins which once served as a kind of domesticated cattle …

Yes, I know, penguins…

I've always had a problem with the penguins, they seem incredibly frivolous in relation to the rest of the story. A strangely off-key addition to what is otherwise a very dark, intense story. Perhaps it's because having grown up in the late twentieth century I find penguins inherently funny, which makes giant blind albino penguins hard to take seriously.

Aside from the penguins, however, this tale is beautifully ominous and brooding. It steadily layers on alien ideas while the strange history of the earth before humanity's rise to prominence, as Dyer discovers it, is perfectly paced and toned as not to bog the reader down in exposition. It's a long read but a great one and one that has seldom been matched, in terms of scope, by anyone. Additionally, 'At the Mountains of Madness' binds the mythos of Lovecraft together. I would posit this story more than any other is the reason Lovecraft is more than just another long forgotten scifi/horror writer from the age of pulp magazines.

It helps that unlike several other major Lovecraft stories, there are few if any troubling aspects to this one in terms of the unpalatable aspects of Lovecraft's fiction. After all, it's not the star spawned horrors and cosmic nihilism that makes Lovecraft uncomfortable reading at times, as much as his politics, racism and sexism. It is perhaps simply because this story doesn't have those problematic aspects of his fiction that this remains one of the most enjoyable reads, remains popular, and often inspires other writers. This is Lovecraft you can enjoy without been reminded what a shit the writer was.

'At The Mountains of Madness' is Lovecraft's tour de force. It has much to unpack not least an entire pre-history mythology for the earth on which much of the mythos of the wider Lovecraft universe is built. It's a story that writers, artists and game makers keep going back to, a deep well of strange, weird brilliance.

As for tentacles, well it has them in abundance and always will because this is Lovecraft at his best without any of the problems he normally brings along with reading him.

THE SCORE: 6 OUT OF 6 TENTACLES REACHING OUT OF A SHOGGOTH THAT HAS BROKEN FREE OF ITS CHAINS, BECAUSE IT HARD TO CHAIN A HOMICIDAL GELATION BLOB.

MYTHOS CONNECTIONS: A great history of pre-human earth, that ties everything together.

LOVECRAFT TWATTRY: Erm, the penguins.

SHOULD YOU READ IT: If you don't read 'At the Mountains of Madness' then I am not sure why you would read any Lovecraft at all.

BLUFFERS FACT: More than one filmmaker has tried to get a movie of this novella off the ground, the most notable and recent attempt being by Guillermo del Toro who sadly failed to get the project off the ground, though he has been trying to get the project funded for over a decade. Del Toro is one of my favourite filmmakers, particularly when he has been allowed to make his vison and not tied by a studio so I hope one day he will.

Until that hopefully happens there are several short film versions of the story kicking about, some noticeably closer to the original than others. Among the best of these (to use the word loosely) is a low budget student project film made by Matt Jarjosa in 2017. All things considered, it's a fine effort on a budget not so much shoestring as sandal toe loop… I stumbled across it (on You tube, where you can find it easily enough if you search Matt's name) while researching for this book and it only has a few hundred views, and it deserves some wider recognition despite its obvious limitations. It's a shadow of what del Toro could achieve with a Hollywood budget of course, but it's oddly wonderful all the same. So, give it a watch and enjoy the shoggoth…

THE SHADOW OVER INNSMOUTH

While many of Lovecraft's stories were published in periodical magazines like 'Weird Tales' in his lifetime, only one was ever published as a book, and even then the whole print run was of only 200 copies each priced at a dollar. It carried many typos and print errors, so many in fact that Lovecraft insisted a corrections sheet be included after the fact. Lovecraft was not even particularly taken with the tale in question and originally had no plans to offer it for publication at all. It was too long for most magazines, hard to split in to more reasonably sized parts as was done with 'Call of Cthulhu' and 'At the Mountains of Madness'. It was derivative of one of his earlier works 'The Festival', and Lovecraft complained about the poor quality of the typesetting and was generally disappointed by the whole enterprise. The publication was a failure and contributed to the collapse of the small publishing house that produced the book. None of which did much to lighten Lovecraft's own view of the story.

These days of course, a good quality 1st edition of this book, which in case you missed the obvious was, 'The Shadow Over Innsmouth' will cost you anything up to $7,000 as they are unsurprisingly highly sought after by Lovecraft collectors.

Despite Lovecraft's own lack of faith and general dissatisfaction with the Innsmouth tale, it is widely considered to be one of his seminal works. It also has within it some of the best action sequences of any of Lovecraft's stories, and this fact alone make it more accessible than many of his stories. There is actually real pace to that action, which helps drag the reader along - something many of Old Tentacle Hugger's tales lack. All the while it maintains the steady building tension and feeling of slowly impending dread that you expect from Lovecraft. The story begins simply enough, with Lovecraft's favourite trope of a narrator retelling his tale after the fact. Robert Olmstead is doing a tour of New England doing government genealogical research when he arrives in the small, dilapidated fishing village of Innmouth, which by coincidence was the birthplace of one of his ancestors. He realises fairly soon that there is something odd about the place, and in the genealogy the people.

They walk with a distinctive shambling gait and have queer, narrow heads with flat noses and bulgy, staring eyes.

As a government researcher, Olmstead is not exactly made welcome by the insular inhabitants, but he starts to gather information on the bizarre history of the town, its links to a strange religious cult 'The Esoteric Order of Dagon'. A cult which he is told by a clerk called Zadok had once practiced human sacrifices and worshiped the 'Deep Ones'. More alarmingly he is told the local population has been interbreeding with the Deep Ones themselves. Olmstead is understandably made a tad unnerved by all this, but finds it hard to lend credence to the fantastical tale Zadok tells him.

Side note. Dear old Dagon, it's oddly comforting to read that name, from way back in January 2017 when I started this little challenge, the first six tentacle story and was only the fourth blog posts. Oh, how happily naive I was back then… but I digress.

Olmstead might well have brushed off everything Zadok told him as no more than a tall tale, if he had not then found himself marooned in the town when the bus he had planned to leave on developed engine problems. Instead, he is forced to stay the night, and after taking a room in the only hotel in the town, he goes back to talk more with the clerk - only to discover the man has vanished. A worrying development as Zadok had also urged him to leave town. Then sometime in the night, as he sleeps in his crappy hotel room, he is woken when someone tries to break into his room. It is at this point the action really starts, as an unnerved Olmstead makes a break for it through the hotel window, into the night.

What happens next is that uncharacteristic bit of pulp action adventure as Olmstead tries to elude the strange inhabitants of Innsmouth, and then an influx of Deep Ones (best described as fish-men, or perhaps merlocks…) who have come up from beneath the waves for their tribute and acts of congress.

All of this makes for a cracking read despite Lovecraft's dismissal of the story. From there on the story spirals towards its conclusion, only slowing down as you reach the epilogue which goes back to Lovecraft's more tried and tested style, where an older Olmstead becomes aware he is undergoing a transformation of his own and his ancestral Innsmouth blood is calling him down to the sea…

'The Shadow Over Innsmouth' is one of Lovecraft most loved tales. It's also one of his most accessible, it has few of his faults (which as we know are many) and ironically the very things about the story that Lovecraft felt were weaknesses are its strengths. That touch of action and adventure meshes perfectly with Lovecraft's brooding dark horror and nail chewing tension. It, along with 'At the Mountains of Madness', and 'The Call of Cthulhu' form a somewhat unholy trinity in some respects as the stories most recognizable by non-Lovecraft fans - they may know little about Lovecraft but these three they have heard of. It has also, like the other two, has inspired artwork, PC games and board games as well as inspiring countless other writers.

(Including a little-known science-fiction writer from the northeast of England, who wrote a story inspired in part by this particular corner of Lovecraft's mythos called 'The Salmon Swims Both Ways' that was first published in 'The Harvey Duckman Anthologies' V5, and later as part of my own anthology 'Cheesecake, Avarice & Boots.')

Of that trinity, 'Innsmouth' is my least favourite. 'Mountains' and 'Cthulhu' have something a little extra about them that this story lacks. But that's like saying it's my least favourite of the original three Star Wars movies. It still remains head and shoulders above much of Lovecraft's other fiction.

THE SCORE: 5 1/2 OUT OF 6 TENTACLES, I WAS TEMPTED TO GIVE IT ONLY FIVE BUT THAT WAS MOSTLY BECAUSE IT CAME STRAIGHT AFTER 'MOUNTAINS', SO I THOUGHT I SHOULD GIVE IT FIVE AND A HALF, POSSIBLY BECAUSE OF ITS DEEP ONE CONNECTIONS THE HALF TENTACLE GREW BACK...

MYTHOS CONNECTIONS: Going right back to 'Dagon', cultists and everything fishy in Lovecraft's lore

LOVECRAFT TWATTRY: In the context of the story there are none, because it's hard to complain about regressive racial traits when the race are fish men...

SHOULD YOU READ IT: Yes, and it's a treat.

BLUFFERS FACT: Robert Olmstead (the narrator) never actually names himself; his name is only known from Lovecraft's notes on the story which were published after his death.

THE DREAMS OF THE WITCH HOUSE

In terms of Lovecraft stories 'The Dreams of the Witch House' is a little odd due to its mixing the cosmic horror that is Lovecraft's staple with hints of the Judeo-Christian concept of the devil. It stands out as the only real example of Lovecraft doing this in any of his cosmic horror tales. Rooting aspects of this story in pseudo-Judeo-Christianity should work well, there is a logic to it, after all explaining things in terms of religion is what humanity has been doing for thousands of years, so seeing the devil in a manifestation of cosmic horror, or the roots of Judeo-Christian myth laying in aspects of Lovecraft's mythology is not only logical but enticing as a concept. Doing so in a story that involves witchcraft and witches, those traditional worshipers of the devil, is also logical. After all, who is to say if a witch is praying to the devil or some cosmic horror that has taken on that aspect. There is so much that could be done with this idea, so much narrative scope... Unfortunately given the way it was done, there are also troubling questions raised by his doing so, but I'll get to that in a moment. The story centres around William Gilman, a student of mathematics and, of all things, folklore at dear old Miskatonic University. Probably the only University in the world where such an odd pairing for a joint degree is ever likely to be studied... As such Gilman takes an attic room in The Mason House in Arkham, a house that bears the local nickname, 'The Witch House' as one of its former residents, Kexith Mason, was to be tried for witchcraft in 1692 before he mysteriously disappeared from a jail cell in Salem. His former residence later developed a reputation for being haunted that persists to the present day the way such rumours do. Rumours linked to the premature deaths of several residents of the house over the last couple of centuries. Residents who, Gilman discovers, all occupied the same attic room Gilman has now found himself living in. A room that he comes to realise is distinctly odd, with an outlandish almost unearthly geometry.

It is at this point that Gilman starts to dream, and such odd dreams they are...

Yes, I know, I was shocked by this turn of events as well...

In his dreams, Gilman is witness to the cities of elder things with their impossible geometric shapes, which start to communicate with him and other oddities. He also encounters a witch called Keziah who has a rat-like familiar called Brown Jenkins which, while having a rodent

body has a human face. But this is only the start, the dreams soon escalate, as does the effect these dreams have upon Gilman in the physical world. Among other things, he goes deaf due to the inhuman sounds he hears in his dreams, as well as becoming slowly emaciated and withdrawn. Eventually, in one dream Keziah takes him to meet 'The Black Man' who implores Gilman to sign 'The book of Azathoth' whence he will be taken to the throne of Asathoth and, as an aside, forced to kidnap a child to sacrifice in the dream…
And it's here the issues start …

…a tall, lean man of dead black colouration but without the slightest sign of negroid features: wholly devoid of either hair or beard and wearing as his only garment a shapeless robe of some heavy black fabric.

'The Black Man' is the allegory for the devil. The epitome of evil in the Judeo-Christian tradition. He is also 'Nyarlathotep', the crawling chaos, the harbinger of 'Asathoth', he who will usher in the age of chaos and destroy human civilization. Now, in aspect, that is all well and good, but specifically throughout this story this cloven-hoofed devil is referred to as 'The Black Man'. Remembering this was written by H P Lovecraft in 1932, in the heart of the era of Jim Crow laws, the rise of fascism in Europe and Lovecraft's racist views, opinions and rhetoric which is well documented. The subtext, whether intentionally or otherwise, is obvious. 'The Black Man' is the harbinger of chaos and destruction, albeit here in the form of Azathoth.

In fairness, Lovecraft's description of 'The Black Man' states he does not have 'negroid' features. It could be argued that this distances the character from any obvious allegory of Lovecraft's views on what he calls elsewhere in his letters and writings 'The negro Problem'. But that's a thin defence when Lovecraft's views are well established and this portrayal of 'The Black Man' as the Judeo-Christian Satan was problematic at best even in 1932. It's difficult to read the story and put that on one side. It is in fact possibly the most obnoxious bit of racism in all of Lovecraft's writing. In previous stories the case, no matter how loosely, could be made that any racist opinions and views expressed were the views of the narrators of those stories. Here, however, it is clearly a view expressed by the writer himself, as here it is the subtext which is expressing the abhorrent views. Perhaps all the worse for the literary sleight of hand in that description above.

Putting the controversy of 'The Black Man' to one side, (and frankly everything about this story could have been better, or at least less horrifying for the wrong reasons, if he was described and referred to differently throughout) 'The Dreams of the Witch House' is a reasonable read. There is a certain obviousness about the ending, and some of the imagery early on in the dreamscape sequences is frankly tedious, but that may be just me, I've never fully got along with Lovecraft's Dreamlands fiction. Certainly, there are aspects of the horror, including some rather visceral images, that are horrifying in the sense you want them to be. Brown Jenkins the man-faced rat eating his way out of Gilman, for example, is particularly nasty bit of imagery in the good way. But the final ending has a predictability about it, there were other ways Lovecraft could have gone with it which would have been far more interesting. But that last is perhaps a niggle of my own. It's a solid enough ending but it's a solid ending to what is ultimately a weak story. Of Lovecraft's later works this is one of the weakest. Perhaps it is better than I give it credit for, I admit I find it hard to get past the whole 'The Black Man' problem, particularity in light of the world as it is today and all that is going on. But even in better times I doubt I would find it easy to stomach the racist subtext. Because of that (but mostly because it's just not the best of stories) it gets a lowly two tentacles. Read it if you feel you must, but if you want my advice, stick on the rock opera, crank the speakers up to eleven and enjoy the story in a much better way…

THE SCORE: 2 OUT OF 6 POLITICALLY QUESTIONABLE TENTACLES.

MYTHOS CONNECTIONS: 'Nyarlathotep', the crawling chaos, the harbinger of 'Asathoth'…

LOVECRAFT TWATTRY: Racism, overt and obvious.

SHOULD YOU READ IT: Listen to the rock opera instead, with the speakers turned up to 11.

BLUFFERS FACT: 'The Black Man' controversy and the desire to distance that controversy from the story as a whole is why when the Lovecraft historical Society commissioned a Rock opera of the 'Dreams of the Witch House', 'The Black Man' was somewhat overtly replaced with Satan in the story.

That album is rather good all things considered, if you like operatic rock music with an entwined story. It's not up there with Jeff Wayne's 'War of the Worlds', or likely to inspire me, in part at least, to write a novel as, Jeff's album did, but what is?

If you like the genre there are worse ways to enjoy the story… Such as reading Lovecraft's original.

THROUGH THE GATES OF THE SILVER KEY

Okay, before we start, let me just reiterate once more, Randolph 'bloody' Carter…

I am, as astute readers may have noticed, not the biggest fan of Lovecraft's 'Dreamlands' stories - with several notable exceptions. Nor am I a huge fan of Randolph Carter in general. The only Randolph Carter story that has done well under my occasionally erratic spotlight is Lovecraft's novella 'The Dream-Quest of Unknown Kadath' and the reasons I like that story are all to do with the greater mythos rather than the story itself. My hopes when it came to this story were not high therefore… Which is slightly odd.

'The Silver Key', a story I loathe, was unsurprisingly the central inspiration for 'Through the Gates of The Silver Key.' It is a direct sequel to that story that was written primarily because a fan of Old Tentacle Hugger, Edgar Hoffmann Price, a writer himself, asked Lovecraft to write it. Hoffmann went further than just asking however, he sent Howard a 7,000-word original draft of the story to Lovecraft, telling the tale of 'what happened next…' to dear old Randolph Carter, after he unlocked the gates at the end of 'The Silver Key'.

Lovecraft's vanity, reasonably enough, was such that he was swayed by the idea, and took that 7,000-word draft and rewrote it into something that ended up twice that length. According to Hoffmann, fewer than 50 words of his original draft remained intact. Despite this, many accredit this tale to both authors as a collaboration. Hoffmann was reportedly very pleased with the resulting tale and full of praise for Lovecraft's reworking of what could be one of the first examples of fan fiction to surface in the zeitgeist.

Despite my trepidation about reading yet another story with Randolph in it, when I first came round to this one, I was looking forward to it. As I said when I wrote of the dreadful 'The Silver Key', I remembered this story fondly… 'Remembered' was clearly the wrong word, at some point, however, in the dim distant past, around the late 1980s, when I was young and impressionable, I did read this particular tale and there was something about it that spoke to me.

I don't remember what it said, and I am fairly sure it lied…

That's one of the problems with re-reading things I read when I was a teenager - a few decades, a whole lot of living and more refined tastes, can mean that stories I loved when I was effectively not much more than a kid don't really stack up anymore. I suspect what I was drawn to back then was the strangeness of the tale. In part, it is very much a psychedelic dream sequence where Randolph becomes just one fragment of a cosmic id, sharing the bodies of other nodes of existence. There are wild, fascinating ideas here, ideas I suspect I'd seldom come across when I first read this story way back in the dim darkness of the past. A past which increasingly is another country...

Fast forward to a more cynical, well-read now, and everything I doubtless found fascinating when I first read this story is still here. But the writing, the descriptions, the plot (what there is of it) and everything about this story aside from the original ideas (only about half of which were Lovecraft's to start with) is awful. The wonder is sucked out of the story and replaced with bland, dull, over written, and frankly boring narrative.

Take for example this passage...

He provided a light-wave envelope of abnormal toughness, able to stand both the prodigious time-transition and the unexampled flight through space. He tested all his calculations, and sent forth his earthward dreams again and again, bringing them as close as possible to 1928. He practiced suspended animation with marvellous success. He discovered just the bacterial agent he needed, and worked out the varying gravity-stress to which he must become used. He artfully fashioned a waxen mask and loose costume enabling him to pass among men as a human being of a sort, and devised a doubly potent spell with which to hold back the holes at the moment of his starting from the black, dead Yaddith of the inconceivable future. He took care, too, to assemble a large supply of the drugs—unobtainable on earth—which would keep his Zkauba-facet in abeyance till he might shed the Yaddith body, nor did he neglect a small store of gold for earthly use.

Maybe that sparks your interest, maybe you are not unlike me as a seventeen-year-old and all power to you if that's the case. I'm not even sure I am like me as a seventeen-year-old. Perhaps my memory confused this story with another when I remembered it fondly. Frankly however my summing up of 'The Silver Key' was:

I'm not saying don't read it, really I'm not, but if you do read it, for the love of all thing scaley don't blame me...

The same applies to this sequel, as does the score it received. Its only saving grace is that this is the last of Randolph Bloody Carter... Well except for another collaboration, 'Out of the Aeons', which he wrote with Hazel Hearld, but as that never appears in the 'Complete Lovecraft', collections, I'm going to forget it even exists... Because it may be a work of utter genius, but I will happily take the risk of that unlikely truth rather than read the words 'Randolph Carter' again...

THE SCORE: 1 OUT OF 6 PITIFUL TENTACLES.

MYTHOS CONNECTIONS: Randolph 'bloody' Carter.

LOVECRAFT TWATTRY: Randolph 'bloody' Carter.

SHOULD YOU READ IT: No, just no...

BLUFFERS FACT: In his literary career, Hoffmann Price produced fiction for a wide range of publications, from 'Argosy' to 'Terror Tales', from 'Speed Detective' to 'Spicy Mystery Stories'. Yet he was most readily identified as a 'Weird Tales' writer. Price published 24 solo stories in 'Weird Tales' between 1925 and 1950, which was somewhat more than Lovecraft. And no, I had never heard of him either...

THE THING ON THE DOORSTEP

It is true that I have sent six bullets through the head of my best friend, and yet I hope to shew by this statement that I am not his murderer. At first I shall be called a madman—madder than the man I shot in his cell at the Arkham Sanitarium. Later some of my readers will weigh each statement, correlate it with the known facts, and ask themselves how I could have believed otherwise than as I did after facing the evidence of that horror—that thing on the doorstep.

That is the opening paragraph of what, for me, is on the face of it, an underrated Lovecraft short story. That strange bunch of notable critics whose opinions on Lovecraft's stories are held in high esteem, almost universally consider it among the poorest of his later stories. Though these are the same critics who consider 'Through the Gates of the Silver Key' to be masterful, so I question the validity of their opinions, not least because this story holds a personable charm to the characters that inhabit it. Interestingly it's also one of the few Lovecraft stories, and certainly the only mythos story, that has a strong female character with agency within the story.
Now I know what you may be thinking, a strong female character with agency in a Lovecraft story…
Finally, we only had to go through 63 other stories to finally get one… Put the bloody flags out, Lovecraft actually managed to get past his misogyny and write a female character at last…
Well don't get your hopes up too far. While Asenath Waite Derby is indeed a strong female character with agency in the story, she's also, not… but we'll get to that.
The story is told to us by Danial Upton, who has indeed unloaded a revolver into the face of best friend, Edward Pickman Derby (Asenath's husband), on his doorstep and done so while Edward was theoretically confined in Arkham's asylum. A violent and uncharacteristic action by a quiet family man, who has borne witness to the strange and gradual possession of his friend by a dead magician, Ephrain Waite, (Asenath's father). While Ephrain died before Asenath and Edward met each other at university, he nevertheless left a long shadow over their relationship. Not least of which is that the initial attraction between the couple was based on a mutual interest in the arcane, Ephrain's field of expertise.

Asenath and her father hail from a small fishing port off the New England coast called Innsmouth (yes, that Innsmouth) and there is more than a hint or two that Asenath's mother was in fact a Deep One hybrid. Asenath herself is described as 'dark, smallish, and very good looking except for over-protuberant eyes' that common trait among the old families of the Innsmouth area...

As time goes by, however, Danial notices his friend beginning to act oddly - his whole personality switching on occasion - after which he would have little memory of preceding events. It is only later that Edward confides in Danial he believes that he is being gradually possessed by his wife, or rather by his wife's deceased father, and that his wife is either possessed by her father's soul, or is acting as a conduit for it. Ephrain is, he concludes, using Asenath's body as a convenient safe haven while he transfers his soul into the body of 'her' husband who is a man of independent wealth... So, what can you say about that, save perhaps...

'Oh for the love of Cthulhu, Howard Philips Lovecraft you utter, utter shite, you finally write a decent female character. A female character that is narratively strong and has agency within the story, and it turns out she's her own father using her/his body as a pit stop while she/he tries to become a man again... You utter fucking arsehole...'

~ Me on reading this story

It's possible you consider the opinion expressed above a little strong... Which it is, I will admit, in the context of a single story. The central narrative idea is interesting, unique and different in terms of Lovecraft's work. It's a well written story, and as an idea its well-executed. As an actual story I have no objections at all, I really quite like it, more than most of Lovecraft's critics it would seem. As a story 'The Thing on the Doorstep' is a good read, it's different enough from his others to stand out, it certainly has memorable, well written characters in it, characters who feel more alive and real than many of Lovecraft's usually stifled characterizations. It also has to be said Asenath is a well written character.... So, taken as a single story this has a lot that is good about it.

But this story is the only story in Lovecraft's entire cannon that contains a strong female character with agency. The only one... And it turns out she is actually a shell inhabited by a man using that shell to try to possess another man.... Her agency exists merely to give agency to her father's spirit... If this was one female character out of many in his body of work then that's not an issue, it is merely an element of the narrative. When, however, it's the only female character of any weight he ever wrote, and her whole agency is as a puppet for her father's intentions and desires, it is unsettling to say the very least and says nothing good about Lovecraft.

To get back to the story itself a moment, Danial notices over the course of time the changes in personality Edward goes through. Edward himself, on the occasions he is himself, suspects he is being possessed by his wife at first and it is only later he comes to believe it's actually the spirit of her father at work. As the story goes on the weight of evidence grows as Edwards's sanity is slowly eroded. Once he is hospitalized things comes to a head when Danial hears a knock at the door, a knock which is familiar as the patterned knock used by Edward whenever he comes to visit. When he opens the door...

Lovecraft's general misogyny is well known from his letters and stories. It is one of those things you may believe you just have to accept when you decide to read Lovecraft, like his racism and right-wing political outlook. When you read his work, you have to be prepared to acknowledge that these things are there and decide if you are willing to see past them and enjoy the stories for what they are. To an extent, I've generally done that throughout this book - while I never glossed over issues, I have focused on the tales themselves. On occasion, however, such as in the case of 'The Dreams of the Witch House' or 'The Horror at Red Hook', it's difficult to see past those issues. With the latter I managed to, with the former I did not. 'The Thing on the Doorstep' is more 'Witch House' than 'Red Hook'. Ironic though it may be that the story with an actual female character in it is the one that screams loudest of Lovecraft's misogyny, but that's exactly what it does.

It's not a bad story, certainly it's not as bad as so many of his notable critics claim, but while their issues are with the story itself, my own remain with the story in context to his wider body of work and frankly I find it abhorrent and hateful, the true horror of this tale is not the tale itself but the misogyny it encapsulates... The story in of itself warrants around four tentacles in my somewhat ecliptic rating system, but taking it in the wider context, and how I feel about that aspect of the tale it gets a big minus from me for the utter shit storm it is...

THE SCORE: -4 OUT OF 6 TENTACLES, OR 4, IF YOU IGNORE THE MISOGYNY.

MYTHOS CONNECTIONS: Minor.

LOVECRAFT TWATTRY: Misogyny, so much of it…

SHOULD YOU READ IT: If you can look past the misogyny yes.

BLUFFERS FACT: Arthur Edward Waite, a real-world occultist, is often cited as the inspiration for Ephraim Waite. A E Waite was for a time a member of the 'Hermetic Order of the Golden Dawn' whose most famous member was Aleister Crowley (occasionally referred to as 'The Great Beast'). Crowley considered Waite a foe within the order and referred to him as 'the villainous Arthwate' in his novel 'Moonchild'.

As to the wisdom of basing characters on renowned real-world occultists, Lovecraft died on the Ides of March (an auspicious date if ever there was one) some three years after writing this story, at the time A E Waite was still very much alive… There could of course, be no connection…

THE EVIL CLERGYMAN

Old Tentacle Hugger had more than his fair share of strange dreams, by anyone's standards. Often these dreams inspired aspects of his stories and occasionally a whole story. 'The Evil Clergyman' however is unique among Lovecraft's collected works because it is not so much a story inspired by a dream as a pure recounting of that dream in its entirety. It's not really a story at all in that respect and was never written down as one. The text is taken from a letter Lovecraft wrote to his friend, Bernard Dwyer, or more exactly the part of a letter in which he recounted a dream he'd had. A dream which, according to the letter, he intended to base a story on. A story he never wrote.

The 'story' came to light after Lovecraft's death when Dwyer brought the story to the attention of 'Weird Tales', who with delightful cynicism published this 'lost' Lovecraft story, capitalising on the increased interest in the writer that developed shortly after his death. This is the same period that many other 'lost' Lovecraft stories materialised from the slush piles of several magazines. The literary equivalent of Elvis getting a UK number 1 single September 1977 with 'Way Down', an eminently forgettable track, because while he was a long out of vogue artist in the UK, his death a month before brought a whole new level of interest in the newly deceased King of Rock n' Roll.

But there you have it, this story, to use the word loosely, is actually just Lovecraft narrating a dream he'd experienced to a friend. While Lovecraft may have gone on to use this as the bases for a fuller tale, what that tale might have become we will never know. Instead, we have this bit of literary grave robbing. A tale that is not really a tale. It is most certainly not the tale the writer would have presented to the world had he chosen to because for one thing it's a really short read that bounds along with little exposition, recounting the dream in its entirety with no real anchor in place. The story has none of H P's later laborious style, no long introduction involving ponderous family histories, tentative connections between the character telling the story and the 'evil' clergyman. All there is here is just a plain story drawn from a dream, cast adrift of contextual constraints. A simple tale, in all regards.

And oddly enough, it's all the better for that.

'The Evil Clergyman' is frankly refreshing when you're wading through Lovecraft's later works in order. It reads much more like his early work in that it grabs you, the reader, quickly, keeps your attention, moves along at pace, and because it's not mired in exposition it stays solidly with the events being described. All of which makes it a fun read and a perfect insight into the place where many of Lovecraft's stories came from, without being mired in the oppressive drone that characterises much of his later work. Instead, it has urgency and a familiar sense of earnestness missing from some Lovecraft stories and a timeless quality to it. It's disturbing in places, but disturbing in the right way because this is a recounted dream, rather than a story inspired by one.

Lovecraft would, I suspect, never have submitted this story to publishers as it stands. It's entirely possible he might never have submitted it at all, but if he had used this as the basis for a story, he would have made it three times as long, there would have been a history of the clergyman who used to live in the attic rather than a mere nod towards his dark reputation. There would have been an explanation of his downfall, of what he was burning and why, of his suicide and all that led to him haunting that place. There would have been exposition aplenty, and layers of brooding tensions. But I suspect it would also lose everything I like about this story in the process.

This is raw Lovecraft, Lovecraft from the source, undiluted by pretension or anything else come to that. Just a story, just an awful chilling horror story of a haunting and evil spirits. Frankly the only thing Lovecraft would have done by writing a story based on this tale would have been to ruin everything good about it.

Now I realise I have said very little about the story itself. To be perfectly honest that's because for me to say anything about the plot would detract from the experience of reading the story. It's a story worth the time it takes to read, which isn't awfully long, It is, however, a little gem amidst the coal of Lovecraft's last few stories… It's not a masterpiece, it's not even a piece at all in any real sense, but it's still good value for its tentacles and I am just thankful Lovecraft never got around to ruining this tale by writing a story based upon it.

THE SCORE: 5 OUT OF 6 DREAMLIKE TENTACLES THREADING THEIR WAY INTO YOUR NIGHTMARES.

MYTHOS CONNECTIONS: None.

LOVECRAFT TWATTRY: None.

SHOULD YOU READ IT: Yes, it is in a strange way a bit of a delight.

BLUFFERS FACT: Just as Elvis was not the only deceased musician to top the charts, Lovecraft was not alone among pulp magazine writers in having his work find renewed interest after his death. His close friend Robert E Howard, who committed suicide a few months before Lovecraft's death, also had works publish posthumously. In Howard's case this included 'Almuric' a full novel published in three parts by 'Weird Tales' in 1939, and in paperback some years later. Doubts over the authenticity of this novel have persisted ever since, with many believing Howard's editor, Otis Kline, wrote the story to capitalise on Howard's continuing popularity. An accusation that has never been thrown at any of Lovecraft's posthumous publications. For all his faults, no one writes Lovecraft like Lovecraft, for which we may be thankful…

THE BOOK

Towards the end of his life Lovecraft had a minor crisis of confidence about his writing. Such minor crises are not particularly unusual among writers in general and it was probably not the first time in his career Lovecraft had a moment… It was, however, probably the last if only because of his premature death. We know this because of a letter he wrote to a friend in October of 1933, in which he wrote the following: I am at a sort of standstill in writing—disgusted at much of my older work, and uncertain as to avenues of improvement. In recent weeks I have done a tremendous amount of experimenting with different styles and perspectives, but have destroyed most of the results

One of these experiments, an incomplete fragment, is this story, 'The Book'. Presumably it was only spared the fireplace because Old Tentacle Hugger saw something in it, though where he intended to take the story, we will never know.

Aspects of the last few paragraphs of this fragment have echoes in 'The Shadow out of Time', which Lovecraft went on to write shortly after this fragment was penned, though most of the concepts involved are very different, the results experienced by the narrator bear some similarity, so it's certainly possible this story is a failed branch of that same narrative tree.

I've said before, with those other posthumously published fragments the publishing ghouls sought out after his death, that we will never know what they may have finally become. As with 'The Evil Clergyman', 'The Book' is clearly unfinished, and later drafts may have changed most of the narrative and style. Unlike 'The Evil Clergyman' this was clearly written as something to be published, even if it is incomplete. It reads as more polished than 'Clergyman', yet perhaps because of this it also lacks something. There is nothing particularly new in this story, if as he claimed, Lovecraft's was experimenting with styles, he didn't go far off the beaten track with this one.

Like other previous fragments, 'Azathoth', 'The Descendant' and others it's a delve into Lovecraft's scrap draw. All writers have them, a folder full of half written, half conceived ideas. My own is mostly in the form of notebooks and a folder on my cloud drive called, oddly enough, 'Scrap'. Is there any value in that folder? Well sure, for me there is. It's a collection of half conceived ideas, and occasionally I get drawn back to them and reshape them into something. What isn't in that folder is any stories. Nothing is complete, it's just ideas, half formed, so beyond myself they are of little or no value to anyone and that is exactly what 'The Book' and all those other fragments are.

All that said, 'The Evil Clergyman', incomplete though it is, it is at least an actual story, with a beginning, middle and end. This fragment on the other hand is merely a beginning, there is a certain intrigue about it, a wistful hunger it inspires in the reader who wants to know more, but that's about it, and its instantly forgotten after you have read the thousand or so words that comprise the fragment, which can be summed up as: A man, who seems unsure about who and what he is, starts to tell you about a book he found in a dark forbidding bookshop. Reading the book he took what it told him and made an arcane circle of some kind and…

And that's more or less all there is to it. It's something for the completist to read perhaps, but even to the completist it is frankly a worthless as an exercise, it isn't a story… So, like those other fragments the publishing ghouls sought out after Lovecraft's death it worth no more than a solitary tentacle. Though to be honest that is a stretch. It adds nothing to Lovecraft's literary legacy, the mythos or the greater wealth of human understanding. It's nothing but an example of publishers being willing to cash in on the vague posthumous fame of a deceased writer to put out any old rubbish in order to sell magazines. If it achieves anything it is that it dilutes the quality of Lovecraft's fiction as a whole. Which is rather sad in the end, when you think about it.

THE SCORE: 1 SOLITARY AND SOMEWHAT POINTLESS TENTACLE OUT OF 6

MYTHOS CONNECTIONS: None.

LOVECRAFT TWATTRY: None.

SHOULD YOU READ IT: No.

BLUFFERS FACT: There is an odd suggestion that 'The Book' is in fact a copy of 'Opps, Mrs Cthulhu: 101 Sexual Positions Involving Tentacles'*

*Actually, that's a lie... Nothing of interest stems from this story, not even an odd Bluffers fact.

THE SHADOW OUT OF TIME

'The Shadow out of Time' is the last and, by many, considered to be the greatest of Lovecraft's novellas. Lin Carter, a Lovecraftaphile if ever there was one, called it 'The greatest achievement in fiction'. Not Lovecraft's greatest achievement, 'The' greatest. Lin is certainly not alone in this high praise, it was rated 'One of the top ten Science Fiction and Fantasy books of 2001' by Cinescape Magazine, which is some achievement for a reprint of a novella that first appeared in a 1936 edition of 'Astounding Stories'. Other commentators have claimed it is Lovecraft's 'Magnum opus', called it 'Awe-inspiring', and said it has an 'amazing scope and sense of cosmic immensity'.

Unsurprisingly Lovecraft himself was not entirely satisfied with it.

Somewhat more surprisingly, I agree with Lovecraft's critics on this one, which flies in the face of almost every other time they load endless praise on one of Lovecraft's works, as you may have noticed. But as stories go 'The Shadow out of Time' is hard to describe with any word other than 'epic'. Though I stop short of rating it quite as highly as some.

The story is told to us by Nathaniel Peaslee, an academic with tenure at the gothic splendour of Miskatonic University in Arkham, and it covers almost twenty years of his life. Peaslee was living the quiet life of academia, mixed with a slightly nosier life of young children when in 1908, quite unexpectedly he was stuck with a strange illness, an illness that led to him falling into a coma for several months. Then just as unexpectedly he recovered, but when he awoke, he was a changed man. Or perhaps if we are being precise here, 'he' wasn't as the man who awoke was, for all intent and purposes, someone else entirely. Or rather something else.

And this is where the epic scope of this story comes into play. Though, and this is my niggle with the story, it takes a while until what is going on is made apparent. Like many of Lovecraft's novellas it's a lot longer than it needs to be, though in its defence this niggle is a little over played, the slow pace of the story does work in its favour, slowly revealing the truth behind events, while laboured, its far less laboured than, for example, 'The Dunwich Horror'.

Peaslee is narrating his story some two decades later, and he equates, certainly to start with, the years after this first wakening in terms of insanity. He, which is to say the man who was now Peaslee, awoke with no apparent memory of his earlier life and driven by mad impulses. Over the next five years the man wanders the globe looking into strange ruins, tracking down obscure ancient books, and becoming something of a polyglot, until in 1913 he is struck once again with a strange illness and falls once more into a coma. Some months later when Peaslee again awakens from a coma he has does so with no recollection of the previous five years. He does, however, remember everything about his life and himself from before his first coma. In short, he is the original Nathaniel Peaslee once more.

What happened to Nathaniel, and to his body in those five years is central to this story. The key to which is held within strange dreams, which he slowly comes to recognise as memories, starting to haunt Peaslee after his second reawakening. Once more the sober academic, Nathanial spends the next several years trying to piece together the events and his travels over those five years from little more than scraps of paper, bank records, ticket stubs and conversations with people he met in the wandering years. He also seeks to reconcile with his family and though his former wife will not entertain him, he grows close to his eldest child. It is through his son, some years later, that Peaslee is invited on an archaeological expedition to the heart of the Australian outback, which is where the mystery of those missing years is finally explained, in the ruins of a city that seems to predate humanity itself.

In the dreams Peaslee recollects living in a strange alien city, populated by even stranger beings, with giant cone shaped bodies and tentacle like appendages with which they manipulate and control the machines of the great city. If this is not strange enough, as the dreams go on, he comes to understand more of these strange beings and their history. They are, he comes to understand 'The Great Race' - or at least the minds which occupy those bodies are. The Great Race themselves perfected the art of mind transference, swapping bodies with other consciousness's across both distance and time. When the civilisation of 'The Great Race' faced an extinction event in their own galaxy, remnants of their race leapt forward in time and space and took control of the cone-like aliens inhabiting the earth some million years before mankind.

And having escaped one extinction… Well naturally they are seeking to do so once more. So, they seek out minds amenable to transplantation and send scouts forward in time. Not just to seek out their next home, but to track records of the past (their future) so they can prepare for what is to come. Hence, in the bodies they borrow they seek out relics of the past to determine where best to mass migrate.

To help them with this, those whose bodies have been 'borrowed' are encouraged to mix and write of their own times and experience. The results of which are kept in a great library of archives deep in the bowls of the city of the Great Race. Through doing this the cone alien that is host to the mind of Peaslee learns many secrets and meets men from across the history of mankind both before and after his own time.

Of course, the question of if this is some grand delusion brought on by a psychotic break still troubles him. Is this all a matter of his mind filling in the blanks of his memory… At least until his son has him invited on that archaeological expedition to the heart of the Australian outback. A dig into the ruins of a city date back to long before humanity rise. A city which is the city once inhabited by the Great Race. A fact Peaslee learns for certain when he finds a book written in his own hand…

There is a lot to unpack in this tale. The scope is enormous, the hints that the Great Race have been interfering with humanity for millennia and will for millennia to come are littered throughout. The view of earth's history, much like that expressed in 'At the Mountains of Madness' encompassed a breath of time that is purposely incomprehensible and describes human history as little more than a footnote in the true history of the planet. For scope alone this story is incomparable to the work of almost any other writer of the time or since. It is by definition, epic in proportions.

It is also a tale that explains in its own way how cults of beings like Cthulhu exist throughout time. Those being used by the Great Race bring back knowledge of the true history of the world buried deep in their psychopathology. Fragments of memories that lead to strange beliefs and obsessions. Was our old friend the mad Arab another of those used by the Great Race, was the Necronomicon written by a mind displaced? Are all those unknown and unknowable things lurking in the darkness aspects of the Great Race interfering.

Which is where a problem lies, as the story itself for all the ideas buried within it, is a trudge at times. Carefully layered though the story is, a good editor could have cut it down by half and lost nothing of that epic scale, because it is the story itself not the way it is laid out that makes it epic. That is, however, my only criticism, which amounts to Lovecraft wrote this story in the style of all later Lovecraft, drawn out and longer that it could be. Yet despite that it remains one of his finest achievements.

THE SCORE: 5 TENTACLES, IN A STARFISH FORMATION BRANCHING OUT FORM A CONE LIKE BODY, OUT OF 6

MYTHOS CONNECTIONS: All of them, the beating heart of the greater mythos.

LOVECRAFT TWATTRY: Surprisingly, none of note.

SHOULD YOU READ IT: Yes, indeed you should perhaps read it first.

BLUFFERS FACT: Among the many 'victims' of the Great Race met by Peaslee in the past, is one Crom-Ya. Who is described as being a Cimmerian chief who lived around 15,000 B.C. who returned to his own time with strange knowledge and powers, raising himself to demi-godhood among the tribes.
It's not a coincidence that Lovecraft's friend Robert E. Howard's best-known creation was, of course, Conan - a barbarian hero also from Cimmeria whose tribe practised the ancestor worship of Crom.

THE HAUNTER IN THE DARK

And so, at last we come to the end of our journey. Sixty-Eight stories written between 1905 and 1936, thirty-one years of stories from Old Tentacle Hugger and in that time, we really have been all over the place, and it all comes down to this… 'The Haunter in the Dark'… a story set in Lovecraft's hometown of Providence, Rhode Island. The only story he ever set in his hometown.

The story behind the story is an interesting one, it's actually a sequel to a story called 'The Shambler from the Stars' by one of Lovecraft's friends, Robert Bloch, who went on to write a third story in the sequence 'The Shadow from the Steeple' in 1950. Bloch and Lovecraft were the kind of friends who took delight in killing off characters based on each other. The main character in 'The Haunter in the Dark', Robert Harrison Blake, who Lovecraft based on Bloch, dies at the end. In Bloch's sequel it turns out Blake did not die at all but was possessed by Nyarlathotep and Blake goes on to kill a character based on Lovecraft. Which, had Lovecraft not been dead for over a decade at the time, we can assume would have amused him.

After all, it's all fun and games until someone loses an eye to the winged horror spawn of Yog-Sothoth.

In this story Blake, who has a long held an interest in the occult, becomes fascinated with an old disused church in the Federal Hill district of Providence, which was an odd choice of location as actually Federal Hill is somewhat bereft of old half abandoned churches. It does however have a large collection of Italian restaurants, is home to a large Italian American population, and at one time held the headquarters of the New England branch of La Cosa Nostra. Which, while not strictly relevant was an odd choice of setting by the Providence born Howard. It seems likely he just wanted an area with a large migrate population and certainly at the time Italian Americans in New England were treated with suspicion by the majority of the population which remained of Anglo-Saxon descent. This was one of the reasons the mafia flourished in the early twentieth century on the east coast cites of America. This was undoubtedly true of Lovecraft who viewed anyone not culturally of protestant northern European ancestry as questionable and inferior. Which made them useful in this story, albeit due to his prejudices.

The disused church, Blake discovers, is avoided by the local Italian migrant population because of its connections to a cult called 'The Church of Starry Wisdom'. There are many rumours about the strange things this 'church' and what its members got up to within the confines of its ancient crypts. Blake lends little credence to the tales of the superstitious, poorly educated locals, though he notes that they all seem to believe the church houses some primeval evil brought forth by the cult before it disappeared several decades ago…

Now, of course when you get told that you should avoid a disused church because it reeks of evil and once housed a sinister cult, the first thing you do is plan to enter it one dark night…

Because why wouldn't you?

So, of course, this is what Blake does, and once he is in the church something draws Blake to ascend its steeple. It is there he finds the long dead skeleton of a reporter called Lillbridge. Blake, who has researched the church, knows the reporter disappeared almost forty years before and it had long been presumed he was killed by the cult who he had been investigating at the time. On the body Blake finds Lillbridge's notebook which strangely enough contains passaged written in Aklo (a fictional language that has been used by many writers before him and which Lovecraft first used in 'The Dunwich Horror'.) There is also a strange object near the body, one which provokes fear in Blake just by looking at it, which he describes as a 'Shining Trapezohedron'.

Now there is an irony for you. A ten-sided dice is one example of a type of Trapezohedron, and they are extensively used in pairs in tabletop role playing games like 'Call of Cthulhu' and occasionally rolled to determine what strange horror from beyond time and space a group of players have accidently summoned…

Guess what happens next…

Aware he has done something he shouldn't have, but not entirely sure what he has done, Blake leaves the church and hightails it to his lodgings. There he spends days trying to translate Lillbridge's notes. The notes tell the pottered history of the 'Shining Trapezohedron' a history that is similar to that recounted in 'The History of the Necronomicon', but each night he feels drawn to stare out of his window at the church across the square, sure he sees movement within the darkness of its interior and hears strange sounds in the night emanating from within the building.

He becomes convinced he has inadvertently summoned a creature that haunts the darkness. A creature that would kill him if it was not being warded off by the streetlights. So as long as there is no inadvertent thunderstorm, that knocks out the cities power grid, well Blakes perfectly safe then isn't he…

Was that a flash of lighting on the hillside…? Is that thunder rolling in after it… Has anyone seen Pitch Black? Where is Vin Diesel when you need him?

'The Haunter in the Dark' is one of Lovecraft's better short stories, it's balanced, tightly written and has that thing many of his later stories lack, pace. There is little new here, but then expecting something new in the last story Lovecraft wrote would be somewhat obtuse.

What is interesting about it, like so many of Lovecraft's stories, is the story behind it. This was written as much to entertain his friends and poke fun at one of them, as to sell to a magazine or further his career. He could not know it would be his last story, but even if he suspected it might be, it reads like a story written by a writer at one with himself. At peace with the many personal demons that beget Howard's life. But perhaps that's just the sentimental romantic in me reading between the lines.

THE SCORE: 5 TENTACLES, GROPING IN THE DARKNESS WAITING FOR THE LIGHTS TO FAIL OUT OF 6

MYTHOS CONNECTIONS: Several, not least the prince of many masks and his master Yog-Sothoth.

LOVECRAFT TWATTRY: His opinions of Italian immigrants notwithstanding, remarkably few.

SHOULD YOU READ IT: Yes, with a light on.

BLUFFERS FACT: Within 'The Haunter in the Dark' Lovecraft mentioned the names of five stories written by Robert Blake: "The Burrowers Beneath"; "Shaggai"; "The Stairs in the Crypt"; "In the Vale of Pnath" and "The Feaster from the Stars" all of which are spoof titles based on stories written by Robert Bloch, just in case Robert didn't realise Blake was based on him…

FINAL THOUGHTS

This marks the end of a long journey for me. In all the plan to read and blog the complete works of H.P.Lovecraft over the course of one year took the better part of four to complete. Perhaps as I read 'The Haunter in the Dark' it was wishful thinking on my part that when he wrote it Lovecraft was in a good place as he came towards the end of his life. For all his many flaws, that he was a troubled soul is evident not only form his biography but in his writings.

It is with some sadness I reached the end of this journey. I'd been living with Lovecraft stories for a long time. Most I read multiple times, and some I had to read again when I was putting this book together because what you write in a flippant blog post often needs to be revised heavily for a flippant book. The mediums are not entirely the same.

But I would be lying if I said the sadness of reaching the end of all this came alongside no little relief that I'd never have to read another story by Old Tentacle Hugger. No more overly languid prose, no more politically unsound opinions, no more bloody Lovecraft…

Except perhaps for fun, I might pick up 'The Rats in the Walls' in a day or so… Because in the end, love him or hate him, Lovecraft left a legacy of stories to the world that live in people's imagination even now and have inspired generations of writers who came after him and will continue to inspire writers for generations to come. Including this one.

Should you read Lovecraft… Well, I've joked in the past that the byline for this book should be 'Lovecraft, I've read him, so you don't have to'. But the truth is you should, and your opinions may be entirely different from my own. This is in the end a book of my opinions, so be guided by them alone at your peril.

Except when it comes to 'Celephais' just stay well clear of that pile of shoggoth spoil, consider yourself warned…

Mark Hayes 2022

ABOUT THE AUTHOR

Mark writes novels that often defy simple genre definitions, they could be described as speculative fiction, though Mark would never use the term as he prefers not to speculate.
When not writing novels, Mark is a persistent pernicious procrastinator, he recently petitioned parliament for the removal of the sixteenth letter from the Latin alphabet.
He is also 7th Dan Blackbelt in the ancient Yorkshire martial art of EckEThump and favours a one man one vote system but has yet to supply the name of the man in question.
Mark has also been known to not take bios very seriously.

Email: darrack@hotmail.com
Twitter: @darrackmark
Blog: https://markhayesblog.com/

Printed in Great Britain
by Amazon